HOW THE PAGE MATTERS

From handwritten texts to online books, the page has been a standard interface for transmitting knowledge for over two millennia. It is also a dynamic device, readily transformed to suit the needs of contemporary readers. In *How the Page Matters*, Bonnie Mak explores how changing technology has affected the reception of visual and written information.

Mak examines the fifteenth-century Latin text *Controversia de nobilitate* in three forms – as a manuscript, a printed work, and a digital edition. Transcending boundaries of time and language, *How the Page Matters* connects technology with tradition using innovative new media theories. While historicizing our contemporary digital culture and asking how on-screen combinations of image and text affect the way we understand information being conveyed, Mak's elegant analysis proves both the timeliness of studying interface design and the persistence of the page as a mechanism for communication.

(Studies in Book and Print Culture)

BONNIE MAK is an assistant professor in the Graduate School of Library and Information Science and the Program for Medieval Studies at the University of Illinois.

Bonnie Mak

How the Page Matters

UNIVERSITY OF TORONTO PRESS
Toronto Buffalo London

© University of Toronto Press 2011
Toronto Buffalo London
www.utppublishing.com
Printed in the U.S.A.

Reprinted in paperback 2012

ISBN 978-0-8020-9760-6 (cloth)
ISBN 978-1-4426-1535-9 (paper)

Printed on acid-free paper.

Library and Archives Canada Cataloguing in Publication

Mak, Bonnie
How the page matters / Bonnie Mak.

(Studies in book and print culture series)
Includes bibliographical references and index.
ISBN 978-0-8020-9760-6 (bound). – ISBN 978-1-4426-1535-9 (pbk.)

1. Books – Format – History. 2. Book design – History. 3. Graphic design
(Typography) – History. 4. Buonaccorso, da Montemagno, ca. 1391–1429.
Controversia de nobilitate. I. Title. II. Series: Studies in book and print culture

Z246.M33 2011   002   C2011-902771-2

University of Toronto Press acknowledges the financial assistance to its publishing program
of the Canada Council for the Arts and the Ontario Arts Council.

  Canada Council   Conseil des Arts
for the Arts   du Canada

 ONTARIO ARTS COUNCIL
CONSEIL DES ARTS DE L'ONTARIO

University of Toronto Press acknowledges the financial support of the Government of
Canada through the Canada Book Fund for its publishing activities.

In memoriam
Leonard E. Boyle, O.P.

Contents

Abbreviations

Libraries

BAV	Biblioteca Apostolica Vaticana, Vatican City
Bib. Laur.	Biblioteca Medicea Laurenziana, Florence
Bib. Naz. Cent.	Biblioteca Nazionale Centrale, Florence
Bib. Ricc.	Biblioteca Riccardiana, Florence
BL	British Library, London
BNF	Bibliothèque nationale de France, Paris
HEHL	Henry E. Huntington Library, San Marino, California
KB	Koninklijke Bibliotheek, The Hague
KBR	Bibliothèque royale de Belgique, Brussels

Printed Sources

BMC   British Museum. *Catalogue of Books Printed in the XVth Century now in the British Museum.* Vols. London: By Order of the Trustees, 1908– .

BSB-Ink   Bayerische Staatsbibliothek. *Bayerische Staatsbibliothek Inkunabelkatalog.* Vols. Wiesbaden: L. Reichert, 1988– .

CIBN   Bibliothèque nationale de France. *Catalogue des incunables.* Vols. Paris: Bibliothèque nationale, 1981– .

Duff   E. Gordon Duff. *Fifteenth Century English Books: A Bibliography of Books and Documents Printed in England and of Books for the English Market Printed Abroad.* Oxford: Printed for the Bibliographical Society at the Oxford University Press, 1917.

ESTC   *English Short Title Catalogue.* At http://estc.bl.uk.

Goff   Frederick R. Goff, ed. *Incunabula in American Libraries: A Third Census of Fifteenth-Century Books Recorded in North American Collections.* Millwood, NY: Kraus Reprint, 1973.

Abbreviations

Acknowledgments

This book has been in the making for almost a decade, and I am pleased to have the opportunity to thank some of the many people who have contributed to its development. Following the trail of the *Controversia de nobilitate*, I spent months in the reading rooms of libraries in the United Kingdom, the Netherlands, Belgium, France, Italy, and Austria, and I am grateful to these institutions for their hospitality. The Huntington Library in San Marino, California, as well as the libraries of the Medieval Institute at the University of Notre Dame and the Pontifical Institute for Medieval Studies at the University of Toronto offered invaluable resources as I continued my research on the North American side of the Atlantic. I was granted the time to revise early drafts of the book as Postdoctoral Fellow of the International Research on Permanent Authentic Records in Electronic Systems (InterPARES) Project between 2004 and 2006, and my thanks go to Luciana Duranti and the School of Library, Archival & Information Studies at the University of British Columbia. Work continued at the University of Toronto in the congenial environments of the Centre for Medieval Studies, the Faculty of Information Studies, and the Coach House Institute. Finally, the Graduate School of Library and Information Science at the University of Illinois made available a supportive space in which to bring the project to completion.

Funding for this undertaking was provided by the Office of the Vice Chancellor for Research at the University of Illinois, the Social Sciences and Humanities Research Council of Canada, the University of Notre Dame, the Andrew W. Mellon Foundation, and Dr Gilbert and Ursula Farfel. Catherine Adam, Fabrice Dehoux, Rossella Giovannetti, and Donato Pineider offered valuable assistance in securing photographic images and the permission to publish them. With regard to the reproduction of copyrighted material, I am pleased to acknowledge the generosity of the Director-General of the Royal Library of Belgium, Patrick Lefèvre, and the Director of the Biblioteca Riccardiana in Florence, Giovanna Lazzi. I am grateful to the Greenwood Publishing Group for allowing me to reprint portions of my essay 'On the Myths of Libraries,' in *The Library*

Acknowledgments

as Place: History, Community, Culture, edited by John E. Buschman and Gloria J. Leckie (Westport, CT: Libraries Unlimited, 2006) in chapter 4.

For their role in the formative stages of the project, I am obliged to Charles Barber, Calvin M. Bower, Theodore J. Cachey, Jr, Semion Lyandres, Laura Dull, and Darin Hayton. I found incisive readers in Brian Cantwell Smith, Heather MacNeil, Jun Luo, Alexander Klein, and Kevin Eldred, and I thank my colleagues at the University of Illinois, Alistair Black, Fernando Elichirigoity, Karen Fresco, Anne D. Hedeman, D.W. Krummel, Jimmy Luu, W. Boyd Rayward, Allen Renear, Dan Schiller, and John Unsworth, for their encouragement. I am indebted to Leslie Howsam, editor of the series Studies in Book and Print Culture, as well as to Jill McConkey, Siobhan McMenemy, and my readers at the University of Toronto Press. In closing, I especially wish to thank Kathleen A. Biddick and Daniel J. Sheerin for their foresight, guidance, enthusiasm, patience, and wisdom.

HOW THE PAGE MATTERS

Introduction

This book is about how the page matters. To matter is not only to be of importance, to signify, to mean, but also to claim a certain physical space, to have a particular presence, to be uniquely embodied. The matter and mattering of the page are entangled in complicated ways as they reconfigure each other iteratively through time.[1] Across cultural boundaries and through centuries of change, the page has emerged as a safeguard for intellectual and artistic achievement. It has been used to share knowledge and communicate ideas from those of Sappho to those of William Shakespeare to our own. Much of what we have learned has been transmitted to us on the page; much of what we have wished to remind ourselves and others of has been broadcast in the same way. The page is a powerful interface between designer and reader, flexible enough to respond to a variety of demands while remaining comprehensible and communicative. The page is now ubiquitous – we flip absently through the pages of a magazine, scribble down notes on a pad of paper, and surf web pages on our laptops, PDAs, or mobile phones – but this ubiquity has led to present-day assumptions about the page and its operation. *How the Page Matters* re-examines these assumptions and focuses attention on the page by tracking the dynamic relationship of material and meaning in the medieval manuscript, printed book, and computational device. The following investigation will thus explore the significance of the page in the development of Western civilization and consider why the interface continues to play such an important role in the transmission of thought.

Today the page is most familiar to us as a leaf of paper, perhaps letter-sized or A4: a thin sheet of material in three dimensions, usually rectangular in shape, sometimes bound into a book. Each page has a *recto* and a *verso*, a front and back side. The height and width of the material regulate the space that may be allotted to text and image on these two sides, and the thickness determines the possibility of inscription upon its edges. From a young age, we are trained to believe that the boundaries of the interface are always identical to the edges of the material platform of the page – namely, that the cognitive space and the physical dimensions of the page are necessarily conterminous.

But the page has not always been circumscribed in this way. Before its emergence as a discrete piece of writing material, the page had an organizational function in the scroll. The Egyptians, Greeks, and Romans of antiquity arranged text and image into columns called *paginae*, or pages, on long rolls of papyrus.[2] The conceptual structure of the page was thus used by scribes to organize ideas graphically, and readers correspondingly developed the manual, visual, and cognitive skills with which to navigate the serial *paginae* of the scroll. Meanwhile, other initiatives in writing technology sought to match the dimensions of the physical material with the dimensions of the *pagina*. These developments made the platform and the conceptual space of the *pagina* coextensive, examples of which may be seen in the rectangular frame of the wax tablet and, later, the folio of the codex or what is now called the page of the book. Although the scroll and the tablet continued to be used in special situations, the codex with its bound pages was adopted as the favoured vehicle for the transmission of thought by the early Middle Ages.

The codex quickly became the customary method for the graphic communication of ideas after the first century AD, and was employed without hesitation through the greater part of the medieval and modern periods. Two millennia later, the codex continues to hold a central place in the transmission of knowledge, and its particular formulation of the page has become embedded as a default in our cultural imaginary. Because of this practical and conceptual longevity, the term 'page' is now commonly used to refer to the simultaneous and coextensive embodiment of the *pagina* with its material platform in the book. But the page need not exclusively be the page of the book. The page can and has existed outside its unique configuration in the codex, and these alternative incarnations have been sites of important developments in writing technology. This study reconsiders the habituated conflation between the page and the page of the codex; the page, I argue, is not always what we may think it is.

How the Page Matters offers a comparative and historical analysis that challenges present-day assumptions about reading, writing, and the production of texts. Chief among these suppositions is the simple coordination between physical platform, mode of production, and historical period: that is, that pages were written by hand on parchment in the Middle Ages, were printed with moveable type on paper after 1455, and are encoded for digital display in the twenty-first century. As the following study will show, these relationships of materiality, temporality, and context operate in creative and dynamic tension. The strategies of the page may be simultaneous, overlapping, mutually responsive, complementary, and even contradictory, and have been domesticated over a period of centuries, not tied exclusively to one particular platform or mode of production. For instance, parchment is still used by printers today; readers decorate the margins of printed pages with notes and drawings; we increasingly write by hand on digital tablets, pads, and other portable devices; and 'born-digital' documents are printed from our computers onto paper. Even as we innovate now in the twenty-first century, we are drawing upon rich traditions in the design of our scripts and typefaces, the layout of text, image, space, and the paratextual devices of title pages, headings, tables, and indices.

The page transmits ideas, of course, but more significantly influences meaning by its distinctive embodiment of those ideas.[3] Discernible in this embodiment is an ongoing conversation between designers and readers. As writers, artists, translators, scribes, printers, booksellers, librarians, and readers configure and revise the page, in each case they leave redolent clues about how the page matters to them and how they wish it to matter to others. The architecture of the page is thus a complex and responsive entanglement of platform, text, image, graphic markings, and blank space. The page hosts a changing interplay of form and content, of message and medium, of the conceptual and physical, and this shifting tension is vital to the ability of the page to remain persuasive through time.

As a foil for exploring the material and the mattering of the page, this study uses a treatise from the fifteenth century entitled the *Controversia de nobilitate*. The *Controversia* is a debate about the origins of nobility, written around 1428 in Latin by the Florentine humanist Buonaccorso da Montemagno. Within two decades of its composition, the text was circulating in manuscript and print, in Italian, French, German, and English translation on both sides of the Alps. More recently, digital versions of the French and English translations have been released on CD-ROM and the Internet. Because the treatise still survives today in these different iterations from the fifteenth to the twenty-first century – on parchment, paper, and computer, and in manuscript, print, and digital forms – it possesses an ideal material history for our examination of the page.

Tracing the development of the page will allow us to see the extent to which many recent explorations of writing technologies have been circumscribed variously by formal, national, or temporal divides. At present, the study of books continues to be enriched with a plethora of detailed analyses of manuscripts to 1450, meticulous investigations of early modern printed texts, careful assessments of digital informational resources, and introspective ruminations about the future of reading. Much of this research is organized by the boundaries of material and time, despite early efforts by James J. O'Donnell and Roger Chartier to show how these divisions might be traversed.[4] The fragmentation of the history of books was encouraged by the work of Lucien Febvre, Henri-Jean Martin, and Elizabeth Eisenstein, which cast the printing press as a major force of change in the development of Western civilization.[5] These scholars created a rift in the traditional landscape of the study of books by characterizing the age of print as a discrete period in history with its own particular culture of readers and writers. For Eisenstein, the advent of the printing press heralded a new epoch in the diffusion of knowledge because a text could apparently be 'fixed' and replicated with no degradation.[6] The era of print was thus distinguished by the circulation of stable and identical texts in contrast to the earlier age of manuscript, which Eisenstein imagined to have suffered from an uneven transmission of progressively corrupt texts. It was contended that the arrival of the printing press freed Western society from the fallibility of hand-copied books and initiated the next phase in communication. Moreover, Eisenstein argued that the standardization of texts that was engendered by printing technology in turn gave rise to a new social order. This order, a specialized group of writers, readers, and artisans, came to understand books in a fundamentally different way from their predecessors, whose intellectual activities, it was believed, had been encumbered by the inconsistencies and deficiencies of manuscripts.

Owing to the labours of Eisenstein and others, the printed book emerged as a cultural artefact that was fit for historical analysis. Bibliographers and textual editors such as D.F. McKenzie and Jerome McGann further constituted the printed book as material evidence of the past by encouraging the exploration of 'bibliographic codes' of particular editions and the investigation of social histories or 'sociologies' of printed texts that identified the particular circumstances of their production, circulation, and reception.[7] Moreover, the complementary notion of a 'print culture' was introduced to define a community that could be studied for its habits of reading and writing. The 'printed book' and 'print culture' were thus circumscribed as approved entities for scholarly investigation; disciplinary recognition enabled historians and literary scholars to understand the printed book as a site for explorations of the use and reception of a text, and also provided warrant for the examination of specific readers and their activities.

But these efforts to demarcate the printed book as a locus for the investigation of reading and writing practices have also fractured the broader history of the codex and communication technologies. The favour shown to the printed book has quietly eroded the significance of its manuscript counterpart, and the privileging of a print culture has likewise diverted attention from earlier developments in the transmission of ideas. More than three decades after its publication, Eisenstein's thesis continues to shape discussions about the history of the writing technologies, with much attention being given to supporting, elaborating, and even refuting the idea of a print revolution.[8] Scholars in the late twentieth century found Eisenstein's correlation of technological change and socio-cultural revolution especially attractive as they struggled to gain perspective on the contemporary shifts in communication that they were themselves experiencing. Like the introduction of the printing press before it, the advent of digital media was thought to signal the beginning of a new age that was to experience similarly profound changes in reading and writing. The death of the printed book was proclaimed as an imminent and inevitable conclusion, with print culture soon to be supplanted by a digital successor. The 'print revolution' and the 'digital revolution' were quickly constituted as comparable if not equivalent discontinuities in the history of books and reading.[9] The reiteration of these notions in both scholarly literature and popular culture established the two 'revolutions' as major signposts in the cultural imagination, and guided the direction of future research by indicating that the history of textual transmission should be viewed in terms of a material or technological division.

In order to examine the traditions of graphic communication across these discontinuities, *How the Page Matters* proposes an alternative history that is organized around the page. Despite its key role in the codex, the page has not yet been analysed in detail,[10] and has therefore escaped being scored by the conventional divisions of medium, language, and geographical area. Reappearing in different contexts through time, the page invites us to bridge these boundaries and explore how and why its communicative space continues to matter, both within and without the codex. The next chapters explore the ways in which the materiality of the page influences its own reception across technology, language, geography, and time by using examples drawn from the *Controversia de nobilitate* and its translations. To establish a footing for this investigation, chapter 1, 'Architectures of the Page,' surveys the different kinds of material platform that have been used in the construction of the page over the past two millennia, as well as the different rhetorical strategies that have been deployed in the layout of text and image. By identifying and examining the functions of different components of the page, the discussion shows how these routinely overlooked elements are critical in the expression of ideas and are indeed an important part of the signifying strategies of the page. Chapter 1 thus begins to uncover the dynamic relationship between the material embodiment of the page and its mattering, and furthermore proposes a way in which to investigate the complex expression of the page which is constituted of both – and more than – form and content.

With the foundations for a historical and theoretical analysis of the page thus established, chapter 2 investigates a range of examples that have been selected from the surviving manuscripts and printed books of the *Controversia de nobilitate* and its translations. The chapter considers how certain elements of the pages of Buonaccorso's text, such as the choice of script, type, image, and physical platform, may be interpreted by different audiences. Although these aspects of the page are often deemed inconsequential or even accidental, the examination reveals how one arrangement of material elements can associate the *Controversia* with a particular tradition at the same time that a different configuration can identify the treatise as a participant in another. By studying the ways in which the construction of the page has influenced the transmission of the *Controversia de nobilitate*, chapter 2 brings to light the fundamental role of the materiality of the page in its meaning and mattering.

Chapter 3, 'The Paratext and the Page,' explores the impact of title pages, dedications, and other paratextual mechanisms upon the trajectory of the *Controversia*. The chapter examines how designers used these devices to consolidate their own reputations, customize the treatise for new audiences, and otherwise direct the reception of the *Controversia de nobilitate*. Paratexts shape the page graphically and cognitively, and chapter 3 tracks the ways in which these devices have exerted pressure on the treatment of the *Controversia*. Building upon the previous chapter, 'The Paratext and the Page' demonstrates that ostensibly minor features of the pages of the *Controversia* can significantly affect the interpretation of the treatise.

Chapter 4 shows that the materiality of the page can be entangled in meanings which resonate far beyond a localized study of a particular text or codex. This chapter explicitly addresses the mattering of the page by examining how the books of the *Controversia de nobilitate* and its translations become implicated in the longer trails of the production and representation of knowledge as they are catalogued and stored in the library. The exploration first raises questions about the function of the library by analysing the description of the book collection in the text of the *Controversia* as a phenotypic response to, and contemporary critique of, fifteenth-century notions of spaces of study. These questions are further pursued in an interrogation of the arrangement of the books of the *Controversia* in the intellectual and architectural spaces of the modern library, specifically, those of the Bibliothèque nationale de France. 'Reading the Library' considers how the principles that govern the library of the twenty-first century can shape the presentation and reception of a late medieval treatise, and thus contribute to a further dynamic of meaning and mattering in the pages of the *Controversia de nobilitate*.

Lastly, chapter 5 offers an investigation of the relationship between materiality and meaning in the newest versions of the *Controversia de nobilitate*. The page in its digital instantiation is yet another phase in the long history of graphic transmission and therefore shares the same lineage as its counterparts in the scroll and the codex. This chapter finds that the latest pages of the *Controversia* are imbricated with multiple strategies of expression. The digitized pages are configured by both traditional and emergent approaches, and informed by both cultural and computational codes. The approaches and codes that underpin Buonaccorso's treatise in the digital environment determine which pages have been made available, how, and why, and together constitute a system that influences the ways in which the *Controversia de nobilitate* now matters.

In our haste to establish a history of the book, we have read the page too quickly. The page has remained a favoured space and metaphor for the graphic communication of ideas over the span of centuries and across different cultural milieux. Handwritten, printed, and digital pages – as well as their hybrid combinations – continue to be generated, circulated, and read today.[11] Yet the page has become transparent, 'disappearing in its very function.'[12] So accustomed to its form, we no longer notice how the page is fundamental to the transmission of ideas and that it shapes our interpretation of those ideas. *How the Page Matters* seeks to remedy this oversight by examining the page as a cultural phenomenon, the product of local circumstances as well as participant in a long tradition of graphic communication and knowledge production. More than a diachronic exploration of the interface, then, this study argues that each page facilitates, circumscribes, and even checks the transmission of thought. The next chapters investigate the dynamic relationship between the materiality and meaning in the *Controversia de nobilitate*, and in so doing will at last draw attention to the significance of the page in the intellectual and artistic traditions of the West.

1

Architectures of the Page

The page has played a central role in preserving the intellectual and artistic traditions of the West for over two millennia. In its long service to the graphic communication of thought, the page has crucially influenced how ideas matter. The page is more than a simple vehicle or container for the transmission of ideas; it is a part of those ideas, entangled in the story itself. The platform of the page, the markings inscribed upon it, and the odours that issue from it together constitute a message. As Don McKenzie has observed, these non-verbal elements have 'an expressive function in conveying meaning.'[1] Yet despite its central role in the transmission of thought, the page often passes without registration or remark. So habituated to its operation, we often overlook how the page sets the parameters for our engagement with ideas.

As interest in the printed book has grown over the last fifty years, so too has interest in its particular version of the page. Much of this research was conducted at the turn of the twenty-first century in response to the prophesies about an imminent 'digital revolution' that was to bring about the demise of the codex. In an attempt to gain perspective on the cultural importance of the book, scholars posited an analogous social transformation in the fifteenth century that they called a 'print revolution.' A discrete era was thus created that began with the arrival of the printing press in the West and, arguably, ended with the universal adoption of computational technologies for the transmission of knowledge. The introduction of the printing press in late medieval Europe and the advent of digital technologies some five centuries later were characterized as profound turning points in history, equally credited with instigating new periods in the production and transmission of information. The reiteration of a print and digital 'revolution' in both scholarly and popular venues etched the paired notion in the cultural imaginary, and furthermore signalled that the history of writing technologies – and the book in particular – was to be understood in terms of technological supersession.

The adoption of a model of supersession allowed the codex to be uncritically divided according to time and manner of production. Intellectual rifts were drawn between manuscripts, printed books, and their digital counterparts, with scholars from different disciplines formulating their own methods of analysis. The physical platform of the codex has consequently been apportioned out for exploration; alternately, in its early instantiations to classical scholars, in its parchment embodiment to codicologists, and in its printed paper form to bibliographers.[2] Thus, how a message has been transmitted in the codex might be investigated by palaeographers who study script and layout in manuscripts, or by graphic artists who study the same in print.[3] If transmitting text, the book might be considered the domain of historians and literary scholars; if transmitting image or notation, the domain of art historians or musicologists.[4] Meanwhile, the examination of digitally encoded texts and online resources has been identified as the field of scholars of new media, information specialists, coders, and the next generation of textual editors.[5]

The page has been explored to some degree in the peripheries of these investigations of the book, but a critical analysis of its role in the transmission and preservation of knowledge – both within and without the codex – is still wanting. By bringing together relevant discussions from across the disciplines, the present chapter seeks to build a foundation for examining the dynamic relationship of materiality and mattering in the page. This particular history bridges the traditional divisions of time, mode of production, and media, as well as the intellectual boundaries that have separated text from image and form from content. To permit an analysis of matter and meaning, the physical and rhetorical strategies of the page must first be identified and disambiguated, although they work together in practice to communicate ideas . For the purposes of clarity, then, the ensuing discussion of the page will be roughly divided into two sections, the first dealing with the broader issues of material and construction, and the second with the more specific issues of *mise en page* or layout, encompassing letter forms, blank space, images, and decoration.

Whether thick, thin, brittle, smooth, dog-eared, or stained, every page discloses a unique identity that has been shaped by cultural forces over time. This identity is susceptible to change across different reading communities, but the material cues provided by the page perdure and are always present in the transmission of ideas. Designers make calculated decisions regarding the size, shape, colour, and quality of the material to suggest to readers what kind of page it is and how they wish it to be treated. Although a handwritten folio of animal skin in a medieval manuscript is as much a page as the leaf of a mass-produced paperback, the characteristics of each communicate vastly different messages about their respective manufacture, circulation, and cultural value. In this way, the construction of the page can be read as evidence of its social history.

The scrolls of antiquity are of particular interest because they show that the page need not always be physically circumscribed as it is in the codex, thus challenging the notion that the page is unique to one particular form. In the classical period, scrolls were made from papyrus, a plant that grew in abundance along the Nile River.[6] The stems of the papyrus reeds could be made into a pliable material for writing, while other parts of the plant were harvested for food and medicine, or used in clothing, baskets, ropes, boats, and sails. Because papyrus was an important resource for communities living around the Mediterranean, changes in the manufacture of papyrus-based products can be considered indications of broader social change. Indeed, E.G. Turner observed a shift in writing material of the first century AD, when the papyrus sheets became larger but were of lesser quality than their forebears: stalks that would previously have been discarded were beginning to be used for writing material in the later period.[7] The use of stems that had once been regarded as substandard suggests that manufacturers were responding to the economic climate of the Mediterranean basin, where the cultivation of papyrus could not keep up with growing demand.

Writing material is constructed from the papyrus plant by gluing long, thin strips of the stem together in two layers, one at right angles to the other. As the strips are pounded together, the papyrus secretes a naturally sticky residue that acts as an adhesive. The individual pieces are thus pasted into a single sheet that is composed of two layers of strips; the fibres run horizontally on one side and vertically on the other. Extant sheets of papyrus are generally of slightly smaller proportions than the modern letter-sized (8½ by 11 inches) page, 25 by 19 centimetres compared with 21.6 by 28 centimetres. The height of the sheet was in part restricted by the natural limitations of the papyrus plant, the usable stems of which rarely exceeded 40 centimetres in length. To create a longer roll of writing material, twenty or more of these sheets would be lined up, one slightly overlapping the next, and pasted together. Egyptian scrolls could be as long as 20 or 30 metres, although their Greek counterparts were more often around 10 metres in length.[8] Additional sheets were appended to accommodate longer texts, and the roll was easily trimmed of excess if necessary. Using a brush to glide over the fibres of the papyrus, scribes painted text and image in columns that were laid out from left to right across the length of the scroll. The columns were usually oriented in a series, sometimes running over the joins of the individual sheets, so that the length of the scroll would be held horizontally and unfurled section by section.[9] Once written or read, the columns disappeared from view as the scroll was rolled up with the left hand and more papyrus was unrolled with the right.

The columns were called *paginae*, or pages, and constituted the chief method of organizing information on the scroll. Although often narrower in breadth, a single *pagina* measures about the same as the text block of a modern letter-sized page. Surviving *paginae* are composed of between twenty-five and forty-five lines, the spacing of which was calculated in accordance with the dimensions of the particular papyrus sheets.[10] For instance, the *paginae* of a small scroll only twelve centimetres high, half the size of an average roll, may still transmit around twenty-five lines. Differences in the layout of the *paginae* appear to be related to the kind of text being transmitted. For verse, many extant scrolls display columns that measure around fifteen centimetres wide, set apart from each other by a margin of about one centimetre. By contrast, prose texts are arranged in narrower *paginae*, about six or seven centimetres in width, separated by a margin of one to one-and-one-half centimetres.[11] In addition to being customized according to the genre of text being transmitted, the design of columns was also influenced by the intended quality of the product. Deluxe scrolls exhibit *paginae* of smaller dimensions that are bounded by wider margins. Furthermore, some *paginae* were executed with a forward-sloping angle, each line of the column inscribed slightly to the left of its predecessor.[12] The overarching commonalities in the disposition of columns suggest that designers understood the *pagina* as an organizational device that set important controls on the transmission of ideas and facilitated successful communication. At the same time, graphic conventions were established to distinguish the luxury product from its more utilitarian counterpart, and this aesthetic variation indicates that the *pagina* was understood as a flexible interface that could be tailored in size, shape, and layout according to the requirements and sensibilities of designer and reader. .

The *pagina* thus emerges in the scroll as a conceptual structure by which information could be organized; it visually divides the long roll of writing material into shorter sections for the effective transmission of ideas. The *pagina* does not necessarily rely on a physical distinction to communicate its boundaries to readers. Instead, the careful arrangement of text and space graphically shows readers where they should read and indicates where they should stop. Designers craft the 'page' of the scroll by juxtaposing text with the absence of text, or image with the absence of image. As the scroll shows, the *pagina* need not be accompanied by an attendant material division. Nevertheless, each *pagina* in the roll possesses its own physicality – one that places it in close proximity to other *paginae*, requires a slow unfurling of the scroll, and encourages a practice of continuous reading.[13]

The scroll could also be configured in a number of ways that allowed its *paginae* to be articulated physically. The concertina-style scroll, for instance, is a long roll that is folded like an accordion, with one *pagina* doubled behind the next. The boundaries of individual *paginae* are reinforced with creases and folds of the material platform; a reader may decide to unfold the entire scroll, thus revealing all the *paginae* at once, or view the columns sequentially, with subsequent *paginae* hidden from view until unfolded. The scroll can also be bound whirlwind-style, a technique in which the roll is cut into pieces of increasing length that are then stacked together and secured along one edge.[14] The early *pagina* was thus circumscribed in different kinds of scrolls as well as in the discrete writing surfaces fashioned from bits of leaf or bark or shards of pottery.

It was, however, in the wax tablet that a physical structure was devised to match and help circumscribe the intellectual unit of the *pagina* materially. The tablet is composed of a wooden rectangular frame, the hollow of which is designed to be filled with a thin layer of tinted wax.[15] The tablet was particularly useful in the drafting of letters, musical notation, and school exercises; letter forms could be inscribed into the yielding wax with a stylus and subsequently smoothed over and erased with the blunt end of the tool. Because only one face of the tablet could be filled with wax, multiple frames were often hinged together with a strip of leather or ring to increase the usable writing surface. This arrangement permitted the transmission of more text, and also allowed the two panels of wax to be closed in upon each other for protection during transportation. The edges of the wax and the frame of the tablet circumscribe the approved space of reading and writing in unambiguous physical terms, and these borders were acknowledged and respected by readers and writers alike. Even when the wax had expired, the depression in the frame was nevertheless recognized as the conventional space of writing; inscriptions can still be seen scratched or written in ink directly in the hollow of the tablet. Like its more familiar modern versions in the tablet computer, PDA, and mobile phone, the frame of the wax tablet marks the edges of the cognitive space of the page, providing clear direction about where information should be written and read.

A similar dynamic is enacted by the page of the codex, a format that began to be adopted in the West around the first century AD. Based on the hinged design of the wax tablet, the codex uses a central spine to bind multiple sheets of writing material together. Whereas the wax tablet only explicitly supports a single *pagina* on one of its faces, the folio of the codex offers space for the graphic transmission of ideas on its *recto* and *verso* – both the front and back sides. Alternative sources for the material of the page soon began to be sought out as the skills of reading and writing spread to areas outside the Mediterranean basin and away from regions that cultivated the papyrus plant.[16] Sheep and goats could be raised throughout most of Europe, and the skins of such animals made for a sturdy support for writing called parchment that was soon widely embraced in the medieval West.[17] Thinner, smoother, and whiter parchments were considered better writing material, as were those produced from the skins of calves or kids. Parchments destined for special products could be coloured with dyes or other pigments, such as those from which the purple pages of the sixth-century *Codex Argenteus* were made.[18]

Although paper had been used as writing material in China almost a millennium earlier, it was not taken up for the construction of the page in the West until the eleventh century.[19] Higher grades of paper were made from crushed and fermented white linen rags; meanwhile, coloured linen, scraps of canvas, or bits of rope were used for products of lesser quality. But even after the introduction of paper, parchment continued to be used for the production of many books and documentary sources throughout the medieval and early modern periods. As shall be explored in the next chapters, the choice

13

to use parchment or paper – when both are available – conveys important information about the history of that particular page, the environment in which it was constructed, and the purpose and audience for which it was intended.

The page as it is now commonly understood may be a single sheet of writing material that physically reinforces the boundaries of the *pagina*. The four edges of the page, perhaps papyrus, parchment, or paper, tell both the designer and reader where the space of communication begins and ends. As a single sheet, the page may stand free of an obvious attachment with others of its kind. The material boundaries of the solitary page not only circumscribe the space of communication, they also circumscribe the message itself; there is nothing more to be read than what is on the page.

Most of the pages that now appear as singletons were once a part of a larger piece of writing material. This larger sheet would have been folded into a booklet, called a gathering or quire.[20] The folds of the quire would subsequently have been cut apart to generate loose-leaf pages, perhaps for maps, calendars, or bills. If the pages are destined for the codex, however, the central fold of the quire is retained while the others are cut open to make – most commonly – eight folia, or sixteen pages. Any number of these gatherings can then be collected, placed in a stack, and sewn together under a binding. In this arrangement, the page is not encountered as an isolated phenomenon. Two facing pages are presented simultaneously in the codex, the back of one folio, or the *verso*, on the left side, and the front of the next folio, the *recto*, on the right. These two facing pages are not part of the same folio and may not necessarily have been part of the same sheet or the same quire; nevertheless, they have an important contiguous relationship.[21] Adjacent and conjoined, they are perceived together by the reader, even if only read one at a time. With each turn of the page, a new pair of facing pages is unveiled at the same time that the previous couple is obscured from view. As a consequence, the recto and verso of the same folio are in close conversation with their facing counterparts, often depending upon this proximal relationship to sustain the rhetorical coherence of their message.

A quire can be prepared with its pages folded and cut before accruing text or image. The designer is, in this case, confronted with the unambiguous physical arrangement of two blank facing pages. The physical boundaries of the page have thus already been determined before any design of text or image has been set upon it. This particular method of book-making was exploited in the Middle Ages, when the copying of a single manuscript was often shared among multiple skilled hands. Quires intended for the same codex could be doled out for different specialized tasks; some workers would write text upon selected pages at the same time that their colleagues were illustrating others.[22] After the pages had been filled with text and decoration, the quires were collected and sewn together under a binding to form the codex.

The disposition of text and image can also occur before the folding and cutting of the quire. In this approach, the *paginae* do not consistently face the same way on the large sheet of material and do not follow in sequential order.[23] In contrast to the previous technique, the *paginae* here are first graphically expressed in ink on the writing material. Only subsequently will each be given its own physical division. The imposition of individual *paginae* on the writing material must be carefully calculated so that text and image will eventually follow on consecutive folia, right-side-up, after the sheet has proceeded through the final stages of being folded and cut. The design of such pages can be challenging for the under-experienced, and quires from the Middle Ages to the modern day show evidence of errors of imposition.[24] The use of these two methods of preparing quires for the codex means that the visualization of the *pagina* can occur in different ways. Products with similar appearances can have significantly different pedigrees, and by attending to their circumstances of manufacture, the genealogies of diverse pages may begin to be laid bare.

The history of the page is one of overlapping methods, materials, and means; the *paginae* of scrolls and codices have worked concurrently for millennia to organize information and facilitate the transmission of ideas, sometimes on papyrus, sometimes on parchment, and sometimes on paper. For instance, the *paginae* of both scrolls and codices were employed in the communication of literary and Christian writing through the first three centuries AD.[25] Although longer texts, especially those of a literary character, were increasingly transmitted via the codex in the early medieval period, the scroll remained the form preferred for the copying of documents by local, imperial, and papal administrations, as well as by communities involved in trade. Letters, contracts, and bills of sale survive on papyrus rolls from the Middle Ages, and the papal chancery continued to use scrolls to issue official documents and bulls.[26] Meanwhile, the exchequer of England adopted animal skin for its scrolls, detailing the royal accounts on rolls of parchment until the nineteenth century. As these different ways of constructing the page developed, so too did the strategies for arranging text and image on the interface. Complex visual patterns of letter-form, space, and image were cultivated in the *paginae* of scrolls, tablets, and codices.[27] But these patterns remained fluid as readers-cum-designers marked up their pages as they were inclined. Thus revised and augmented by different hands over time, the page emerges as evidence of its own production, performance, and consumption. The markings on the page are a part of the 'cultural residue' left by a battery of authors, scribes, artists, booksellers, book owners, and readers, and can be read as a compelling narrative about the social history of thought.[28]

Words on the page are regularly understood to transmit information through language, but they can convey meaning in other ways. Scholars such as Johanna Drucker, Armando Petrucci, and Stanley Morison have explored the visual dynamic of writing in a variety of contexts, from its epigraphic manifestations on monumental architecture to its typographic instantiations on paper.[29] They found that specific letter forms can infuse a text with social or political suggestion. By generating a particular visual expression, the shapes of letters may, for instance, exploit the authority of an established tradition or diverge self-consciously from conventional patterns.[30] Because the decisions surrounding the deployment of one style of script over another are influenced by social, political, and economic forces, letter forms can be considered part of a broader cultural discourse about the production and transmission of ideas. The disposition of letter shapes may thus be used as a way to explore reading and writing communities.

Likewise, the structures for arranging these letter forms in manuscripts and printed books are graphic indications of how designers visualized ideas and organized them for themselves and other readers. The processes of thinking and reading, then, may be discerned in part from the clues offered by the page. For instance, early Christian copyists and readers developed a method of dividing their texts into paragraphs and chapters to facilitate the consultation of passages from scripture. These designers of the early page also split long lines of prose text into shorter units, arranged as lines of poetry – *per cola et commata* – to aid reading and understanding.[31] Meanwhile, the canon table correlated similar passages of different Gospel texts, and headings helped the readers navigate the codex. These developments indicate shifts, perhaps in reading practices or in readership. When books began to be employed in great numbers by university communities in the twelfth century, designers reallocated their attention to the systematic ordering of information on the page.[32] Scholarly readers often needed to refer to multiple texts at once, and therefore demanded an organizational apparatus in support of their particular reading activities. Sophisticated patterns of ruling were developed to divide the page into units that were conceptually and graphically distinct. This layout permitted designers to set commentaries and glosses adjacent to the passage that was being explicated, and thus transmit a number of different texts in a single *pagina*. The page became an intricate weaving of narratives as scholars and students read their standard texts while consulting the accompanying marginal and interlinear glosses. In the thirteenth century, Vincent of Beauvais discussed the importance of arranging and organizing information on the page in the *apologia* to his compendium, the *Speculum maius*. Vincent explains that he hopes to aid his readers by dividing the *Speculum* into shorter, labelled sections. As Malcolm Parkes has noted, many of the surviving manuscripts of the *Speculum maius* preserve the same pattern of disposition, suggesting that Vincent and his copyists recognized the headings, running titles, and tables to be a critical part of the work that contributed importantly to its transmission.[33] From early Christian manuscripts, to glossed university texts, to liturgical books with illustration and music, the rich variations of the medieval *mise en page* indicate that the interface was understood and exploited as a field of engagement that could be reconfigured as needed.

Although the study of the word is central to many current explorations of books and their materiality, a consideration of its absence is equally valuable. Unmarked zones of the page are purposeful, and participate critically in the communication of ideas.[34]

Blank space is crucial to the activity of reading, and especially silent reading, because it enhances the legibility and comprehensibility of the page.[35] Without these saccadic pauses that allow the eye to skip quickly across a line of text, the process of reading can take more than twice as long. The broader significance of space on the page has been explored by Paul Saenger, who observed that the separation of words in the seventh century was a visible manifestation of the shift from oral reading practices to silent ones.[36] Furthermore, the spaces between words, between lines, and around the text block can be understood as visual and cognitive breaks, employed by designers and readers as a way to moderate the pace of engagement with the page. By leaving space on the page unfilled, designers provide openings for readers to pause and consider the thoughts that they have encountered. Readers are given the opportunity in these zones to contemplate, consider, and question ideas, and may even be encouraged by the empty spaces to add their own thoughts to the page.

Like blank space, image and decoration also work as visual avenues of exchange with readers.[37] The placement of images on the page, for example, is a sign from designers about the value of the illustrations and how they are meant to be read. Illustrations may be designed to displace or replace letter forms, especially if they have been positioned in the centre of the page. In the marginal zones of the page or woven into the letter forms themselves, images can propose an interpretation that is complementary, supplementary, or even contradictory. Meanwhile, images may have no explicit connection with a particular text when isolated on their own pages. Bound in the codex, however, images are placed in proximity to other elements – perhaps letter forms or decorations – and are perceived by readers in terms of this relationship. Moreover, illustrations can refer to the world beyond the page and participate in a wider conversation about the book that involves the social status of the particular codex, its designers, and its owners.[38] For instance, the inclusion of more images in religious books of the later Middle Ages has been identified by scholars as an indication of the emergent practice of private devotion.[39] The designers of Books of Hours catered to their growing audience with a *mise en page* that complemented the activity of personal prayer. Accommodating different reading abilities in the lay population and various methods of devotion, the pages of these customized and portable manuscripts feature rich illustrations, as well as special rubrics, instructions, and prayers.

The layout of printed text has similarly been theorized in the last decades by Gérard Genette and D.F. McKenzie.[40] By analysing the material and graphic elements of the printed book, both scholars sought to develop an understanding of these materials that took into account the circumstances of their production. The scholars identified different visual and verbal cues for critical examination, calling them paratexts and bibliographic signs. These signs include typefaces, title pages, prologues, epilogues, dedications, and chapter headings. The visual and verbal cues are manifest inside, outside, and around the text proper, appearing simultaneously with the text and configuring the reading experience in fundamental ways. Because writing is designed to 'produce effects, dictate a posture, and oblige the reader,' its examination – and the investigation of paratextual devices in particular – can serve to supplement broader explorations of the communication of knowledge.[41]

Similarly, the use of digital technologies in the transmission of ideas has led scholars to begin considering algorithmic code as a culturally pregnant means of shaping the display of text and image. Studies in the areas of new media and digital humanities have shown that the computational code enabling our interaction with information is not neutral, but instead constitutes an intellectual system.[42] This cognitive system establishes patterns in which ideas are presented, organized, and accessed in the digital environment. The entire expression of the digital page is built upon relationships that are both created and concealed by computational code. As Adrian Mackenzie has characterized it, the algorithms underpinning the digital transmission of ideas 'concatenate different regions and neighbourhoods of relations' and hide 'unexpected complexities and inconsistencies.'[43] Understood in this way, the digital page – much like pages in other media – becomes evidence in the longer history of the transmission of thought.

The page is an expressive space for text, space, and image; it is a cultural artefact; it is a technological device. But it is also all of these at once. The ensuing chapters will explore the page as a careful integration of physical and cognitive architectures by using a hybrid approach adapted from methods that have already been established in different disciplines to study the book and book-related issues. The following discussion therefore combines the tools of palaeographers, codicologists, art historians, literary critics, and new media theorists to examine the complicated synthesis of rhetorical, intellectual, and physical elements of the pages of a fifteenth-century treatise. This treatise, the *Controversia de nobilitate*, has been transmitted in manuscript, print, photograph, and microfilm, and on computer across diverse linguistic, geographical, and cultural boundaries. As the next chapters will demonstrate, designers and readers have imagined the text with different configurations of materials, letter forms, spaces, and images. In so doing, they have proposed their own interpretations of the *Controversia de nobilitate* and shaped its reception through six centuries of history.

The *Controversia de nobilitate* was written in Latin around 1428 by Buonaccorso da Montemagno, and provides a wealth of evidence to support an investigation of the page.[44] Multiple copies of the treatise survive in handwritten, printed, and digital forms. Over a hundred manuscript copies from the fifteenth century are preserved today in libraries across the Italian peninsula, from the Biblioteca Ambrosiana in Milan, to the Vatican Library, to the Biblioteca Nazionale Marciana in Venice. In addition, a number of translations of the *Controversia de nobilitate* survive from the same period. The Italian and French translations are extant in handwritten copies, and the *Controversia* was printed in Latin, Italian, French, German, and English before 1501. More recently, two versions of the *Controversia* have appeared in the digital environment, Jean Miélot's fifteenth-century French translation on CD-ROM and the English translation of 1481 in an online database.

Originally from Pistoia, Buonaccorso da Montemagno moved to Florence, where he worked as a jurist, diplomat, and scholar.[45] He was one of a number of writers in the humanist milieu of Florence to take up the question of nobility, which he did in the *Controversia de nobilitate*. Whether nobility was endowed by birthright alone was a debate of some interest in the fifteenth century, a part of the humanist revival of classical themes. Indeed, both Plato and Aristotle had explored the nature of an elite social class. In the *Nicomachean Ethics* and the *Politics*, Aristotle recognized that good family connections and wealth were important for the acquisition of virtue, but so too were rational thought and contemplation.[46] Similarly, in the story of the *Controversia de nobilitate*, Buonaccorso explores whether a noble character is only passed down through birthright or whether it must be cultivated with labour and outstanding civic service. He stages the traditional question as a debate in ancient Rome between two suitors, Publius Cornelius Scipio and Gaius Flaminius, who are competing for the hand of the virtuous Lucretia. To determine which man is worthy of being her husband, Lucretia and her father ask the suitors to engage in a debate about their respective nobility. They must argue their cases in front of the senate, and Lucretia will marry the man who is deemed the winner of the contest.

The *Controversia* is organized as two extended monologues, with Cornelius speaking first. Cornelius contends that nobility can only be passed through the bloodlines. He argues that virtue is inherited, transferred from parent to child. Because he is of a highly ranked family, Cornelius says that nobility is in his blood and bones, and can be detected through a close inspection of his countenance. He uses the public statues and memorials of his ancestors as evidence of his personal nobility. These are to be understood as visible records that remind the public of the debt owed his family and, by extension, him. Moreover, Cornelius believes that his conspicuous wealth should garner him much esteem. Arguing that prestige follows fortune, he enumerates the properties left to him by his family, including the country estates where he spends his time on leisurely pursuits. He also provides an inventory of the material goods – magnificent family heirlooms, opulent furniture, sumptuous jewellery – that would be available to Lucretia should she choose to marry him. She would have an easy and relaxed life with him, he declares, with no material care in the world. Servants would meet her every need, and she would pass her days unencumbered, hunting, singing, and playing music in the company of her maidens.

Countering Cornelius's argument, Flaminius contends that nobility does not travel through bloodlines and therefore cannot be assumed by familial association. Instead, nobility must be attained by each individual and, furthermore, renewed continually through work. In support of his argument, he cites cases in which poor men achieved respect and gained social status on the basis of their own merit. For instance, Flaminius says, Servius Tullius and Marcus Porcius Cato were of humble families, the former being a son of slaves; both distinguished themselves through their military prowess to become two of the most highly regarded men of Rome. Flaminius adds that lowly origins did not hinder Socrates, Euripides, or Demosthenes from achieving great repute. He also provides examples to illustrate that poverty need not preclude nobility. To make his point, he recalls the story of Lucius Quintus Cincinnatus, a farmer who was eventually nominated to the esteemed office of dictator by the Roman senate. Flaminius argues that like these great men, he has also distinguished himself in his military service to Rome. More recently, he has turned his attention to the study of philosophy with Latin and Greek masters. He contends that his books and library are important signifiers of virtue; they are material evidence of his nobility to be contrasted with the rich home furnishings of Cornelius. Flaminius says to Lucretia, '[In my home,] you will see my library filled with books, in which I have placed all my hope. These are indeed illustrious household goods.'[47] To counter the inventory of jewellery and heirlooms offered by Cornelius, Flaminius gestures to the collection of books in his library. Thus presented to bear witness to the virtuous character of its owner and his home, the library emerges as an important symbol in the debate about nobility and more broadly indicates the appeal of such a space to Buonaccorso and his contemporaries.

Over the course of six hundred years, Buonaccorso's treatise has been copied, recopied, and translated in various ways. Yet the text of the *Controversia de nobilitate* has remained remarkably consistent. The most dramatic changes to the *Controversia* are in the design of its pages. The material fluidity of texts in general has been noted by Henri-Jean Martin, who writes: 'Even in periods of apparent stability, ... traditional texts were ceaselessly revised, adapted, translated, and changed in their physical aspect to bring them into line with the spirit of the times and to make them appeal to a specific public. The presentation of written texts – one might say, the 'staging' of the written work – never stopped evolving.'[48] As will become evident in the next chapters, Buonaccorso's treatise continues to be reincarnated in different guises for different audiences. An examination of the history of the *Controversia de nobilitate* reveals that designers are even today 're-staging' Buonaccorso's composition for their readers. These material variations mark important shifts in the perception and use of the treatise; the differences in the materiality of the page are differences in meaning.

Designers have used a range of materials as well as an assortment of letter forms, colours, and combinations of text, space, and image to propose their own interpretations of Buonaccorso's story. Outfitted with different paratextual codes, the *Controversia* can be presented as a rhetorical exercise, a courtly romance, a scholarly tract, or a precious relic. These ways of reading the *Controversia de nobilitate* are further reinforced by the parcelling of the treatise with texts of more established repute: the pages of the *Controversia* are placed in close proximity to aspirational ones in hopes of consolidating a particular identity for Buonaccorso's treatise. The different material contexts of the *Controversia de nobilitate* have accrued for the text multiple, varied, and overlapping identities. These guises are still in force today and establish the grounds upon which the treatise is received and understood.

Whether a product of manuscript, print, digital, or hybrid technologies, the page of the *Controversia de nobilitate* constitutes a thick network of expressions that continues to be augmented as it passes through history. Readers interpret text, space, and image as they are inclined, but the meanings that they formulate are predicated upon the materiality of each carefully designed page.[49] The page is thus an interface, standing at the centre of the complicated dynamic of intention and reception; it is the material manifestation of an ongoing conversation between designer and reader. The page has borne witness to this rich exchange for centuries, and will continue to do so for many more. For its long-standing participation in the transmission of knowledge in the West, we shall begin our exploration of how the page matters.

2

Reading the Page

Over the past five centuries, the *Controversia de nobilitate* has been copied in a multitude of ways, each instantiation presenting the treatise in a new light. Designers have rewritten Buonaccorso da Montemagno's debate by hand, translated it, printed it on parchment and paper, imagined it with illustrations, microfilmed it, and encoded it for digital access in an effort to communicate with new audiences through time. The construction of the page, including the layout of text, space, and image, all help to embody a message. Consequently, every page of the *Controversia de nobilitate* can be read as material evidence of an ongoing conversation between designer and reader. This chapter, 'Reading the Page,' explores how letter-form, space, and image have shaped the transmission and reception of the *Controversia de nobilitate*. By analysing a handful of examples from the *Controversia*, the investigation will track the ways in which the graphic layout of the page can propose different identities for Buonaccorso's treatise, and consider the significance of these identities for designers and readers.

The *Controversia de nobilitate* was written by Buonaccorso da Montemagno around 1428. In the treatise, Buonaccorso explores whether a virtuous character can be earned through study rather than endowed through the traditional avenue of genealogy. Like others in the humanist circles of Florence, Buonaccorso was interested in classical scholarship and drew from these sources for the topics and structures of his compositions.[1] He followed guides such as the *De inventione* of Cicero, the *Institutio oratoria* of Quintilian, and the *Rhetorica ad Herennium*, and adapted from them the rhetorical forms of the dialogue and the *controversia* for the *Controversia de nobilitate*.[2] The *controversia* is a type of declamation that was commonly employed to rehearse judicial oratory, structured as a pair of speeches for and against an imaginary defendant. Stock themes and settings established an unobtrusive backdrop against which writers and orators could highlight the construction and argumentation of their cases. The creativity of both the classical and fifteenth-century rhetorician was therefore expressed by the unconventional use of historical characters or the clever juxtaposition of modes of argument.[3] Working within the parameters of the *controversia*, Buonaccorso staged his debate in the classical past, using the names of such legendary characters as Lucretia, Cornelius Scipio, and Gaius Flaminius to vivify the story.

Classical models were employed not only in designing the form of the *Controversia de nobilitate*, but also in developing its content. Indeed, whether nobility could be attained through hard work had been discussed as early as Plato and Aristotle. Because of their exposure to these classical sources, humanist readers were already familiar with the topic and arguments of Buonaccorso's debate. However, in order for the *Controversia* to be accepted and succeed as a treatise in humanist circles, its material expression needed to match its classicizing content and rhetorical structure. As Buonaccorso's treatise was copied and recopied in and around Florence, the pages were configured so that the *Controversia* would be recognized as a particular kind of text. A product of and for the humanist milieu, the *Controversia* was engineered to look the part. The manuscripts of the *Controversia* declare themselves participants in the classicizing tradition by verbally communicating the likeness to readers, of course, but also graphically. The graphic correlation of the *Controversia de nobilitate* with existing manuscripts in humanist circles constituted an assertion about the identity of Buonaccorso, his treatise, and its audience. At the same time that the content of the *Controversia* recalls classical tropes favoured by humanist readers, the page of the *Controversia de nobilitate* employs visual tropes favoured by the same audience.

One of the most distinctive characteristics in the manuscript tradition of the humanists is a particular style of letter forms called the Humanistic hand. The Humanistic script was developed in Florence around 1400 by Coluccio Salutati, Niccolò Niccoli, and Poggio Bracciolini.[4] Letter shapes in this classicizing style are characteristically round and wide, and the vertical strokes that are manifest in letters such as *d* or *p* – called ascenders and descenders – are long, extending beyond the main body of the letter. The script recalls earlier models of writing, specifically the Carolingian hand that was in use between the eighth and twelfth centuries, which itself was based on classical archetypes. As humanist scholars revisited classical themes and motifs in their compositions, they further emphasized this relationship with the past by using the Humanistic script. The script enabled the humanists to display a connection with those whom they considered their intellectual forebears. In proposing this link with classical scholars and scholarship, the humanists hoped to add a sense of authority to their own work. The pages consequently served as a verbal and visual reference to classical sources, transmitting claims about the scholarly apparatus of the humanists, as well as their intellectual pedigree and social aspirations. As the treatises were copied, circulated, and recopied in the Humanistic hand, the association between the texts and the script that was at first an assertion became fixed more securely in the cultural imagination of those inside and outside humanist milieux.[5]

A variety of Humanistic hands, from formal book scripts to rapid cursives, were used to transmit the *Controversia de nobilitate*. An example of one of these hands can be found in the fifteenth-century manuscript Florence, Biblioteca Riccardiana, MS 660 (plate 1).[6] The manuscript is one of a handful of copies of the *Controversia* that survive on parchment.[7] A product of good quality, this incarnation of the *Controversia de nobilitate* has benefited from more attention to detail than some of its contemporary counterparts on paper; in this way, the parchment material of the page may be taken as an indicator of added care and thus social value. Characteristic of the Humanistic style of writing, the *d* has a tall vertical ascender; the *g* is written with two compartments; and the tall *s* is used. The *ct* ligature that binds the two letters together is a custom adopted from the earlier Carolingian hand. The *a* has two compartments; this execution of the letter-form is sometimes used to distinguish the formal book-hands from their cursive variations, which use a single-compartment *a*.[8] The regular occurrence of blank space gives the page a look of graphic consistency, and a great effort has been made to create visual uniformity in the text block of twenty-six long lines. The words of the treatise have been generously spaced to ensure maximum legibility, abbreviations are rare, and capital letters articulate the body of the text. Opening the *Controversia* in MS 660 are the Square letter *A* and Rustic majuscule letters, which recall epigraphic sources that date from at least the fourth century.[9] The implicit association of the initials with the culture of ancient Rome reinforces the link with the past and, by extension, helps to bolster the claim of the humanists to a specific intellectual heritage that was rooted in antiquity.

Scripts are fluid and subject to cross-fertilization, and the hand in MS 660 displays a familiarity with the cursive variations of the Humanistic script that were being practised by many scholars, clerks, and copyists in the fifteenth century. In contrast to book-hands, cursive forms of writing are designed to facilitate speed. They are executed in a running line, and are thus characterized by an emphasis on the horizontal axis rather than the vertical.[10] Cursive hands were primarily employed for documentary purposes in business and administration, but began to be adopted in more general use towards the latter part of the fifteenth century. A cursive hand is found in the manuscript Florence, Biblioteca Riccardiana, MS 671 (plate 2).[11] As witnessed in the previous example, the *d* has a straight, vertical ascender, and the tall *s* is again used. In addition, the ampersand is employed to indicate *et*, and the *ct* ligature is in evidence. In contrast to the double-compartment *a* of the book-hand in MS 660, the *a* with a single bow, which can be executed with more speed, is preferred.

Because the cursive joins letter shapes together, the style of writing is often considered more difficult to read than a formal book-hand that individually articulates each letter. Moreover, there is a greater tendency to use abbreviations while writing in a cursive, which can contribute to misreadings. To mitigate the disadvantages of the cursive hand, the designers of MS 671 arranged for generous amounts of blank space to be left on their pages. Although the dimensions of this paper manuscript are greater than those of the parchment example discussed earlier, the size of the text block has not been expanded accordingly.[12] The ruling of the paper page in MS 671 accommodates a large margin around the text block and substantial space between the lines; as a result, there is more blank space on the pages of MS 671 than on those of MS 660. The liberal amount of blank space aids the reading of the cursive hand and grants the page an appearance of order.[13]

Although it may seem a given that a text written by a humanist should be copied in a Humanistic hand, this correlation is a deliberate invention of identity. The purposeful creation of a humanist guise for the *Controversia de nobilitate* can be perceived more clearly when the pages of MSS 660 and 671 are juxtaposed with those that transmit Buonaccorso's debate in another style of writing. The majority of the extant manuscripts of the *Controversia* employ Humanistic scripts, but there are an important few that do not. The existence and survival of the *Controversia* in other hands suggest that the connection between a text and the particular script with which it is transmitted is contingent, the result of a decision influenced by socio-cultural, political, and economic factors. The Gothic script was the dominant style of formal writing in the West from the twelfth to the fifteenth century, having emerged about three hundred years before the development of the Humanistic hand. In contrast to the broad, round forms of the Carolingian and Humanistic scripts, the Gothic hand is characterized by angular, narrow letter shapes that appear to have been compressed laterally.[14] This compression is accentuated by letter-biting, or the fusion of adjacent letters. Moreover, in contrast to the ascenders and descenders of the earlier Carolingian and the later Humanistic hands, those of the Gothic hand are squat, staying close to the main body of the letter-form. Another distinguishing feature is the use of feet, decorative markings that are added to the extremities of letters; feet may be employed to give the page a strong sense of visual uniformity.

A mixture of Gothic and Humanistic letter-forms can be seen on the pages of some manuscripts of the *Controversia* that date from the fifteenth century.[15] For instance, the hand in Florence, Biblioteca Riccardiana, MS 779 is a hybrid cursive that draws upon both styles of script (plate 3).[16] Gothic and Humanistic letter-forms are written adjacent to each other throughout the text. The single-compartment *g*, typical of the Gothic script, is employed even within the same word as the double-compartment *g* of the Humanistic hand. Humanistic influences can also be detected in the straight-backed *d* in contrast to the Gothic sloped-back *d*, which is also in evidence. The predilection for the tall *s* shape is a Humanistic tendency, while the stylized *v* is characteristic of the Gothic hand.

Buonaccorso's treatise is copied in a cursive variation of the Gothic script in London, British Library, Harley 1883 (plate 4).[17] The sloped-back *d* is again in evidence, and notable features in this example include the horned *g* and *p* that add a calligraphic look to the page. The *a* is of the single-compartment variety, consistent with the cursive shape of the letter forms. The opening initial *A* is decorated with a pen drawing of a fish. Other large initials are executed in red ink, visually demarcating the significant breaks in the text. Red ink also highlights the presence of capital letters throughout the text. As was the convention in the north, the text is arranged in two columns, here consisting of forty lines each.[18] The two-columned format provides a generous allotment of blank space on the page and, as Albert Derolez has observed, embodies a particular aesthetic of verticality that was especially appreciated by the designers and readers of Gothic manuscripts.[19]

Despite the differences in the *mise en page* of Buonaccorso's treatise, the story of the *Controversia de nobilitate* remained intact as it travelled across the Alps. Furthermore, the debate continued to be copied with the same texts with which it had circulated on the Italian peninsula, such as Cicero's *De inventione*, as well as letters, orations, and translations of Greek authors. The copying of these same works in Gothic hands suggests that there was no fundamental link between classical and classicizing texts and their disposition in the Humanistic script. The cultural information that was encoded in the Humanistic hand did not resonate in the north in the same way that it did on the Italian peninsula. There was no pressure to create or perpetuate a specifically humanist identity for these texts, their writers, or their readers. The examples of the *Controversia* of northern provenance therefore show that the connection between a text written by a humanist and the use of the Humanistic script for its transmission was not predetermined; the copying of the *Controversia* in Gothic hands suggests moreover that the association of humanistic writings with Humanistic hands was a conscious and careful fabrication of identity.

When the *Controversia de nobilitate* began to be printed towards the end of the fifteenth century, designers continued the tradition of paratextual devices that had been established in its manuscripts. These new printed editions were not necessarily preferred by readers over manuscripts, as the latter continued to be generated in some number into the following century.[20] The simultaneous manufacture and circulation of the *Controversia* in manuscript and print indicates that the different products were serving different functions. Copying by hand was considered an efficient method of transmitting texts even after the introduction of printing technology, and indeed remained a more desirable method of communication in some milieux. In its manuscript forms, the dissemination of the *Controversia de nobilitate* was regulated by a network of friends, acquaintances, and colleagues. Thus controlled through a system of referral, the selective distribution of the treatise was designed to help Buonaccorso build and consolidate his status in humanist circles. Meanwhile, those who did not have the connections to procure the *Controversia de nobilitate* in its manuscript form could purchase a printed copy from a local bookseller. The printed editions of the *Controversia* allowed Buonaccorso's debate to reach a broader audience, but these copies were by no means interchangeable with their manuscript counterparts. As Brian Richardson has noted, printed books had a social significance that was different from that of manuscripts. 'Circulation by hand-writing, when carried out by amateurs, ... had the advantage of being free of any taint that might derive from association with the printing industry ... Publication in print might also expose an author to accusations of vanity.'[21] The two products thus possessed their own individual social status and meaning; the materials were a part of different networks of textual transmission and consequently were read in different communities. In this way, the circulation of the *Controversia* in print allowed Buonaccorso to forge relationships with readers beyond those with whom he was socially and professionally connected.

Although participating in different systems of textual transmission and circulation, the printed editions of the *Controversia de nobilitate* on the Italian peninsula were generally executed with the same graphic codes as their manuscript counterparts, including Humanistic letter forms. The pages of the edition of 1480, printed in or around Florence, display a type that employs formal Humanistic letter shapes (plate 5).[22] The straight-backed *d* is again evident, as are the double-compartment *g* and the *ct* ligature. The *a* is of the double-compartment kind, similar to that favoured in book scripts. The edition of 1480 is in octavo format, noticeably smaller than the contemporary manuscripts of the *Controversia*.[23] Twenty-three long lines are printed on each paper page, bounded by generous margins. The words and lines are spaced well apart, rendering this instantiation of the *Controversia de nobilitate* highly legible.

Also following manuscript convention, northern editions of the *Controversia de nobilitate* show a predilection for the Gothic type and a *mise en page* of two columns. For instance, the 1473 edition of the treatise from Cologne uses a type inspired by Gothic letter forms (plate 6).[24] The typically Gothic squat *d* and the '2'-shaped *r* are scattered throughout the text. The long *s* has a characteristic shoulder to the left. The double-compartment *a* suggests some formality. Few abbreviations are used, and letter-biting can especially be detected in the combinations of the letters *be* and *pe*. The separation of words and the regular use of capitalization help to articulate the body of the text and increase its legibility. Recalling the manuscript tradition in northern European circles, the printer has arranged the text of the *Controversia* in two columns. The layout exploits the generous size of the larger quarto page, which shares similar dimensions with those of a modern letter page.[25] Although this copy of the *Controversia de nobilitate* may now be categorized as a product of the printing press, both handwriting and print have been used in its manufacture. Red ink has been added by hand to decorate initials and accentuate capital letters throughout the treatise. Manuscript and print technologies are thus shown in an intimate relationship on the page; the fifteenth-century designers worked with knowledge of both techniques, making use of the advantages of each. The preceding examples show that the page has long been conceived as a flexible interface that can be the product of multiple technologies and can host a range of visual and verbal agendas. The pages of the *Controversia* thus challenge assumptions about textual transmission and circulation, as well as the applicability of the model of technological supersession that has dominated the study of books in the last decades.

The incarnation of the *Controversia de nobilitate* in Gothic, Humanistic, and hybrid hands and types indicates that the treatise was not universally understood by contemporaries as the exclusive domain of a single style of script, and was not understood to be limited to a single identity. The *Controversia* does not dictate in which hand or type it will appear. Although the text was composed by a scholar who was interested in a classicizing intellectual movement, the graphic expression of the *Controversia de nobilitate* is the result of a consideration of many factors that may have had little to do with Buonaccorso himself. Designers of the treatise selected a tradition in which to situate their version of the text, and accordingly customized their redaction with the appropriate paratextual devices. In this way, the style of the letter forms proposes an identity for the treatise, its designers, and its owners, and visually communicates important cultural information to readers, and indeed, to literary scholars and historians of the book.

Further evidence of the contingent relationship between text and script is provided by the manuscripts that preserve the Italian translation of Buonaccorso's treatise in Humanistic hands. Giovanni Aurispa undertook an Italian translation of Buonaccorso's treatise shortly after 1428, calling it the *Trattato della nobiltà*.[26] By the middle of the century, the *Trattato* was circulating in and around Florence in Humanistic and hybrid Gothic-Humanistic hands.[27] Designers evidently had no compunction in associating a text in the Italian vernacular with the newer letter-forms of the humanists. Examples of a formal Humanistic script can be found in surviving manuscripts of the *Trattato della nobiltà*, including Florence, Biblioteca Riccardiana, MS 2544 (plate 7).[28] Typical of the Humanistic book-hand, the letter forms in this example are round and well spaced. Other notable characteristics include the long ascenders and descenders in the letters *d*, *l*, and *p*, and the tall *s*-shape. The double-compartment *g* is employed with regularity, as is the ampersand for *et*. The *a* is of the double-compartment type, consistent with the tendency of formal book-hands. There is no biting of letters and abbreviations are rare. The ruling pattern enables thirty long lines of text to be written onto each page, with generous margins on all sides. In this example, the title of the *Trattato* has been written with red ink to distinguish it from the main body of the text, and a maniculum in the margin draws attention to the blue two-line initial at the opening of the treatise.

The history and historiography of the Humanistic script were debated by palaeographers and bibliographers in the early twentieth century,[29] and the significance of this style of script grew more complicated as humanism came to be understood as a cultural movement that marked the transition between the Middle Ages and Renaissance.[30] Through the course of these disputes, the Humanistic script became intimately connected with the transmission of classical and classicizing Latin.[31] But from the examples of the *Controversia de nobilitate* in Latin and its Italian translation, it is evident that there were important exceptions to this graphic polarism. A classicizing text in Latin by a humanist could be transmitted in Gothic hands as well as Humanistic ones. Meanwhile, the translation of the *Controversia* in the Italian *volgare* did not circulate exclusively in Gothic hands, but chiefly in Humanistic ones.[32] What emerges from the foregoing survey of the manuscripts of the *Controversia de nobilitate* and its Italian translation is that the treatise was malleable enough to support a variety of visual and material expressions, and that designers routinely capitalized on this flexibility as they constructed different pages for it. Because each graphic expression of the *Controversia de nobilitate* was engineered to be compelling to a specific audience, the page may be read as a response to contemporary social, political, and economic pressures.

The multiple and varied instantiations of Buonaccorso's debate raise questions about the validity of the supposition that the Humanistic script was an absolute sign of a new approach to reading, writing, and thinking in the Latin language.[33] The *Controversia* in Latin was transmitted in Humanistic, Gothic, and hybrid hands through the end of the late Middle Ages. Meanwhile, its translation in Italian, the *Trattato della nobiltà*, circulated at the same time in Humanistic and hybrid scripts. From at least the mid-fifteenth century, then, designers of the manuscripts did not associate the Humanistic hand exclusively with Latin literature. In light of the evidence offered by the manuscripts of the *Controversia* and *Trattato*, the Humanistic hand might instead be more precisely considered a graphic proposal of a new approach to reading and writing, of intellectual difference, and of scholarly heritage. The social and cultural assertions embodied in the Humanistic hand were immediately exploited by the designers of the *Trattato della nobiltà*. The designers of the *Trattato* adopted the emergent conventions of the humanists in hopes of fabricating credibility for a literary tradition in the vernacular. Not only was the *Trattato della nobiltà* copied in Humanistic scripts, so too were the texts with which it was packaged, including Leonardo Bruni's *Novella di Antioco*, Dante's *Vita nuova*, the letters of Boccaccio and Petrarch, as well as orations, poems, and songs in the *volgare*. Even before humanists had established the Humanistic script as a visual code for their scholarly work in Latin, designers were already appropriating the aesthetic to add prestige and authority to texts in the *volgare*.

Meanwhile, north of the Alps, other designers were working to cultivate a heritage for the *Controversia de nobilitate* in its French translation. Buonaccorso's debate had been translated into French by Jean Miélot, a clerk at the court of Burgundy, by 1450.[34] Instead of perpetuating the humanist identity that had been constructed for the *Controversia* on the Italian peninsula, the designers of *La controversie de noblesse* chose to imitate the look of the literary tradition in the French vernacular that had been developing for at least a century.[35] In this guise, Buonaccorso's treatise was introduced to yet another audience. The new look appealed to the sensibilities of the courtly elite and enabled *La controversie de noblesse* to gain a broader readership in northern circles.[36] As A.J. Vanderjagt has remarked, Buonaccorso's treatise thus 'made a transition from a civic, humanist culture to the princely political culture of the court of Burgundy ... This is remarkable and it shows just how completely the cultural meaning of this text was changed at the ducal court.'[37] At the same time that the *Controversia de nobilitate* was circulating as a rhetorical exercise in Latin, its French translation was being read as romance in an explicitly aristocratic context. By adopting the graphic codes of the literary tradition in the vernacular, designers were able to make *La controversie* into a product that was recognizable to, and resonated with, courtly readers in the north.

In the manuscript tradition of romance, one of the favoured scripts is the *bâtarde*, a cursive form of the Gothic hand.[38] By using the Gothic *bâtarde* in the manuscripts of *La controversie*, designers presented the text as a courtly literature in the French vernacular. To help manufacture a heritage for Buonaccorso's treatise that it did not yet possess, the designers packaged *La controversie de noblesse* with new companions. In extant manuscripts, *La controversie* is found with courtesy texts that discuss the proper conduct of ladies and gentlemen.[39] These didactic works include Lucian's *Débat de honneur*, Diego de Valera's *Traité de noblesse*, and a collection of tracts on chivalric, heraldic, and institutional matters that begins with a piece entitled *Comment on doibt faire ung nouvel empereur*.[40] By offering *La controversie* with other discussions of nobility in the vernacular, the designers were able to create a pedigree for the treatise that was readily identifiable by readers in northern circles. The graphic codes of the page were configured to communicate what *La controversie* was and how the treatise should be understood: namely, as courtly didactic literature.

Illustrations helped further to locate *La controversie* in this literary tradition. From the late thirteenth century, many French romances, including histories and didactic pieces, were accompanied by extensive systems of illustration. These programs often begin with depictions of authors and royal patrons, and continue with a series of miniatures that is woven through the rest of the text. In her study of *Le Conte de Graal (Perceval)* by Chrétien de Troyes from the early fourteenth century, Sandra Hindman investigated the cycle of fifty-four miniatures preserved in one particular manuscript.[41] She found that a miniature could, on average, appear as frequently as every five folia in the manuscript of 272 folia. Other handwritten copies of the same text preserve twenty-six, fifty, fifty-one, and fifty-two miniatures respectively.[42] These books and other such illustrated manuscripts had already set the graphic conventions of courtly romance at least a century before Miélot embarked on his translation of Buonaccorso's treatise.

In order to position *La controversie* in this established genre of vernacular literature, the designers imagined Miélot's translation with illustrations. In conjunction with the other cues of the page, the miniatures of *La controversie de noblesse* constituted a pattern that would be acknowledged as a conventional sign of courtly romance. The illustrations help to form an expression that resonates with the reader; the parchment page, the system of miniatures, and the Gothic *bâtarde* all generate a look for *La controversie de noblesse* that was and is still identifiable as romance.[43]

In the deluxe versions of *La controversie de noblesse*, miniatures decorate the prologue and signal movements in the plot line within the main narrative section. Like blank space, illustrations visually break the flow of the text and can provide interludes for the reader. As Brigitte Buettner writes, 'Miniatures lured because they produced a rhythmical sequence, a *musica* that punctuated the text and introduced visual pauses where the gaze could rest, remember, learn, relish.'[44] Designers thus used the miniatures strategically; not only did the illustrations consolidate an identity for their product, they also had an editorial function, designating and underscoring shifts in *La controversie*. The placement of the images in the text enabled designers to signal where the audience should pause, reflect, and consider. With these illustrations, then, designers continue to direct the ways in which readers interact with the treatise and shape how *La controversie* is understood.

One of the earliest manuscripts of *La controversie de noblesse*, Brussels, KBR, MS 9278–80, from around 1449, exhibits a sophisticated arrangement of text, image, decoration, and space (plate 8).[45] The dimensions of the parchment are large, substantially greater than those of the modern letter-sized page.[46] Nevertheless, the text block is composed of a conservative twenty-seven lines. Designers have adopted the Gothic *bâtarde* in keeping with the visual tradition of courtly romance. In this example, cursive secretary elements of the hand include the pointed or prickly aspect of letters; the clubbing of the tall *s*, which amplifies the contrast between thick and thin strokes; the horned *g*; and the angular bow of the *d*. Although a cursive hand, the *bâtarde* was of a high grade and could be used in products of good quality. Red ink is used to distinguish headings from the main body of the text and adds an element of distinction to the page.

A large portion of the page is occupied by a miniature that ostensibly depicts the opening scene of the treatise. Lucretia, her father, and the two suitors – all dressed in fifteenth-century attire – engage in conversation.[47] The castle walls form a proscenium that frames the stage for the characters. Visible, too, are the roof and turrets of the castle that differentiate the interior and exterior spaces of the miniature. Architectural elements thus help to distinguish the spaces of the image; they moreover divide the illustration from other features of the page. Immediately beneath the miniature, an eight-line initial draws attention to the opening of the treatise. The letter is physically raised from the surface of the parchment with the application of layer of gesso.[48] This decorative technique exaggerates the three dimensions of the page and creates a complex topography for the reader to navigate. A rich blue background distinguishes the initial from its surroundings, but the letter also extends beyond this framing device to move into the space of the text. Vacillating between visual and verbal modes, the initial embellishes the page as it reminds the reader of its semantic relationship with the letters that follow. Finally, a border brings text, image, and decoration together and consolidates their simultaneous effect. The visual guidelines aid readers who must locate themselves in relation to the illustration and begin to make sense of the page, but these cues also constitute a way in which designers may elicit an ideal response from their audiences.

Similar graphic strategies have been employed in a presentation copy of *La controversie de noblesse*, Brussels, KBR, MS 10977–9, copied in 1460 (plate 9). This manuscript is smaller than the previous example, about the size of a modern letter-page, but transmits a well-proportioned text block.[49] Each parchment page has been ruled for thirty lines of text. The hand borrows from the cursive secretary, and includes notable characters such as the angular bow of the *d* with its looped ascender, the horned *g*, and the clubbed tall *s*. Red ink distinguishes headings from the main text. The opening page of the treatise is decorated with a large illustration, again intended to depict Lucretia, her father, and the two suitors. Colonnades and archways organize the different zones of the image. In the foreground, a stepped wall creates a threshold between the miniature and the reader, delineating the space of the image and consequently the space of the reader. As the wall cuts away, the reader is permitted a glimpse of the interior scene in which the characters of *La controversie de noblesse* appear in conversation.

The miniature is a contrived and deliberate show, and moreover participates in the staging of the page as a whole. An ornamental border of flowers and greenery encloses the miniature, the decorated initial, and the text. This band of decoration provides a control for the page by separating the space of *La controversie* from that of the reader.[50] The division between the treatise and its audience is further emphasized by the liberal margins. The blank space functions here as an anchor that may be grasped physically and conceptually by the reader. With this margin, the reader can safely make the cognitive leap into the illustrated scene without losing a sense of the physical platform of the page. The blank areas allow onlookers to reconcile their own reality as they grapple with the *pagina*; these are spaces to remember where one exists as a reader. Here it is perhaps most evident that the page acts as an interface, mediating between multiple worlds. The page is the point of contact between author, designer, text, image, and reader.

In print, the French translation of the *Controversia de nobilitate* continues its visual ties with the conventions of courtly literature. Colard Mansion printed his paper edition of *La controversie* with a translation of Lucian's *Débat de honneur* in 1476, in a type that shares letter shapes with the cursive Gothic *bâtarde* (plate 10).[51] Characteristic features include the angular bow of the *d*, the looped ascenders, the '2'-shaped *r*, and the clubbed tall *s*. The Gothic tendency of biting is particularly manifest in the combination of the letters *d* and *e*. Although some of the editions of the *Controversia de nobilitate* were being printed in a double-columned format in the north, as discussed earlier in this chapter, Mansion chose to print the French translation in long lines as it was often laid out in vernacular manuscripts. Up to twenty-three lines of text appear on a page in his quarto edition of *La controversie de noblesse*.[52] The text block is divided into sections, and these breaks are highlighted by headings. Furthermore, blank spaces have been left throughout the text to accommodate the addition of decorative elements, such as initials or paraph marks to be inked by hand. Again, scribal and print strategies are conceived in a complementary relationship; manuscript and type are intended to share the space of the page as they contribute to the final product. In the copy held in Paris,[53] the possibilities of handwriting have been exploited by a rubricator. Red initials, marks, and lines were added by hand, and this articulation of the different paratextual elements functions both as ornamentation and an aid for reading.

By adopting the bibliographic conventions found in romance manuscripts, designers of the pages of *La controversie* graphically asserted the membership of the treatise in the tradition of courtly literature. Although a faithful translation of the story of the *Controversia de nobilitate*, the French translation was incarnated as a courtesy text. The designers repackaged Buonaccorso's composition and gave *La controversie* a different intellectual heritage from the one that it had as the *Controversia de nobilitate* on the Italian peninsula. After being recopied with the material accoutrements befitting French literature, the treatise eventually attained the status of an accepted exemplar. That is, designers in the fifteenth century employed the conventions of Gothic letter forms, coloured inks, and illustrations to propose *La controversie de noblesse* as a member of the literary tradition, and their books of *La controversie* are now used to perpetuate the visual and material identity of the romance genre. Even today, the manuscripts and printed books of *La controversie* continue to reinforce the association between courtly vernacular literature and a specific set of graphic codes and paratextual devices.[54]

'Reading the Page' has explored the ways in which the variations in the pages of the *Controversia de nobilitate* and its translations enabled Buonaccorso's debate to transcend geographic boundaries and appeal to diverse audiences. Designers took a flexible attitude towards the 'depiction' of the text, repackaging it in a variety of ways.[55] But these new looks also constitute different interpretations of the *Controversia de nobilitate*; a new materiality indicates a new meaning. The page thus shapes the reception of the text by suggesting a tradition in which it belongs and a context in which it should be read. Designers encode an identity into their pages of the *Controversia*, and the treatise cannot be read without the simultaneous communication of this proposal. Transmitted in each copy of the *Controversia* is therefore not only the story of the treatise, but a story about its visualization, production, circulation, and preservation. The next chapter will explore in detail some of the paratextual signs that accompany the *Controversia de nobilitate*, and consider how the devices might be read as assertions about the status of the author, patron, designer, reader, codex, and the text itself.

3

The Paratext and the Page

Scribes, printers, translators, editors, and booksellers have all left their indelible marks on the pages of the *Controversia de nobilitate*. These designers shape the readerly encounter with a variety of paratextual devices, and thus propose ways to understand the fifteenth-century treatise on nobility.[1] As Buonaccorso da Montemagno's debate was recopied, a paratextual apparatus composed of title pages, prefaces, headings, and epilogues began to be woven into the *Controversia*, eventually becoming an integral part of the text.[2] These devices are legitimized by their proximity to the treatise and wield interpretative power over it. Indeed, readers rarely regard the title of a book with suspicion, or interrogate its chapter divisions. The paratext says, 'The text is thus,' as if it were a statement of fact. Authorized by its own presence, the paratext is trusted because it exists.

Chapter 3 examines some of the paratextual mechanisms that configure the *Controversia de nobilitate*, presented in the order in which the reader might encounter them. First, an array of introductory materials prepares the audience for the reading experience. Title pages, prefaces, and prologues visually and verbally fabricate a context for the treatise, even if the pages are only leafed through or skimmed. Then, headings and subdivisions contour the graphic performance of Buonaccorso's composition; they punctuate important moments in the story and thereby affect in what manner the treatise will be read. Colophons and epilogues draw the debate to a conclusion and are positioned to leave a final impression of the text upon the reader. The following consideration of the paratexts of the *Controversia de nobilitate* is by no means exhaustive, but may serve as an introduction to the kinds of conversations that can and have occurred – and will continue to occur – between designer and reader on the page.

The French translation of the *Controversia de nobilitate* was printed by Antoine Vérard in 1497 as part of a collection of didactic texts that includes Diego de Valera's *Traité de noblesse*.[3] Reinforcing the association of *La controversie de noblesse* with courtly romance literature that had been proposed in its manuscripts, Vérard selected a type that was similar to the Gothic script and opted for large pages of vellum as a platform.[4] Because printing on parchment involved much more labour and expense than printing on paper, Vérard's choice of material helped to communicate the quality that he envisioned for his product. The combination of type, material, and contiguous texts served to align his edition of *La controversie* visually and materially with the tradition of romances.

In one particular copy of the edition, currently shelved as Paris, BNF, Vélins 411–13, Vérard divided the collection of texts into three parts and created illustrated title pages for each.[5] Inscribed on the rectos of these folia are the titles '*Le gouvernement des princes,*' '*Le Tresor de noblesse,*' in which *La controversie de noblesse* appears with Diego de Valera's *Traité de noblesse*, and '*Les fleurs de Valere le Grant.*'[6] Beneath each title is the phrase 'Pour le roy,' referring to Charles VIII, King of France, for whom this compilation was apparently intended. The versos of the folia transmit full-page illustrations, framed by rich borders that have been ornamented with the gold fleurs-de-lis of the House of Valois. The first title page depicts the ceremonial presentation of a book (plate 11).[7] A figure on bended knee, whom the reader might presume to be Vérard, offers a book – the suggestion is this particular codex – to his royal patron. At a respectful distance, a number of courtiers watch the transaction take place. Despite the rhetoric of the image, the illustration is not a record of a historical moment; the scene is a fiction. When the title page was composed, the book had not yet been offered in this way to Charles, if indeed it ever would be. The title page is instead a performance with a specific function: the image visually links Vérard with his royal patron, and both of these men with the codex. If nowhere else, the men are connected by their depiction on the title page.

The complex and peculiar dynamic between patron and designer is, in part, made visible in this title page.[8] Although the figure of Vérard is shown in a deferential pose, the illustration is a powerful way for the designer to establish and preserve his own association with the book and the treatise that it conveys. Moreover, it is in Vérard's capacity to preserve the royal name of his patron with this same device.[9] By codifying the name and likeness of Charles in the book, Vérard helped to consolidate the legacy of the king. In return, the image of the royal patron valorizes the codex as a kind of relic, and furthermore bestows social status and prestige upon Vérard.[10] With patron and designer thus anchored in the paratext, this copy of *La controversie* sustains the idealized relationship between King Charles, Vérard, and the book. The circulation of the title page reinforces Vérard's proposed relationship with royalty in the communal imagination and continues to preserve the alliance even today, long after the deaths of both men.

An illustration with a similar performative function may be found on the title page that introduces *La controversie de noblesse*. In the image, a scholar is shown at work in his study (plate 12). The industrious figure copies from an exemplar by hand; a lectern, a book-wheel, books, and an assortment of writing instruments surround him. The placement of the illustration on the title page suggests that the scene has a direct connection with the text that follows. But of course Vérard's edition has been – in the main – printed, not copied by hand as is suggested in the miniature, and moreover without the personal involvement of Buonaccorso or Jean Miélot. By invoking the conventional figure of the author-scribe, the illustration is designed to validate and guarantee the authenticity of the contiguous text. Scholar portraits of this type find their roots in early depictions of the evangelists and ancient philosophers, and Vérard's title page to *La controversie de noblesse* participates in this long iconographic tradition.[11] In employing such a portrait, Vérard sought to add an air of authority for *La controversie* and the codex as a whole. Furthermore, the use of a stock image allowed Vérard to repurpose the illustration for deployment in other products, which he did in at least three other instances.[12] This scholar-portrait and its compatriots in BNF, Vélins 411–13 were therefore not developed to function uniquely in conversation with *La controversie de noblesse* or the accompanying texts. Although the images do not overtly explicate the works that they preface, they offer another kind of contextual framing. The title pages constitute a mechanism by which Vérard continues even today to assert an identity for the book, its readers, its owners, its patron, and indeed, himself. In this way, the title pages may be read as a self-conscious effort to signal prestige.

The paratextual effect of the title page is made clear when this instantiation of *La controversie de noblesse* at the Bibliothèque nationale de France is compared with another of the same edition, now held in London by the British Library.[13] The latter copy did not receive the same finishing work as its counterpart. The three sections *Le gouvernement des princes*, *Le Tresor de noblesse*, and *Les fleurs de Valere le Grant* are bound together sequentially, without the special treatment of decorated title pages. Thus, the same edition of the same collection of treatises could be packaged in a different way to become a different product. Although the text of *La controversie* may be called the 'same' in the sense that the pages of the two copies were likely issued from Vérard's press shortly after one another with little alteration to the formes that were used for printing, it cannot be said that the two codices – the two products – are identical. Vérard's title pages are therefore an example of the capacity of paratexts to change the material expression of a book and, consequently, its meaning. At the same time that the copy in Paris appears to be a lavish presentation edition of courtly romance for Charles VIII, the copy preserved in London is a fine but otherwise unremarkable collection of didactic texts in the French vernacular. By packaging *La controversie de noblesse* in different ways, Vérard modified how the text, its pages, and its identity were and are to be understood.

Turning past the title pages, the next paratextual form that a reader might encounter is the dedication.[14] While ostensibly directed to a single person, dedications are always constructed to be read by others. As Gérard Genette has noted, a dedication is aimed as much at the attentive reader as it is to the dedicatee. He writes: 'Whoever the official addressee, there is always an ambiguity in the destination of the dedication, which is always intended for at least two addressees: the dedicatee, of course, but also the reader, for dedicating a work is a public act that the reader is, as it were, called on to witness … The dedication always is a matter of demonstration, ostentation, exhibition.'[15]

Dedications are performances; they are designed to be read by others as much as – if not more than – the person who is explicitly mentioned. Readers are offered a scenario in which they can enjoy the company of the esteemed dedicatee by holding and perusing the codex. They might imagine that the dedicatee has touched the same pages and read the same words. As the book passes through different hands, each reader re-performs the dedication and reactivates its paratextual function. The dedication exploits the ability of the page to serve as an intermediary between different social or even temporal worlds. That is, the paratextual device brings together the two otherwise unrelated figures of the dedicatee and reader into the same time and space as the author and the text;[16] all are drawn into an eternal present. Furthermore, the invocation of a person of prestige communicates to the reader that the treatise and the codex have a certain authoritative importance. By suggesting that the treatise is under the protection of the dedicatee even as it continues to be reproduced, subsequent copyists or readers may be discouraged from making substantial changes of their own. In this way, the dedication can also function as a mode of protection. Similar to the author-portrait, then, the dedication may be perceived to offer a guarantee of quality and thus act as a safeguard for the text.

A vivid example of the dedication can be found in Antoine Vérard's printed edition of *La controversie de noblesse*. As discussed above, the title pages of the collection in Paris carry inscriptions to Charles VIII, but not all copies of Vérard's *La controversie* have been equipped with these paratextual devices. However, the dedication is repeated in the body of the text so that it will still accompany the versions of *La controversie de noblesse* that are not embellished with title pages. The dedication is embedded in a paragraph in which Vérard asks Charles to render judgment in the contest between Cornelius and Flaminius. Vérard writes: 'I send this translation to you, sir, who, through your great virtues and courage have lately worked to establish peace in your kingdom of France … And it will not be a difficult thing for you – the legitimate source and root of nobility, and to whom all the noblemen not only of this kingdom but of all others must appeal – to judge, determine, decide, and settle which of these two should be called the most noble.'[17] Given the unresolved nature of the contest of *La controversie de noblesse*, Vérard suggests that the king, whom he identifies as a source of nobility, is in the best position to render a decision in the debate.[18] Vérard imagines himself in the same time and space as his patron, indicating to the reader that he is in direct conversation with Charles. In this passage, Vérard verbally insinuates himself into the court of King Charles even as he did visually in the illustration. Like the figure of the king on the title page, the name of Charles adds value to the codex and establishes it as a product of high quality. The dedicatory paragraph consolidates Vérard's proposed association with Charles as the text is read and reread. Although the title pages are not duplicated in the less extravagant version of *La controversie* in the London copy, the dedicatory passage is. Vérard has thus woven his relationship with the king of France into the treatise to increase the likelihood that the connection would become fixed as an integral part of Buonaccorso's text. Vérard uses the dedication to garner prestige for himself and his handiwork, and sustains the proposition of both with the paratextual device. In this way, the copies of *La controversie* that are not directly linked with the original dedicator and dedicatee nevertheless continue to memorialize them.

Despite the best efforts of a designer, other factors could intervene to reshape the force and trajectory of the dedication. Two different dedications are extant in the manuscripts of the *Controversia de nobilitate* in Latin. A single manuscript of the *Controversia* now held in London preserves an inscription to Carlo Malatesta, Lord of Rimini.[19] Carlo had at one time been allied with the people of Florence, where Buonaccorso lived and worked, but died shortly after the *Controversia* entered circulation. The majority of the surviving manuscripts of the *Controversia* carry a dedication to Guidantonio Montefeltro, papal vicar and Lord of Urbino from 1404 to 1443.[20] The coexistence of multiple inscriptions has been explored by John A. Buchtel, who observed that the rededication of a work was common after the death of the first dedicatee because the author would be in need of ongoing patronage.[21] The rededication of the *Controversia de nobilitate* therefore suggests that a new patron was sought out after the death of Carlo. Moreover, because the dedication was updated with the name of Guidantonio, it seems that the paratextual device continued to have an important and active function even after the initial release of the *Controversia*, and that it worked to garner status for those involved in the subsequent production and dissemination of the text, as well as to confirm the place of the patron as a valued member of the elite.

Although the dedication to Guidantonio is by far the most prevalent in the extant manuscript sources, more often transmitted in the printed editions of the early modern period is the dedication to Carlo. For instance, Giovanni Casotti printed the dedication to Carlo in 1718 in his facing-page Latin and Italian translation of the *Controversia*.[22] The influence of Casotti's edition can be seen in later studies of the *Controversia de nobilitate*; the dedication to Carlo is repeated and reinscribed in twentieth-century scholarship, while the one to Guidantonio is, for the most part, overlooked.[23] In 1952, Eugenio Garin states in his prologue only that Buonaccorso dedicated the *Controversia* to Carlo Malatesta, and it is not until 1991 that the dedication to Guidantonio resurfaces in a translation by Albert Rabil, Jr.[24] Thus, the dedication to Carlo was transformed when the *Controversia de nobilitate* began to be printed in the early modern period. Not only was the near-extinct dedication revived and resurrected in print, the association with Carlo became crucially embedded in the modern history of Buonaccorso's treatise and has consequently shaped scholarly perspectives on the text, its author, its audience, and Quattrocento Florence.

Moving into the main body of the *Controversia de nobilitate*, one of the next paratextual devices that the reader might encounter is a network of internal titles, or section headings.[25] Headings are visual and verbal signposts that contour the shape of the text and the look of the page. Frequently accompanied by blank spaces to distinguish them from the rest of the text, these internal titles can provide visual and cognitive interludes for the reader while providing instructions and interpretive clues.[26] Gérard Genette has observed that, in contrast to the title of a treatise, which enjoys a broader currency and circulation, section headings are seldom accessible to anyone except readers, and their content often only makes sense to someone who is already engaged with the text.[27] Internal titles are directed towards the audience and therefore might be considered unambiguous evidence of the communication between designer and reader.

The designers of the manuscripts of Buonaccorso's treatise in Latin had limited interest in developing a robust cycle of headings. A series of simple titles occasionally marks the prologue, the oration of Cornelius, and the oration of Flaminius. When section headings have been included, they are short and descriptive, such as 'The oration of Publius Cornelius Scipio.'[28] Although written in the same ink as the main text, the headings are visually distinguished from the rest of the page by one of two means. In the first technique, designers employ blank space to separate the headings from the main text (plate 3). The text block has been broken up to create special zones for these titles. The headings are thus clearly distinguished from the main text with blank space. In the second method, designers rely upon punctuation to separate the headings from the main text. In lieu of blank lines, punctuation marks, usually sets of double virgules ('//'), are employed to differentiate the section title from the narrative.[29] In both methods, designers create visual and verbal waymarks on the page for their readers. The section titles articulate the shape of the text visually at the same time that they do so cognitively; they offer pauses to temper the rhythm of reading. Thus, by highlighting particular moments in the *Controversia de nobilitate* with headings, designers control the opportunities for readerly reflection.

The manuscripts of the *Controversia de nobilitate* in its Italian translation preserve a more extensive system of headings than their counterparts in Latin. The apparatus in the *Trattato della nobiltà* supplies a narrative description to aid the reader and, perhaps, the casual browser. For instance, one manuscript begins, 'The debate about nobility that was argued by two young Romans in the presence of the Senate, and how each claimed to be nobler than the other,'[30] and the speech of Cornelius is prefaced with 'The oration of Publius Cornelius Scipio, in which he speaks about his nobility.'[31] Another manuscript opens the first speech with the heading 'Being the question just put to the senators, Publius Cornelius wishes to show that he is nobler and that Lucretia should be his wife, and thus begins his oration.'[32]

In addition to creating interludes before and between the orations, the headings of the *Trattato della nobiltà* impart further details about the progress of the debate. These entries are interspersed throughout the body of the text and closely follow the arguments presented in the *Trattato*. The phrase 'Another argument from Publius Cornelius Scipio that nobility exists through riches'[33] helps to explicate the argument of Cornelius for the reader. Likewise, the mid-line heading 'Flaminius's example in support of his argument'[34] prefaces the list of Rome's unlikely heroes provided by Flaminius, while on the next folio, 'Flaminius's argument demonstrating that poverty does not make a virtuous man ignoble'[35] breaks up his lengthy catalogue of examples. The detail of such headings permits the less attentive or less skilled reader to follow the shape of Buonaccorso's composition and indicates a difference in the kind of readerly engagement that was occurring with the text in its incarnation in the *volgare*.

In addition to providing more signs on the page for visual orientation, the headings offer a way of understanding the *Trattato della nobiltà*. The manuscript tradition of the Italian translation capitalizes on the ability of these paratextual headings to function both graphically and verbally on the page. The internal titles break the text block with regularity, increasing the legibility of the treatise while also serving to track the argument. The use of internal titles to summarize and explicate the *Trattato* was part of a growing strategy in the presentation of texts in the *volgare* in general, and may have been related to broader changes in reading practices.[36] Paul F. Grendler has observed that literacy rates in Italy remained below 40 per cent for men and 20 per cent for women even into the sixteenth century, and half of this reading demographic was proficient in both Latin and Italian.[37] Readers for texts in the Italian vernacular were drawn from diverse social and economic circles, and could include members of the educated elite, women of nobility, and the clergy, all of whom might also be literate in Latin, as well as merchants, artisans, and shopkeepers, who were usually not. Moreover, the regional differences in dialect on the Italian peninsula could render someone with proficiency in one local vernacular a reader with only elementary skills in another dialect. The audience for books in the Italian vernacular was therefore partly composed of new readers and new writers.[38] Designers and booksellers responded to the needs of their diverse audience by providing an extensive reading apparatus that offered assistance to less experienced readers and navigational tools for more experienced ones. The convention of lengthy headings that was established in the manuscript tradition of the *Trattato* and other such texts in the Italian vernacular flourished in the hands of later editors and printers. As Brian Richardson writes, 'Many editors did their best from the 1530s onwards to make it easier for readers to understand and imitate the key model texts … by providing glossaries, annotations and other sorts of practical help and advice.'[39] The partiality for narrative headings in the Italian tradition can be especially detected in a sixteenth-century manuscript of the *Trattato della nobiltà*, in which a protracted two-page summary of the story prefaces the treatise.[40] By the end of the sixteenth century, the predilection for summary in the *volgare* had become a formalized process, and more space was appropriated for the expanded notes.[41] Editorial control was asserted graphically on the page with this important paratextual apparatus. Printers moved the growing descriptions to the margins and advertised them as special features of the codices; meanwhile, booksellers could claim that their particular annotations were more comprehensive or more accurate than those of their competitors.[42]

In contrast to the traditions in Latin and Italian in which headings were written in the same ink as the text, the headings in the manuscripts of *La controversie de noblesse* were almost always inscribed in red. The rubricated section titles in French are embedded in the main text without the blank space or punctuation that was used in the manuscripts in Latin.[43] Colour was thus employed in *La controversie* to differentiate the headings from the main body of text. The content of the section titles remains consistent in the surviving manuscripts, and falls between the conventions in the manuscripts of the *Controversia* and those of the Italian translation. Headings in *La controversie de noblesse* include 'Here ends the prologue of the author, and the title of this declamation of nobility that was argued long ago before the senators of Rome,'[44] 'Here Publius Cornelius speaks against Gaius Flaminius before the senators of Rome,'[45] and, 'The oration of Gaius Flaminius follows.'[46]

In the printed editions of 1476 and 1497, Colard Mansion and Antoine Vérard used types that were similar to the style of the Gothic *batârde*, a script seen in many manuscript versions of *La controversie*. The speeches themselves are introduced with headings that transmit more detail than their Latin counterparts. For instance, Vérard opens with the printed phrase 'On this topic, here follows the translation of a controversy and debate of two courageous men, competing for the beautiful Lucretia in marriage.'[47] Although the exemplars of *La controversie de noblesse* in manuscript used red ink to draw attention to these headings, Mansion and Vérard had to balance the graphic conventions of scribal traditions with the extra time and cost involved in printing in red.[48] Both printers depended instead on blank space to set off the section titles, a technique employed in the manuscripts of the *Controversia* and its Italian translation, the *Trattato*. Their approach to the *mise en page* allowed subsequent designers the flexibility to insert rubrication and other decoration in these spaces by hand: for instance, the copy of Mansion's edition now held in Paris preserves underlining, initials, and other handwritten marks in red that were used to increase the visual impact of the headings (plate 10), and the copy of Vérard's edition has been embellished with red and blue paint to ornament the headings and articulate breaks in the text.[49] The headings included in the early printed editions of *La controversie de noblesse* are therefore important examples of how handwriting and printing were understood to be complementary technologies for the disposition of text in the fifteenth century.

Designers thus developed different systems of internal titles to mark the text and its pages in the traditions of the *Controversia de nobilitate* in Latin, Italian, and French, in both manuscript and print. The network of headings provides relief on the page, interrupting the course of the text and its reading. The section titles constitute graphic and cognitive breaks but also control them; in these spaces, the reader is encouraged to pause, to reflect upon what has passed, and to anticipate what is to follow. The visual fragmentation of the page was, however, not a strategy that was employed by all designers of the *Controversia de nobilitate* and its translations. Indeed, the designers of the printed editions in German envisioned the layout of the page differently.

The *Controversia de nobilitate* was translated into German as *Von dem Adel* by Nicolaus von Wyle and circulated in his anthology of translations of humanist treatises.[50] Other texts in the collection of eighteen *Translationen* include German versions of *De duobus amantibus*, dialogues from Petrarch's *Remedia utriusque fortunae*, and orations and epistles of Poggio Bracciolini. The first edition of the *Translationen* was printed by Conrad Fyner in 1478.[51] Partly historiated or decorated initials are scattered throughout the collection, articulating the text that otherwise continues uninterrupted for two hundred folia. Recognizing that this layout could constitute a hostile reading environment, designers of subsequent editions of Wyle's translations began to use running titles to help readers find their place in the volume.[52] These headings, located atop the pages, provide readers with navigational cues as they move through and around the book. In his edition of 1510, Johannes Bryse printed the header 'Die xiiii translation' in the top margin of the versos of the folia carrying the translation of the *Controversia*, and its German title 'Von dem adelusz alten hystorien' atop the corresponding rectos.[53] These are welcome additions to the daunting blocks of forty-one lines that stretch on unbroken for 150 folia. Using a similar approach, Heinrich Stayner printed the *Translationen* in 1536 (plate 13).[54] The treatises in the *Translationen* are preserved here in a large format; the dimensions of the folia exceed those of a modern letter page. Moreover, the book is composed of over two hundred of these substantial folia. The reader cannot but be impressed by the monumental column of words on each page, as well as the collective weight of the pages themselves. Like Bryse, Stayner chose to include running titles in his edition. The header 'Der Vierdtzehend Translation' is printed along the top of the verso, indicating to the reader that the translation of the *Controversia* is the fourteenth text in the collection. On the recto, the corresponding title of the treatise appears. Furthermore, foliation in bold Roman numerals helps readers orient themselves in the long anthology, and is distinguished graphically from the Gothic typeface of the main text.[55] The configuration of the page of *Von dem Adel* is unlike the expressions of the *Controversia* witnessed in its Latin, Italian, and French traditions. Here, systems of headings and patterns of rubrication have been eschewed in favour of running titles and foliation. The apparatus in Stayner's edition, for instance, allows readers to peruse texts out of sequence and navigate different selections quickly. The paratext of the German editions indicates that emphasis was laid on understanding the treatises individually and comprehending their respective positions in the codex.

Running titles had fallen out of use in the early part of the Middle Ages when monastic *lectio* became the predominant model for reading. Reading, understood as a spiritual exercise, emphasized the slow and steady contemplation of a single text.[56] With this approach, readers were less likely to be in need of reminders of their location in the larger context of the book. By the twelfth century, however, other customs of reading were on the rise. The development of universities fostered analytical modes of engagement with text, especially in the urban, scholarly communities.[57] Texts were once again being consulted for reference purposes, and books consequently needed to be equipped with features such as indices and chapter headings to accommodate these reading practices.[58] Different paratextual apparatuses were thus modified or created for diverse audiences. As a part of broader changes in the design of books, German printers began to use running titles and foliation in their editions in the late fifteenth century. Miriam U. Chrisman has suggested that an emergent lay culture in the German-speaking lands 'pursued its own goals in terms of knowledge and had its own distinctive values,' and audiences for *Von dem Adel* may have demanded devices in support of their particular reading activities.[59] With this customized expression, *Von dem Adel*, along with other humanistic works and a growing number of books in the German vernacular, continued to find readers despite the social instability and religious reforms of the sixteenth century.[60]

As readers approach the conclusion of the *Controversia de nobilitate*, they might on occasion find supplementary material appended to the debate. In many medieval manuscripts, a colophon is frequently attached to the end of a work; this short passage often includes the name of the author of the text that was copied, the name of the scribe, and the date and place of copying. The names preserved in this device could enjoy the same longevity as those embedded in the dedication, discussed earlier.[61] The colophon thus commemorates in perpetuity those who had contributed to the development of the book or, at least, the figures who assumed such a position.

The designers of the manuscripts and printed books of the *Controversia* knew that any text that they added to Buonaccorso's treatise had the potential to become a permanent fixture of the text and circulate with it. Anticipating that he would be able to preserve the advertisement of his role in the transmission of *La controversie de noblesse*, Jean Miélot, the translator, included his name in the colophon. The closing inscription of the French translation credits both Buonaccorso, the author, and Miélot, the translator. It reads: 'This was made and composed by a famous doctor of law and great orator named Buonaccorso of Pistoia. Then, by the order of the very noble, very powerful, and very excellent prince Philip … the controversy or debate about nobility was translated into French by Jean Miélot, the least of the secretaries of that lord, in the year of grace

43

1449.'[62] With this colophon, Miélot attached his name to all subsequent copies of *La controversie*. His name is repeated not only in the manuscripts of the treatise, but also in the later printed editions of Colard Mansion and Antoine Vérard. Using this paratextual device, Miélot was able to document his involvement in the production of *La controversie de noblesse* and create a legacy for himself and his work.

Similarly, the printer William Caxton shows his hand in the epilogue that he added to the English translation of the *Controversia*.[63] Although he does not claim responsibility as author or translator of the *Declamacyon de noblesse* – he is neither – Caxton presents himself as the mediator of the text. Furthermore, he heightens the importance of his own contribution to the *Declamacyon* by omitting the name of Buonaccorso.[64] Caxton only makes a vague reference to an anonymous author of the *Declamacyon*, 'myn auctour.' He writes in his epilogue: 'As touchyng the sentence dyffynytyf gyven by the Senate aftir thise two noble knyghtes had purposed and shewed theyr Oracions I fynde none as yet pronounced ne gyuen, of whiche myn auctour maketh ony mencion of in his book / Thenne I wolde demaunde of theym that shal rede or here this book. whiche of thies tweyne that is to saye Cornelius Scipio and Gayus Flammyneus was moost noble.'[65] By asking the reader to play judge in the debate in the same way that Vérard did with King Charles, Caxton takes on a role of authority and makes his connection with the *Declamacyon* overt. He implies that he is in a position to intervene in the presentation and transmission of the text. With this paratextual manoeuvre, Caxton writes himself into the history of the *Declamacyon*. As Mark Addison Amos has argued, Caxton is 'not quite usurping the author's role of dictating the terms of the literary creation, but [is] consciously and self-consciously assuming to himself the ability to dictate its reception.'[66] Caxton reveals his presence to the reader in the epilogue, crafting his identity as a producer of the text and suggesting in his own terms the extent of his influence in the reproduction and circulation of the *Declamacyon*.

After concluding the passage with a prayer for the late Earl of Worcester, John Tiptoft, Caxton adjoins the phrase 'Explicit per Caxton' (plate 14).[67] This colophon is placed centrally and prominently on the final page. Additional emphasis is provided by generous amounts of blank space that separate the *explicit* from the foregoing text. This phrase and its visual expression are unambiguous assertions about Caxton's contribution to the production of the text and the book, and 'ascribe a unified – if not quite yet sacred – agency to a collaborative text.'[68] The name of the printer is intended to be clearly impressed upon the audience; 'Caxton' is the last word that the reader sees. Although Caxton does not presume to replace Buonaccorso as the author of the *Declamacyon* or take up the position of the translator, he is able to show how the edition is nevertheless his product, and that he continues to play an important role in the transmission of the text even as it circulates. As Joseph Grigely characterizes it, 'Iconic signatures do not so much say "I was here" as they say "I'm still here."'[69] Indeed, the colophon still communicates Caxton's presence to the reader, preserving his involvement in the transmission of the *Declamacyon* now six hundred years later.

Meanwhile, the name of Buonaccorso and his involvement in the composition of the *Controversia de nobilitate* are completely erased in the German translation of the treatise.[70] There is no mention of the author in the paratextual devices that accompany *Von dem Adel*. Nicolaus von Wyle, the translator, usurps Buonaccorso's role with this omission. However, the names of the authors of other texts in Wyle's anthology are notably present; Petrarch and Poggio Bracciolini, for instance, are mentioned. The inconsistent invocation of authors in the *Translationen* suggests that the name of Buonaccorso held no currency in the northern circles in which the editions circulated.[71] The names that were made explicit, such as that of Poggio, were part of an important paratextual strategy for Wyle, the designers, and booksellers of the *Translationen*. Like those included in dedications and other such paratextual devices, these names were thought to furnish the text with a sense of authenticity and confer prestige upon the codex. The names that were deemed worthy of mention communicated elite associations to readers, and were deployed to endow the book with a high social standing and, thereby, increase the value of the product.

The epilogue could thus be exploited in different ways and by different participants in the production, reproduction, and translation of the *Controversia de nobilitate*. Designers understood that the epilogue could become a permanent appendix to the treatise and consequently used the space to preserve personages and deeds in perpetuity. Scribes, copyists, translators, printers, and booksellers could generate prestige for their version of the text with the addition of the name of a renowned writer; meanwhile, with the inclusion of their own names, the designers could establish and secure their personal legacy. The colophon and other such mechanisms were therefore employed to create and codify reputations. These paratextual devices could manufacture pedigrees for the *Controversia de nobilitate* and the book in the same way that they could for writers, translators, printers, booksellers, and even readers.

The foregoing two chapters have explored the ways in which the pages of the *Controversia de nobilitate* and its translations were designed and redesigned with different paratextual cues for a variety of ends. The judicious insertion or omission of a name could establish, usurp, or erase a legacy. Furthermore, the use of a certain style of script or visual pattern could assign an identity to the treatise and the codex as a whole, and even play a role in the consolidation of a tradition. The multiple guises of the *Controversia de nobilitate* and its translations will figure largely in the next chapter as the discussion investigates how the codices are collected, catalogued, and arranged in the library. In the same way that the pages are able to construct or suggest affiliations for the *Controversia*, so too can the books in which they are bound generate associations for the treatise. Depending on their arrangement in the library, the handwritten and printed codices of the *Controversia de nobilitate* may confirm the propositions intimated by the expressions of their pages, or they may expand the interpretive horizon of Buonaccorso's debate. The influence of the identities of the *Controversia* and its translations is therefore not constrained locally; the pages can be used as a way to understand, classify, and present both text and codex as participants in the broader world of information. By tracking Buonaccorso's treatise as it is organized in the library, the following chapter considers how the page of the *Controversia de nobilitate* may be entangled in longer trails of meaning and mattering.

4

Reading the Library

Chapter 4 follows the trail of the *Controversia de nobilitate* into the library to explore how the pages of Buonaccorso da Montemagno's treatise are incorporated into places and spaces of knowledge. The discussion first begins in the fictional library of the *Controversia* itself, where it is argued that books can attest to the character of their owner. As the library is folded into an understanding of nobility that was designed to rival traditional genealogical models, the activity of reading and the spaces associated with reading take on a broader cultural significance. A phenotypic expression of and response to contemporary ideas about study, the *Controversia de nobilitate* indicates that intellectual work and the places supporting such pursuits had already begun to be recognized as a way of negotiating social status by the early part of the fifteenth century. A closer examination of the library in Buonaccorso's treatise, then, will set the stage for a consideration of libraries more generally and the arrangement of the books of the *Controversia de nobilitate* within them.

The first oration of the *Controversia* outlines the conventional understanding of nobility, in which a noble character is considered to be hereditary, passed on from one generation to the next. In this speech, Cornelius argues that he is noble by birthright, and submits as proof the public monuments that honour his ancestors. Numerous triumphs and arches commemorate the past deeds of his family and remind the people of Rome of the debt owed to Cornelius's family. Cornelius contends that he, in an analogous way, is a human memorial of his ancestors and their accomplishments, keeping the virtues of his family alive within him. Like a monument, his body preserves achievements of the past in a timeless present.[1] Cornelius claims: 'There are as many magnificent monuments displaying the nobility of my ancestors as are permitted to any mortal. Thus the possession of nobility itself has been left to me as an inheritance, in that the very images have been implanted by my ancestors as a hereditary possession. Their descendants continue to perpetuate their natural characters, and in their faces the physical characteristics of their ancestors continue to be reflected. I have their blood, their limbs, their form joined in my body.'[2] For Cornelius, nobility is transferred through the bloodlines as if it were an artefact, remaining untouched and unchanged as it moves down through the generations. Cornelius argues that the virtues of his ancestors are now collectively instantiated in him and visible in his outward appearance. His countenance, limbs, and body all bear witness to his noble ancestry, he says, and accordingly bear witness to a noble character.

To counter Cornelius's theory of overt and physiognomic displays of nobility, Flaminius turns the discussion inward, arguing that a noble character must be cultivated by each individual with constant work. For Flaminius, this work is the application of his mind. His pursuit of knowledge is meant to show that he is continually working to develop his virtues. Flaminius explains that he absorbs himself in study while his rival is occupied with the leisurely activities of hunting, singing, and dancing. Cornelius has depended solely on the noble deeds of his ancestors to establish his character, Flaminius contends, neither displaying any of the virtuous qualities of his forebears nor distinguishing himself through his own activities.

Flaminius submits for consideration a personal library as evidence of his scholarly labours. He argues that the books in the library are indicators of the kind of man he is and thus attest to the nobility of his character. As Maria Ruvoldt explains, 'The objects displayed in a study were expressions of the self, material manifestations of the variety of their owner's interests and, by extension, evidence of his virtue.'[3] If each book is understood as proof of virtue, Flaminius's library transforms into a vault of evidence. Moreover, the books are understood as commodities that will be shared in marriage in the same way that furniture and other household goods will be shared. Flaminius offers the use of his library to Lucretia, inviting her to participate in her own process of character building. In the closing of his oration, Flaminius exhorts, 'Let me lead you, sweet, chaste Lucretia, into my peaceful home; although it is not full of unnecessary adornments, nonetheless it glitters everywhere with virtue, order, joy, and modesty. There, in the first place, you will see my library filled with books, in which I have placed all my hope. These are indeed illustrious household goods.'[4] Flaminius underscores the peace and tranquillity of his home with the noisy chatter that characterizes the household of his rival. In the oration of Flaminius, then, Buonaccorso provides a sketch of the ideal domestic setting in which the library holds a prominent position. By using the ownership of a library as a viable alternative in an argument about nobility, Buonaccorso indicates that multiple systems for the evaluation of prestige were active in the same social network and that the adoption of a scholarly identity was a credible way to improve one's standing. A model for building such an identity is thus offered in Flaminius's speech.

At the same time that Buonaccorso was exploring the cultural significance of books and libraries, so too were his contemporaries. Benedetto Cotrugli, perhaps a Flaminius of sorts in real life, promoted the idea of a domestic space that was dedicated to reading. Cotrugli had ascended the social ladder to become an influential man of affairs in the court of Naples. By 1458, he had completed a four-volume text on the life of the ideal merchant. In *Della mercatura e del mercante perfetto* (Of Trading and the Perfect Trader), Cotrugli suggests that the home of a merchant should have a library for personal use and an office in which business affairs are conducted. He describes how the two rooms should be spatially distinct. Cotrugli writes: 'You ought to have a *scrittoio* in the *solar* on the first floor, suitable for your needs … which should be separate [from the rest of the house] without causing disturbance to your family on account of the strangers who come to the house to contract business with you … He who delights in letters should not keep his books in the common *scrittoio*, but should have a *studiolo*, set apart in the most remote part of the house.'⁵ In clear terms, Cotrugli distinguishes office space from study space, as well as the respective work that occurs in them. The office and *studiolo* are two different rooms with explicit purposes. Cotrugli imagines the domestic library as a quiet, isolated place of study and contemplation. The ideal *studiolo* is thus a refuge from the noise of business activity and chatter of daily household routines.

Even before Buonaccorso and Cotrugli, the connection between solitude and reading had been developed at length by numerous writers. Petrarch, for example, notably explored the models of the *vita activa* and the *vita contemplativa* – the active life and the contemplative life.⁶ The active life was that of the engaged citizen who was involved in politics, commerce, and the social affairs of the state. The introspective life, by contrast, was characterized by a spiritual withdrawal. Petrarch's notion of the *vita contemplativa* that was later recalled by Cotrugli is itself rooted in the romanticized life of the scholar that had been developing since antiquity. The ideal especially gained momentum after the seventh century, when the *Rule of St Benedict* established reading as a part of the daily labours of those who were living in religious houses. As the *Rule* was adopted and augmented in the customs of different communities across the West, the contemplation of texts came to be understood and valued as an important part of monastic routine.

Reading could be organized as a communal activity or an individual endeavour in the monastery.⁷ According to the *Rule*, sacred texts were to be recited during mealtimes. One monk would read passages aloud to the others while they ate together in the refectory. Readings were also performed in the church in front of the entire congregation as part of the daily liturgy. Meanwhile, the provisions for individual reading allowed monks to borrow books from the communal library. These books would be read as part of the quotidian rituals in the cells of the monks or, more frequently, in the cloister. Located next to the church, the cloister was the chief meeting place of the monastery, usually constructed as an arcaded walkway of four long corridors that enclosed a central courtyard. The cloister afforded natural light, fresh air, and a proximity to nature, all considered conducive to meditative reading. However, reading in the cloister also meant exposure to the elements. The less-than-ideal conditions are described on the flyleaf of a manuscript by a monk at Ramsey Abbey: 'As we sit here in tempest, in rain, snow and sun, / Nor writing nor reading in cloister is done.'[8] Despite the realities of cloistered life, the idea of undisturbed reading in a tranquil and secluded setting persisted in the imagination and continued to be cultivated by writers and artists through the late Middle Ages.

Quiet space for reading, eventually embodied in the library, became an integral part of the scholarly ideal. Models for such an isolated place of calm in the home were developed by Buonaccorso and his contemporaries through the course of the fifteenth century. For example, Leon Battista Alberti outlines some of the practicalities of a domestic library in the *De re aedificatoria* (1450). Alberti recommends that wood panels be installed in a room that has been designated for reading. The panelling acts as a barrier of insulation from heat and cold, and can moderate the temperature of the room.[9] Similarly, Angelo Decembrio's *De politia litteraria* (1464) provides an account of the ideal design and furnishing of a library. Echoing Cotrugli, he writes that the library should be located in a secluded part of the house, away from the noise of the household and of neighbours. Moreover, he observed that the light perfume of flowers or scented wood panels could be used to freshen the air in the library, while the books themselves should be protected from dust and direct sunlight, as well as from marauding mice, cats, and dogs. Finally, Decembrio recommends that the books should only be taken out of their cupboards one at a time to be read.[10]

These fifteenth-century narratives are unmistakably influenced by classical scholarship and follow the tradition established by Vitruvius's treatise on architecture.[11] As early as the first century BC, Vitruvius advised that light and fresh air were important considerations in the construction of a library. He suggests that the ideal villa should be built facing east in order to benefit from the morning light, which would protect books from mildew. He writes: 'Bedrooms and libraries ought to have an eastern exposure, because their purposes require the morning light, and also because books in such libraries will not decay. In libraries with southern exposures the books are ruined by worms and dampness, because damp winds come up, which breed and nourish the worms, and destroy the books with mould, by spreading their damp breath over them.'[12]

Once the library had been built, there were other concerns to which to attend, including the arrangement of its contents. A personal account regarding the upkeep of the library can be found in the letters of Cicero, who owned book collections in Rome, Antium, and Tusculum. Cicero describes how he needed to hire assistants to provide specialized support for his chief librarian. He asks his friend, Atticus, to send some staff members to help with the labelling, cataloguing, and repair of the books of the library in Antium. When the organization of his library was finished, he writes to Atticus: 'And now that [chief librarian] Tyrannio has put my books straight, my house seems to have woken to life. Your [assistants] Dionysius and Menophilus have worked wonders over that. Those shelves of yours are the last word in elegance, now that the labels have brightened up the volumes.'[13] Cicero's letter suggests that a library could set the temperament of the home, and that a well-organized collection could inspire a lively household. Classical writers thus set the foundation for the notions of scholarly activity which their medieval successors would later refine. Plans and designs of the archetypal study, as well as recommended practices of reading, all continued to be developed and amplified through the Middle Ages. At the centre of the ideal was a well-designed library in a quiet part of the home, equipped with an orderly collection of books and the proper accoutrements for study; such a space indicated a happy household and an owner of good taste and character.

As different facets of the scholarly model were being explored in textual narrative, artists were developing similar tropes in visual form. One of the earliest illustrated models of the scholar is found in the image of Ezra in the *Codex Amiatinus* from the early eighth century. In the portrait, Ezra is seated at a desk. Behind him is his bookcase, the cupboard doors of which are left ajar to reveal a collection of books. This image of Ezra served as the inspiration for many portraits of the evangelists that are still extant in manuscripts of the early Middle Ages.[14] Together, these illustrations helped to formulate the scholar's ideal pose in visual terms: he should be working at his writing desk with books, pens, and other similar accessories to hand.[15] By the fifteenth century, the trope of the scholar-scribe was beginning to be exercised in other media. An abundance of paintings from the Quattrocento attests to the force of the scholar and his study in the imagination. Jerome, in particular, was often represented in such a setting.[16] Numerous portraits of him, including *St Jerome in His Study* of Colantonio of around 1450, *St Jerome in His Chamber* by Antonello da Messina of around 1460, and the engraving by Albrecht Dürer of 1514, consolidated the visual trope of the scholar-portrait. In these images, Jerome is always seated at his desk, surrounded by all the accoutrements of reading and writing, including a pair of spectacles, an assortment of inkwells, pens, penknives, pen cases, scissors, and candles.

Portraits of this type adorn both manuscript and printed copies of the French translation of Buonaccorso's *Controversia de nobilitate*. In addition to the illustration on Vérard's title page discussed previously (plate 12), an early manuscript of the treatise is decorated with an image that shows a scholar at work in his room, his bed visible behind him (plate 15). Recalling the idea of the monastic cell, the chamber functions as a space both of sleeping and of working. The figure is fully engaged in the process of copying from an exemplar that is pinned above his writing desk. The requisite equipment of a pen, penknife, and inkpot are all in evidence. Miscellaneous papers are strewn about the room and books lie carelessly on the floor – perhaps, it is suggested, left out for quick reference. It appears that the scholar is so absorbed in his work that he has allowed his fire to die out. There is a casual disorder to the room as the scribe remains focused on his labours.

Although the viewer seems to have caught the scholar in a candid moment, the air of spontaneity in these portraits is a contrivance. As Harry Berger puts it, such images document a pose of not-posing; they constitute 'a gaze that exhibits itself to be seen.'[17] The illustrations are rhetorical fictions that seek to recall the ongoing tradition of scholar-portraits. At the same time, however, the illustrations are representations of, or responses to, a particular social and intellectual atmosphere; they are cultural products of their time. The images thus divulge something of the circumstances of their manufacture. Namely, the popularity of the scholar-portrait suggests that there were circles in which prestige was accorded to scholarly activity, or, at least, the appearance of it.

From this perspective, the story recounted by Buonaccorso in the *Controversia de nobilitate* emerges as more than a simple contest between the stasis of the monument and the vitality of the library. Even as the library emerged in the fifteenth-century home, it had already become a memorial; it could at once fabricate and commemorate an intellectual heritage for its owner. The library thus symbolizes scholarly activity whether or not any such work is taking place. In the same way that the monuments of Cornelius recall his genealogical connections, the library is used to advertise Flaminius's intellectual connections. According to Flaminius, the accumulation of books in the library may be understood as the amassing of virtues. As this sentiment gained support in the late medieval period, the domestic library and its books soon became collectible objects. The possession of books was considered a mark of high social standing by some because it indicated that the owner had both the means to acquire the books and the leisure to enjoy them.[18] By the beginning of the sixteenth century, Caroline Elam has noted, the identification of the study or *studiolo* with collecting had become so intimate that its association with the activity of reading was, in many cases, lost.[19] In later periods, the *studiolo* became exclusively a space of collection and exhibition: a gallery, cabinet of curiosity, or *wunderkammer*.

A fine example of the scholarly performance is the *studiolo* of Federico of Montefeltro in Urbino. The *studiolo*, completed around 1476, is a small space, measuring approximately 3.6 by 3.4 metres.[20] Its walls are veneered with illusionistic inlaid panels that depict furniture and other ornaments suitable for a study (plate 16). A bank of benches seems to line the walls of the room. The cupboards above them appear with their doors artfully left ajar. Assembled on the shelves is an assortment of musical and astronomical instruments, hourglasses, inkwells, and pieces of armour. Books are also featured among the faux furnishings. The names of Roman writers, such as Cicero and Vergil, are visible on the fore-edges of the codices, helping to complete the ideal space for the classicizing pursuits of a humanist.[21] The apparent disarray suggests that Federico has only been distracted from his studies momentarily. Like the scholar-portrait, the *studiolo* is configured as a performance staged for an ever-present audience.[22]

In addition to the inlaid panels, a series of portraits also contributes to the scholarly atmosphere. Paintings of twenty-eight famous men line the walls above the marquetry, and include such personages as Plato, Boethius, Euclid, Jerome, Thomas Aquinas, Dante, and Petrarch. These portraits, arranged in two rows with lay personalities in the upper register and their ecclesiastical counterparts in the lower, correspond roughly to the important fields of study at the time: the *quadrivium* of astronomy, music, arithmetic, and geometry, part of the *trivium*, including logic and rhetoric, as well as moral philosophy, poetry, law, and medicine.[23] The pretence of an intellectual heritage is overt here; Federico imagines himself in the company of these writers and scholars, and, perhaps, as one of them. Indeed, it has been conjectured by some experts that a double portrait of Federico and his son had even been placed in the series of paintings.[24]

Despite the scholarly atmosphere generated by the inlaid panels, Federico's *studiolo* does not function as a study or library. The room was not designed as a place in which to keep books or to read them. There is scant storage, and very little natural light illumines the room. Nevertheless, outfitted with all the appropriate accoutrements for scholarship in *trompe l'oeil*, the *studiolo* was constructed to look like an ideal study. Because it is situated on the upper floor of the *palazzo*, between the duke's dressing room and the audience room, the *studiolo* is easily associated with personal space and contributes to the illusion that the room reflects Federico's character. Federico's *studiolo* may be presented as a quiet retreat from the world, but the room is always on exhibition and exhorts the viewer to imagine its owner at work here.[25] There is important play between 'showing' and 'not-showing' in the *studiolo*. The room is a theatrical space of self-exhibition, a monument and a memorial to study that permits Federico to broadcast his erudition. With the *studiolo*, Federico has acquired an intellectual heritage.

Federico's books were not stored in the *studiolo*, but in a large room on the main floor of the palazzo.[26] Like the *studiolo*, the library functions in a performative way; visitors to the palazzo must pass by the library on their way to the grand staircase that leads up to Federico's rooms, perhaps catching a glimpse of the book collection as they do so. The location of the library adjacent to the entrance hall recalls Flaminius's description of his own study, which he says will be seen 'in the first place.' Moreover, reminiscent of Cicero's letter, 'well-ordered' shelves were said to have lined the long walls of the room.[27] Another account offers further details about the arrangement of the library, relating that books were piled on top of each other, three or four codices high, in eight cupboards of seven shelves each.[28] The manuscripts themselves were bound with coloured materials, such as silk, linen, and leather, some highly ornamented.

By the time of his death in 1482, Federico had amassed around a thousand books, in both manuscript and print, including a copy of the *Controversia de nobilitate* that was dedicated to his father.[29] Federico owned six hundred books in Latin, over one hundred in Greek, and around eighty in Hebrew. He also collected works in the Italian vernacular by writers such as Dante and Petrarch. The holdings of his library were organized according to the classification scheme of the seven liberal arts, the *trivium* and *quadrivium*, that had been established in the early Middle Ages. Many libraries of the Quattrocento were arranged in this manner, including the private collections of Francesco Sforza, Francesco Gonzaga, and Piero di Cosimo de' Medici.[30] One of the earliest extant inventories of Federico's library is the *Indice vecchio*, compiled around 1487.[31] The *Indice* lists the sacred writings of the collection first, beginning with bibles and psalters, followed by the Church Fathers and philosophical works. Next are the books on medicine, law, mathematics, and cosmography. The final section of the inventory lists the books that have been classified as history, poetry, and grammar. Federico's copy of the *Controversia de nobilitate* appears in this last category, among histories and panegyrics.[32] Grouped with other disputations, the treatise thus understood according to its form; also in this category were invectives and laudatory pieces. In Federico's library, the *Controversia de nobilitate* was considered a work of rhetoric.

Thus classified, the *Controversia de nobilitate* was likely read as an exercise in composition, an application of the lessons garnered from classical writers on rhetorical style. Contemporary evidence, moreover, suggests that the treatise was appreciated for the quality of its form. After Buonaccorso's debate began to be circulated in Florence around 1428, Poggio Bracciolini responded with his own discussion of nobility, the *De nobilitate*. Poggio's tract prompted such a lively reaction – from both supporters and detractors – that he was subsequently compelled to write a defence of his work. Upon comparing the two treatises, Lauro Quirini shared his thoughts about the two writers in a letter to Pietro Tommasi. He writes: '[Poggio] tried to demonstrate that he was the first Italian to discuss nobility, although in reality another man had not only discussed it before him but had done so more intelligently and eloquently. Did [Poggio] think the learned were so blind that they would not find out sooner or later that Buonaccorso da Montemagno, the best of orators, wrote two declamations on the subject prior to Poggio …? [The Genoese] judged Buonaccorso's orations elegant and worthy of immortality and accused Poggio of plagiarizing from them.'[33] Lauro's letter indicates that treatises like the *Controversia de nobilitate* and *De nobilitate* were distributed throughout the humanist community for examination, comparison, and discussion, and were indeed designed to stimulate such activity, for this was how a scholar's reputation could be established or consolidated.[34] The works were evaluated closely with special attention paid to their rhetorical form. In this way, the circulation of texts was carefully controlled as part of a broader system of negotiating social status, and the sharing of ideas was correspondingly constrained as writers sought to establish and secure their reputations in the humanist milieu and in society at large.[35]

Over the last sixty years, historians have cited the *Controversia de nobilitate* as a crucial piece of evidence in the development of fifteenth-century civic humanism. Because the dialogue suggests that Flaminius could elevate his social status based on his service to the state and individual merit, it has been argued that the *Controversia* is a typical demonstration of Quattrocento civic pride and constitutes proof of the rise of the mid-dle class. Scholars such as Hans Baron, Quentin Skinner, and Alexander Murray have understood the text as an indication of the changing intellectual climate in the Italian city-states and especially in Florence.[36] They contended that interest in the *Controversia* reflected a wide-spread sentiment in the fifteenth century that rejected the idea that nobility was exclusively associated with genealogy or familial wealth. The growth of a mercantile class, the scholars believed, accounted for the popularity of this alternative model in which social rank could be improved though political activity.

But the appeal of the *Controversia de nobilitate*, reincarnated as *La controversie de noblesse*, in the courts of northern Europe indicates that the treatise could induce a more flexible reading than one that constituted an espousal of humanist ideals characteristic of fifteenth-century Florence. Attempting to reconcile the concurrent popularity of the *Controversia* in the Florentine civic and Burgundian courtly spheres, A.J. Vanderjagt expressed doubt that Quattrocento humanists had the earnest intention of promoting equality. He contended instead that those who supported linking nobility with personal virtue were acting primarily out of self-interest.[37] Moreover, Vanderjagt argued that Buonaccorso incorporated enough courtly associations in the *Controversia* that the text would resonate with an audience north of the Alps. The dedicatory letter to Guidanto-nio, duke of Urbino, combined with the setting of the debate, allowed the *Controversia* to be construed as a courtly romance. According to Vanderjagt, then, the treatise should be more accurately classified as a 'cliffhanger between civic rhetoric and court literature.'[38]

The multiple identities of Buonaccorso's debate have consequences that reach far beyond the ways in which the treatise might be understood by individual communities of reading. As the preceding discussion has shown, the *Controversia de nobilitate* can be read as a rhetorical exercise, as it seems to have been in Federico's library in Urbino and more widely in Quattrocento Italy, or, in the twentieth century, as an earnest discus-sion of Florentine humanist ideals about the equality of men. Meanwhile, in its French incarnation, the treatise is part of the corpus of courtly vernacular literature in which it is still considered a member today. Changes to the material configuration of the page and codex have enabled Buonaccorso's treatise to assume different guises in different reading communities, and it is according to these identities that the books of the *Controversia de nobilitate* are currently catalogued, classified, stored, preserved, read, and used in the modern library. In the library, the pages of the *Controversia de nobilitate* become mate-rial participants in broader traditions of knowledge. At the same time, however, they help to reinscribe the divisions between the disciplines, and shape how categories such as 'humanism' or 'romance literature' are now understood. The pages of the *Controversia* therefore not only influence the reception of the text locally, but also affect the ways in which divisions of knowledge continue to be distinguished on a grander scale.

The entanglement of the *Controversia* in the disciplines of knowledge is perhaps nowhere more evident in than in the modern Bibliothèque nationale de France, where the classification of information is rendered in spatial terms.[39] The logic for the organization of the treatise – conceptually in the catalogue and physically in the library – is found in the pages of the *Controversia de nobilitate*. The proposals set out by the designers in the fifteenth century are taken as incontrovertible statements about the membership of the *Controversia de nobilitate* in the disciplines of knowledge. By examining how the Bibliothèque nationale has chosen to organize and handle the *Controversia* and its translations, the remainder of this chapter explores the ways in which Buonaccorso's debate is reimagined and deployed in the library. The following discussion shows how the pages of the *Controversia de nobilitate* participate in multiple systems of classification, are transformed into representatives of different categories of knowledge, and even come to signify knowledge itself.[40]

The Bibliothèque nationale de France (BNF) currently holds twenty-two manuscripts and early printed editions of the *Controversia* and its translations.[41] Aside from the more recent editions of the text, there are ten manuscripts and four early printed books in Latin, three manuscripts of the French translation, and examples of the two fifteenth-century editions of *La controversie de noblesse* printed by Colard Mansion and Antoine Vérard. The BNF also preserves a copy of the edition in German by Conrad Fyner and a printed edition of the *Declamacyon de noblesse* by William Caxton. The different books have been separated variously according to their mode of production, subject area, and value in the Bibliothèque nationale. By grouping the copies of Buonaccorso's treatise in these ways, the BNF locates the *Controversia de nobilitate* in different areas in its particular institutional landscape of knowledge.

The most apparent division separates the handwritten incarnations of the *Controversia* from their printed counterparts. This split arises from the assumption that a significant cognitive and cultural change took place with the introduction of the printing press.[42] Yet a decisive break cannot be discerned in the material history of the *Controversia de nobilitate*. Both manuscript and printed versions of the treatise were produced and read concurrently throughout the fifteenth century and into the next, with designers readily adapting for use in print the strategies of visualization that had been established for the *Controversia* in manuscript. In the BNF, the overlapping and simultaneous histories of the manuscripts and printed books of the *Controversia* are overlooked in favour of a different story – namely, the arrangement of books according to their mode of production. Mode of production is thus presented as a valid way by which to classify materials in the BNF. Because the library has created the explicit categories of manuscript and print, the codices of the *Controversia de nobilitate* can now be identified, understood, and evaluated according to their technology of transmission.

The intellectual division between the handwritten and printed versions of the *Controversia de nobilitate* in the BNF is further legitimized by a corresponding geographical division. The manuscript copies of the *Controversia* are preserved at Site Richelieu, an eighteenth-century building near the Louvre in the centre of Paris. Meanwhile, all printed editions of the *Controversia* are stored some five kilometres away in the thirteenth district in the Bibliothèque François Mitterrand at Site Tolbiac. This geographical separation of the books and their readers is amplified by the different operational principles of the buildings.[43] The routines exercised in the two locations underscore the different approaches to materials, information, and knowledge. For instance, manuscripts are granted special treatment in how they are catalogued and handled. Particular rituals govern the *Controversia de nobilitate* in Site Richelieu, ostensibly to ensure the safety and preservation of the manuscripts. Entry to the reading room is regulated: readers are carefully monitored and their belongings are inspected. The printed editions of Buonaccorso's debate, by contrast, are thought to be more stable. The apparent homogeneity of printed books is used to justify a broader approach to their classification, handling, and preservation. The perceived sameness of print led to the BNF's decision to relocate all such material to Site Tolbiac, where the printed editions of the *Controversia* and its translations are grouped according to subject matter.

In the Bibliothèque François Mitterrand at Site Tolbiac, the online catalogue provides the first line of access to the holdings, and creates emergent relationships for Buonaccorso's composition and its translations. The system places the printed copies of the *Controversia de nobilitate* in such categories as Catholic theology, philosophy, natural law, ethics, and literature, often depending on contiguous texts for guidance.[44] This particular arrangement of the *Controversia* offers new ways in which the treatise might be understood. In the catalogue, a copy of the *Controversia* becomes a member and representative of an intellectual discipline with which it may have traditionally had little association. Different codices of the *Controversia de nobilitate* are assigned in this way to diverse subject areas, and the conceptual reshuffling encourages alternative ways of interpreting Buonaccorso's treatise. The online catalogue is as much generative as it is restrictive; even as the catalogue limits some ways of interpreting the *Controversia*, it broadens the range of possible meanings for the treatise. Sustaining multiple and different identities is nothing new for the books of the *Controversia de nobilitate*, but these identities take on a striking spatial dimension in the Bibliothèque François Mitterrand, which is a vivid incarnation of the intellectual divisions that it uses to order books and knowledge. The building embodies its classificatory scheme, its four towers representing a specific subject area: Law, Science, History, and Literature. Because of the way that the *Controversia de nobilitate* has been catalogued, the printed editions of Buonaccorso's treatise span these disciplines and are intended to be correspondingly stored in at least two different towers. The *Controversia* thus challenges the rhetoric of order proposed by the architecture of the Bibliothèque François Mitterrand and reveals the ambiguity of institutional systems of control.

Aside from being divided according to mode of production and subject, the books of the *Controversia de nobilitate* find themselves further differentiated by yet another way of understanding the treatise. Many of the printed editions of Buonaccorso's text and its translations in the Bibliothèque François Mitterrand have been designated as rare. These 'rare' editions of the *Controversia* were printed around the end of the fifteenth century and the beginning of the next. Date, material, or other factors, such as the presence of the signature of an author, artist, or owner, might earn a codex this special status. These copies of the *Controversia de nobilitate* are thus distinguished from their peers as being extraordinary and are housed separately from the general collection in the Rare Books Reserve. The Reserve presents the *Controversia* in another context. For instance, the 1473 edition of the *Controversia de nobilitate* in Latin and Antoine Vérard's 1497 copy of the French translation are grouped together as equally rare. The 1473 edition is un-illustrated, and printed on paper. Meanwhile, Vérard's edition is printed on parchment, ornamented with illustrated title pages, and dedicated to – and was destined for – King Charles VIII of France. Although the 1473 version of the *Controversia* is not outfitted with the same material cues as Vérard's edition, it now attains a comparable status by its designation as rare and its inclusion in the Reserve collections of the Bibliothèque François Mitterrand.

The architecture of the library aids in emphasizing the difference between the 'rare' books of the *Controversia* and their 'non-rare' counterparts. Located in Room Y on the mezzanine of the library, the Rare Books Reserve is physically isolated from the rooms that are designated for scholarly research on the lower level, or the *rez-de-jardin*, as well as from the spaces that are designated for public access on the upper level, the *haut-de-jardin*. Thus installed between the two main floors, the Reserve avoids identification with one zone or the other, and is able to devise its own identity in the Bibliothèque François Mitterrand.[45] In this in-between space, Room Y can formulate its own approach to the administration of reading activities. Namely, the digital system that governs movement in the rest of Site Tolbiac is eschewed in favour of the traditional routines of the Manuscripts Room of Site Richelieu. Like the Manuscripts Room, entry to the Reserve is controlled through a process of personal interview, and access to the collection is granted by special permission. Readers register for seats and submit requests for books in person at the front desk rather than by computer. The unusual procedures of Room Y communicate to readers that they are in an exclusive space and have access to a special collection of materials. These intellectual and physical signals oblige readers to make certain associations for the books within the Reserve as well as for those without. It is understood that the codices in the Rare Books Reserve are valued more highly than their counterparts located in other parts of the library. By circumscribing Room Y with conceptual, physical, and procedural distinctions, the Reserve bestows upon its holdings and readers a privileged status that influences the ways in which all the books of the library, including the *Controversia de nobilitate* and its translations, are understood.

Despite the intentions of the designers of its books in the fifteenth century, the trajectory of the *Controversia de nobilitate* may be influenced by unforeseen social pressures that recontextualize the treatise, consequently affecting the way that it is read.[46] As 'Reading the Library' has shown, the *Controversia* and its translations have acquired additional ways of mattering in the BNF: the codices of the *Controversia de nobilitate* are manuscripts or printed editions; they can be rare or ordinary; and they participate in different disciplines in the humanities and the social sciences. In these new configurations, the books in turn help to shape broader categories of knowledge. The associations and affiliations of the *Controversia de nobilitate* are multiple, simultaneous, overlapping, fragmentary, and changeable; entangled in these complex and sometimes contradictory relationships, the books of the *Controversia* are nevertheless tied to the construction of literary genres, canons, and historical epochs.

The display of books is an important part of the design of the library, and the codices of the *Controversia* – along with many other printed materials – are meant to be arranged in the towers of the Bibliothèque François Mitterrand as signifiers of knowledge. This story is, in part, intimated in Buonaccorso's very text. As the books of Flaminius became signs of virtue in the fictional debate with Cornelius, so too do the books of the *Controversia de nobilitate* function in an analogous way at Site Tolbiac. The towers of the building have been conceived to exhibit the accumulation and sedimentation of a collective intellectual heritage.[47] Measuring seventy-nine metres in height and designed in the form of opened books, the towers are colossal assertions about the possession and control of information. The books of the *Controversia de nobilitate* become a part of the visual and material expression of the Bibliothèque François Mitterrand; they are deployed as indicators of learning, and used to symbolize virtue as part of the scholarly performance that Buonaccorso's own text had described. In this way, the codices of the *Controversia* are enfolded into the library as part of its monumental representation of knowledge.

The ideal library is recalled with great familiarity in other parts of Site Tolbiac. The four towers are connected in a rectangular shape around an interior garden; the configuration of the long passageways is a self-conscious reference to the monastic cloister. The cloister was the regular place of reading and writing in the monastery, its arcaded walkway providing readers shelter from the elements while granting access to sunlight, fresh air, and a proximity to nature, all of which were thought to facilitate the contemplation of texts. In an imitation of the colonnade of the cloister, the glass-encased corridors of the Bibliothèque François Mitterrand offer secure vantage points from which readers may gaze upon the trees, grass, and flora of the central garden. The green space at the heart of the library plays a key role in the ideal. In the courtyard, according to the architect, Dominique Perrault, 'We have created a mystical place beyond all known references ... – the soft protection of undergrowth, with its aromas and rustling sounds, the reunions with oneself, and with another world.'[48] By replicating the layout of the cloister, the courtyard of the Bibliothèque François Mitterrand summons the notion of the idealized life of the scholar-monk that had been of great interest to writers in the Middle Ages. The allusion to this traditional motif that has been a part of the cultural imaginary for centuries garners authority for the architectural assertions of Site Tolbiac. The reference to the medieval cloister serves not only to substantiate the intellectual character of the new library, but also to indicate the long-standing tradition to which this space belongs. By evoking notions of a scholarly heritage, the Bibliothèque François Mitterrand establishes a foundation upon which it can declare possession of a body of knowledge, exert control over it, and regulate access to it.

Like the page and the book, the library transmits a message about its own complicated history. The architecture of the Bibliothèque François Mitterrand is purposely designed to recall and participate in a scholarly ethos, but the recapitulation of traditional tropes discloses an urgent desire to convince onlookers of a heritage of erudition. Like the monuments of Cornelius, the building and its collections are thought to embody the combined intellectual achievement of a nation, passed down from one generation to the next. Meanwhile, like the library of Flaminius, the Bibliothèque François Mitterrand is an assertion of a learned identity that is intended to establish and consolidate a social, cultural, national, or even international standing.

The idealized notion of scholarly life has been cultivated for centuries in narrative, image, and architecture, entangling within it the *Controversia de nobilitate*. From Flaminius's invocation of the library in the debate, to the addition of scholar-portraits in the manuscripts and printed editions of Buonaccorso's treatise, to the incorporation of the codices in the architectural expression of the BNF, the *Controversia de nobilitate* has borne witness to, participated in, and promoted the development of the scholarly model. The foregoing discussion has explored how manuscripts and printed editions of the *Controversia de nobilitate* can be caught up in broader vectors in the disciplines of knowledge. The strategies that shape the making of meaning in the library of the twenty-first century may thus be influenced by – among others – manuscript, printing, and digital technologies; historiographical and literary debates; cultural ideals and conventions; as well as emergent attitudes about reading, writing, and information management.

The next chapter will continue this exploration as designers cultivate a presence for the *Controversia de nobilitate* in the digital environment. The digital pages of the *Controversia* transmit codes that are unique to their material and mode of production, but the interfaces nevertheless show vestiges of established traditions of textual transmission. As the page divests itself of some of the constraints of its more conventional instantiations, its expression still evokes familiar practices of reading and writing. Further, the digital instantiations of the *Controversia de nobilitate* are subjected to the same disciplines of knowledge that mark their parchment and paper counterparts, and are additionally shaped by the mission of the online exhibition, database, or catalogue for which they were encoded; these agendas affect readerly interpretation, and thereby influence the fortunes of the treatise. In the digital environment, then, the *Controversia de nobilitate* continues to be shaped from within and without.

5

The Digital Page

Digital pages are complex interfaces that provide a point of contact between designer and reader. Like their analogue counterparts, these pages communicate verbally, graphically, aurally, and tactilely, and are constructed in a material way that influences how they are read and understood.[1] Each page is a unique combination of visual expression and physical platform, and it is with this dynamic relationship that the page transmits information and contributes to the making of meaning. As the discussion shifts to examples of the *Controversia de nobilitate* in emergent media, the entanglement between the material and mattering of the page continues to be of central importance. Treating the digitized pages of the *Controversia* as further manifestations of the *pagina*, or the conceptual division of the page, this chapter follows Buonaccorso da Montemagno's medieval treatise into the twenty-first century.

Although the digitally encoded page may imitate the look and behaviour of counterparts in parchment and paper, it has its own distinct materiality.[2] Computational technologies open new avenues for the transmission of information even as they foreclose others. For instance, multiple *paginae* can now be presented simultaneously in one place, organized in dynamic and responsive configurations. Meanwhile, a single digitally encoded *pagina* may appear to stretch beyond the physical dimensions of the hardware, consequently demanding that the reader scroll in different directions to navigate its borders. The boundaries of the digital page, like those of the *paginae* in the papyrus roll, need not be coextensive with the boundaries of the material platform; the digital *pagina* is not always conterminous with a computer monitor or the screen of a hand-held device. Furthermore, the unique materiality of a digital page enables the interface to support relationships with its siblings that are unlike those that exist between the contiguous pages of a codex. Because the connections between digital pages are predicated on grounds that are often computational in nature, the assumptions regarding the construction of the book and the composition of the pages cannot always be applied directly to new media. As Roger Chartier has observed, the digital representation of written artefacts 'radically modifies the notion of contextualization because it substitutes distribution in a logical architecture – the software that organizes a database, electronic files or key words – for the physical contiguity among texts put together in the same printed object.'[3] In addition, the computational codes of the digital page are themselves shaped by cultural, political, and economic pressures, as well as contemporary approaches to the transmission of text . The digital page and the circumstances of its incarnation, including its collection and configuration in an online exhibition, database, or archive, are thus open to critical evaluation; it is this materiality from which meaning is made.

Having examined handwritten and printed examples of the *Controversia de nobilitate* on parchment and paper, the investigation now turns to the digital incarnations of Buonaccorso's treatise. Chapter 5 offers possible ways of understanding and analysing the newest versions of the *Controversia de nobilitate* which have been shaped by manuscript, print, computational, and other technologies for the transmission of information. The English and French translations of the *Controversia*, the *Declamacyon de noblesse* and *La controversie de noblesse* respectively, began to circulate in digital form in the early part of the twenty-first century. Both products are complex technological translations, employing the conventions of textual editing and facsimile reproduction to imitate the bibliographic signs of fifteenth-century manuscripts and incunabula.[4]

Textual criticism has been an influential force in the transmission of ideas in the last century. As part of a philological enterprise, early scholars collected multiple versions of a text and organized them systematically according to date, similarity, and quality.[5] The oldest surviving manuscripts were used to reconstruct an exemplar of a text from which all subsequent copies were supposed to have been derived. Earlier witnesses were usually deemed more valuable because of their antiquity; later manuscripts were stigmatized by virtue of their differences and considered 'a priori bad.'[6] Drawing upon different portions of different manuscripts, the resulting edition might embody an idealized version of the text that may never have existed in a single incarnation. Other scholars, preferring to avoid overt editorial intrusion, designated a best-manuscript or copy-text which they transcribed and then supplemented with the variants from other surviving versions of the text.[7] Meanwhile, as the techniques of lithography and photography were refined through the eighteenth and nineteenth centuries, designers were able to use imaging technologies to offer visual simulations of illuminated manuscripts and other materials.[8] By the twentieth century, colour and digital photography could be employed to create facsimiles that showed such detail as the fine grain of the writing material and other characteristics of the page. In contrast to textual editions, then, a facsimile can provide readers with a visual imitation of unique objects. Although the digitized *Declamacyon de noblesse* is by no means a critical edition of the text and the digitized *La controversie de noblesse* is by no means a comprehensive facsimile of a manuscript, the latest versions of Buonaccorso's debate nevertheless align themselves with these recognized methods of reproduction. By adopting the rhetoric of the edition and facsimile, the designers indicate how their products should be located in the broader spectrum of textual transmission and thereby understood.

The English translation of Buonaccorso's treatise, the *Declamacyon de noblesse*, appears in a database of English material printed before 1700. This database, called *Early English Books Online* (*EEBO*), uses both the textual edition and the facsimile reproduction as models for its transmission of text.[9] *EEBO* offers searchable full-text transcriptions and digitized images that take microfilmed copies of early English printed books as exemplars.[10] Thus, the digitized *Declamacyon* in *EEBO* is based on a microfilm of one of the surviving copies of William Caxton's edition of 1481, currently shelved as London, British Library, IB.55045.[11]

In its full-text instantiation, the digitized *Declamacyon* is displayed in a sans-serif typeface. The text is arranged in a single column in long lines. Signs that refer to Caxton's edition have been carefully included; for instance, virgules ('/') are used to indicate where the lines of text are broken on the printed page. Meanwhile, each new paragraph in the full-text edition corresponds to each new page of the codex. Hyperlinks are positioned between these paragraphs to allow the reader to call up the matching images that have been digitally encoded from the microfilm. These cues remind readers of the connection between the full-text version of the *Declamacyon* and the printed edition that it uses as an exemplar, even as the treatise is mediated through microfilm. The paratext of the *pagina* makes clear that the digitization has a predecessor in a printed book; this relationship is preserved and even foregrounded as if *EEBO* were presenting a diplomatic edition – an exact transcription – of the *Declamacyon* as it appears in British Library, IB.55045.[12]

At play in the digitally encoded version of the *Declamacyon* are the intellectual assumptions associated with transcription. The activity of transcription is fraught with the same dilemmas whether performed in an environment dominated by manuscript, print, or digital technologies; a careful transcription still constitutes an assertion by an editor about the text. That is, by dividing the text and assigning particular values to words and phrases, the designers exert influence upon how readers engage with and understand the treatise in its digitally encoded instantiation. The searches that readers may conduct depends on how a text has been marked up with code. As Stephen Ramsay has stated, these tags are 'not merely structural delineations, but patterns of potential meaning woven through a text by a human interpreter.'[13] Moreover, Peter Robinson observed from his own attempts to develop online scholarly editions that 'transcription is a fundamentally interpretive activity. It is not at all a simple recording of what is on the page. It is forever an act of translation.'[14] The strategies that mark the traditional page can be thus re-enacted in its digital counterpart. In the same way that scholars propose a particular reading of a text in the traditional critical edition, *EEBO* offers its particular interpretation of the *Declamacyon*.

In a peculiar twist, the signs that link the full-text version with Caxton's printed edition are expunged from the 'print-friendly' version of the digitized *Declamacyon*. The paragraph breaks that had indicated the beginning of each successive page in the printed edition are collapsed, and the paragraphs themselves conflated. Moreover, new paragraph breaks are introduced in the 'printable' view; these breaks have no correlation with the layout of text in Caxton's version, but instead emphasize moments of rhetorical significance in the debate. By configuring the debate verbally and visually with these new cues, the designers offer yet another editorial interpretation of the *Declamacyon*. The print version thus stands at a remove from Caxton's printed edition. Indeed, any of the printed copies that are generated from *EEBO* will have more in common with their on-screen counterpart than their incunabulum exemplar of 1481. The printed page that is issued from the 'printable' view is governed distinctly by computational codes; even as the *Declamacyon* returns to printed form, it is irrevocably marked by the logic of *EEBO*.

The *Declamacyon* in its full-text and print-view versions purposefully commingles the respective spaces of the story and the reader. The designers present the text in a way that looks unmediated so that the audience is seemingly put in direct contact with the text. Moreover, the full-text and print versions of Buonaccorso's treatise in *EEBO* encourage the reader to make a conceptual elision; although these digitally encoded editions of the *Declamacyon* are not facsimiles – visual imitations – in the traditional sense, they are designed to be construed as faithful reproductions of their exemplar. As Bernard Cerquiglini writes, 'Tempted by the diplomatic copy, these editions [of medieval texts] have been drawn into the fantasy of the facsimile, of honestly providing in the most complete form all the intact data.'[15] The fantasy of the facsimile is made more credible in new media because digital technology often seeks to conceal the presence of its own mediation. Nevertheless, the interface, however unmediated it may appear, is a careful construction. The aesthetic of transparency, or immediacy as J.D. Bolter and Richard Grusin have called it, generates the illusion that the *Declamacyon* has been protected from editorial intervention.[16] The design of such a page is meant to garner authority for *EEBO*'s edition of the *Declamacyon* by capitalizing on the uncritical supposition that digital technology is neutral, 'indifferent to the subjectivity of … personal idiosyncrasies,' and that it can produce 'not just more observations, but better observations.'[17] The designers have thus produced a page for the *Declamacyon* that is an artful pose, one that authenticates as it proposes a reading of the text.

The *Declamacyon* is also transmitted in *EEBO* more explicitly as a facsimile, instantiated as a series of digitized images. These images are hybrid products of print, microfilm, and digital technologies. Engineered according to a principle of visual fidelity, the facsimile purports to offer a simulation of the *Declamacyon* as it appears in London,

British Library, IB.55045. The images allow the digital *Declamacyon* to imitate the look of its fifteenth-century counterpart, but it is clear that there are important differences. More than inconsistencies in visual similitude, these differences point to changes in the underlying rhetorical, cognitive, and physical structures of the page.

The traditional facsimile often shares the same platform as the artefact that it seeks to imitate; namely, a traditional facsimile is a codex that imitates a codex. In the digital environment, however, images displayed on screen are used to do the same work. The digital version is computational, the result of algorithmic code.[18] Because the process of constructing a digital facsimile differs from that of the traditional facsimile, the two products are underpinned by different systems and therefore shape the making of meaning in different ways. Furthermore, even as the facsimile imitates the visual tradition of an exemplar, it is marked by a social history of its own.[19] Questions regarding the difference in materiality between the original and its reproduction are often dismissed as inconsequential, but this cognitive slip is promoted by the rhetoric of the facsimile itself. After all, facsimiles look like the 'real thing' because they have been designed to look like the 'real thing.' Although an illusion of virtuality is central to any facsimile, this particular kind of artifice has been especially refined in the codes of digital reproductions. Both hardware and software are complicit in the illusion. As Bruno Latour and Adam Lowe have remarked, 'The association of digitality with virtuality is entirely due to the bad habits given by only one of its possible outputs: the … screen of our computers.'[20] The facsimile is designed to imitate, to emulate, to reproduce; it encourages readers to overlook the ontological rift between the facsimile and the object that is being imitated, and nowhere more acutely than in the digital environment.

The disjunction between the logic of the codex and the logic of the computer can be detected as two facing pages of the *Declamacyon* are flattened and welded together on the *pagina* of the facsimile, first in microfilm and again in *EEBO*. The physical distinction of the two pages is replaced with visual continuity. Moreover, this continuity is taken as the organizing principle of the facsimile as *EEBO* shapes Caxton's printed page into a new cognitive unit.[21] In this configuration, the prologue of the *Declamacyon* is fused together with the conclusion of the treatise that was bound before it on f. 98v. The facing pages of f. 98v and f. 99r from the 1481 edition are now subsumed under a single page number, both simultaneously indicated by and accessed on *EEBO*'s page 99. In this way, the three-dimensional page opening of the codex is replaced by its simulacrum; the nuanced relationship of contiguity and physical difference in the facing pages of the printed edition is replaced with visual continuity in *EEBO*'s document images. These are not simple substitutions that engender little effect, but instead represent significant changes in the communicative process.

The material shift in the way that the *Declamacyon* is configured, reconfigured, and transmitted has important consequences for how readers understand what is being conveyed. Even as different images of the *Declamacyon* are called forth from the database by the reader, the *pagina* exerts the editorial voice of *EEBO*. The paratext declaims *EEBO*'s proprietorship of the *Declamacyon* with an ever-present banner across the top of the page. The banner reminds readers that the *Declamacyon* belongs in the context of *EEBO*, is read in *EEBO*, and is able to be read because of *EEBO*. The designers thus dislodge Caxton from his central role in the history of the *Declamacyon*'s transmission. Marginalized from this history, too, is Buonaccorso. *EEBO* identifies the *Declamacyon* primarily by the first text of the printed edition in which it is bound, the *On Old Age* of Cicero. The reference beneath the images of the pages of the *Declamacyon* credits Cicero as author, lists a translation of *De senectute* (On Old Age) as the title, and acknowledges the British Library as owner of the printed exemplar. With these paratextual devices, the treatise is arranged and presented in a new way. *EEBO*'s *Declamacyon* is not a simple surrogate for the book that is shelved under London, British Library, IB.55045; instead, it is an interpretation of the microfilm of a single copy of Caxton's edition that possesses its own distinct materiality and social history.

As computational codes work within the digitally encoded versions of the *Declamacyon* to make the text legible and comprehensible to readers, they also moderate the circumstances in which the treatise is to be made visible. These codes direct the dimensions of the *pagina*, the shape of the letter forms, the size and quality of the images, and the arrangement of other paratextual mechanisms of the *Declamacyon*.[22] In this way, both digitized versions of the *Declamacyon* are also systems by which the treatise is ordered and the behaviour of its readers is shaped. In the foregoing examination of the *Declamacyon* in *EEBO*, the digital *pagina* emerges as a thoughtfully encoded contrivance, much like any of its predecessors and contemporaries in other media. Although computational, the codes that underpin *EEBO*'s *Declamacyon* are still influenced by contemporary attitudes towards the visualization, transmission, and preservation of ideas. Thus, the algorithms and protocols that enable the *Declamacyon* to be read and used online constitute evidence of their own manufacture, as well as broader movements in the communication of information.

Having been based on a particular microfilm of a particular codex, *EEBO*'s versions of the *Declamacyon* are no more accurate or reliable than any other witness of Caxton's edition. Nevertheless, the digital instantiations of the *Declamacyon* achieve a privileged status as a part of the *EEBO* database. They enjoy a modern distribution, inscribed into a canon of early printed materials that now circulates in many scholarly environments. As the versions of the *Declamacyon* in *EEBO* are circulated, read, and downloaded, their digital processes are inscribed into twenty-first-century narratives about the treatise. *EEBO*'s incarnations of the *Declamacyon* will come to provide the dominant reading for the English translation of Buonaccorso's debate; they will be the versions that are the most often referred to and the most often cited. As readers copy, annotate, save, print, and interact with the text in different ways, the editions of the *Declamacyon* in *EEBO* will assume the role of exemplars and inspire other instantiations of the treatise in manuscript, print, digital, and hybrid forms. This particular understanding of the *Declamacyon* will feed back into the textual tradition and consequently influence the trajectories of the *Declamacyon*, Caxton's edition, and the *Controversia de nobilitate* in general.[23]

As the previous chapters have shown, pages and books that transmit the same words do not always transmit the same story. Each embodiment of a text communicates with readers in its own way. Digitized texts are likewise not homogeneous. These materials are coded with computational instructions that are shaped by specific circumstances of manufacture and, as a result, constitute unique methods of communication. The preceding discussion of the *Declamacyon* in *EEBO* has revealed that the same service can provide two distinct incarnations of a text, each employing individual strategies of expression. Although both versions can be described as 'digital,' the term does not adequately identify their commonalities or differences. Similarly, the digitally encoded French translation of Buonaccorso's *Controversia de nobilitate* demands a separate analysis, for it, too, bears the signs of its own process of production. *La controversie de noblesse* in its digitized form was conceived as part of a different initiative, and is marked with a set of codes that diverges from those that structure the editions of the *Declamacyon* in *EEBO*.

Digital versions of *La controversie de noblesse* have been published by the Royal Library of Belgium as part of a project to showcase the fifteenth-century collection of the dukes of Burgundy. The series of CD-ROMs, called the *e-Librairie des ducs de Bourgogne* (*eLDB*), offers an illustrated survey of the books of the ducal library.[24] The library's collection had been cultivated over a number of generations in the late medieval period, and was enlarged especially by Philip the Good, who held the title of duke of Burgundy from 1419 to 1467. Among the deluxe books that Philip commissioned were the illustrated manuscripts of *La controversie de noblesse* that are now preserved in the Royal Library of Belgium.[25] The success of the digital reassembling of the ducal library depends upon the ability of the *eLDB* to convince readers that it offers accurate visual reproductions – facsimiles – of the books. Using images of high resolution, the *eLDB* generates a sense of historical authenticity for its collection. Readers are encouraged to suspend their scepticism and consider the digitizations as unmediated reflections of fifteenth-century manuscripts.

Images from the manuscripts of *La controversie de noblesse* may be found on volume 2 of the five-set *eLDB*.[26] In total, volume 2 preserves nine images from two different manuscripts of the translation by Jean Miélot. Eight of the sixty-six pages of the treatise in the manuscript Brussels, KBR 9278–80 have been digitized, five of which are decorated with half-page miniatures. Complementing these is the image of a single page of *La controversie* from a second manuscript, Brussels, KBR 10977–9. In this discontinuous configuration, the *eLDB*'s versions of *La controversie de noblesse* are not intended to

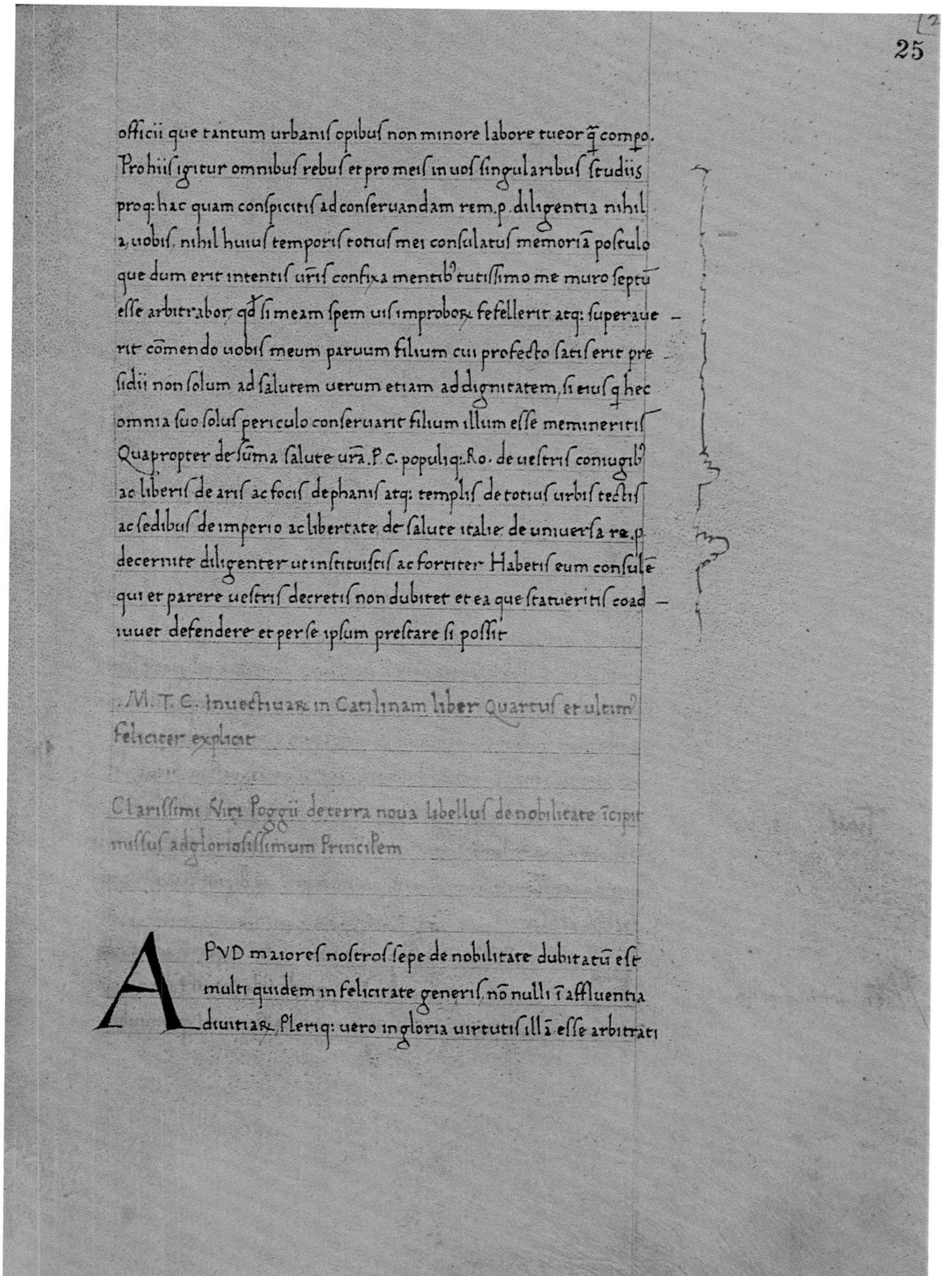

officii que tantum urbanis opibus non minore labore tueor q̄ compo.
Prohii igitur omnibus rebus et pro meis in uos singularibus studiis
proq: hac quam conspicitis ad conseruandam rem. p. diligentia nihil
a uobis, nihil huius temporis totius mei consulatus memoria posculo
que dum erit intentis uiris confixa mentib' tutissimo me muro septu
esse arbitrabor; q̄ si meam spem uis improbos fefellerit atq: superaue -
rit comendo uobis meum paruum filium cui profecto satis erit pre
sidii non solum ad salutem uerum etiam ad dignitatem, si eius q̄ hec
omnia suo solus periculo conseruarit filium illum esse memineritis
Quapropter de suma salute ura. P. c. populiq: Ro. de uestris coniugib'
ac liberis de aris ac focis de phanis atq: templis de totius urbis tectis
ac sedibus de imperio ac libertate de salute italie de uniuersa re. p.
decernite diligenter ut instituistis ac fortiter. Habetis eum consule
qui et parere uestris decretis non dubitet et ea que statueritis coad -
iuuet defendere et per se ipsum prestare si possit

.M. T. C. inuectiuar in Catilinam liber Quartus et ultim°
feliciter explicit

Clarissimi Viri Poggii de terra noua libellus de nobilitate icipit
missus ad gloriosissimum Principem

A PVD maiores nostros sepe de nobilitate dubitatu est
multi quidem in felicitate generis, no nulli i affluentia
diuitiar. Pleriq: uero in gloria uirtutis illa esse arbitrati

Plate 1 The *Controversia de nobilitate*, ascribed to Poggio Bracciolini, on parchment in a Humanistic book-hand. Florence, Biblioteca Riccardiana, MS 660, f. 25r. By permission of / Su concessione del Ministero per i Beni e le Attività Culturali. Further reproduction prohibited.

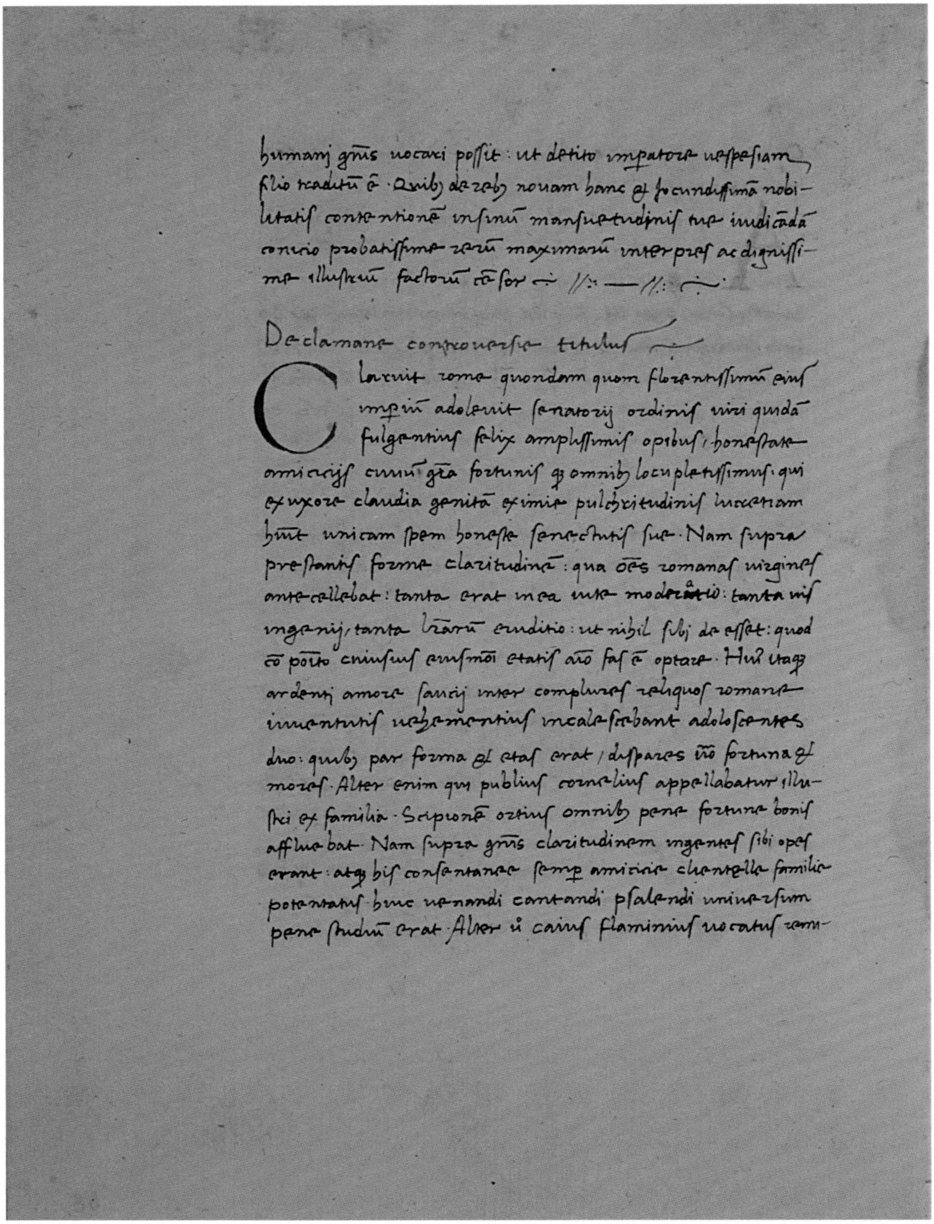
humani generis vocari possit: ut devicto imperatore vespesiam
filio traditum est. Quibus de rebus novam hanc et iocundissimam nobilitatis contentionem in sinum mansuetudinis tue iudicandam
commisi probatissime rerum maximarum interpres ac dignissi-
me illustrium factorum censor.

Declamatio controversie titulus

Claruit rome quondam quom florentissimum eius
imperium adolevit senatorij ordinis viri quidam
fulgentius felix amplissimis opibus, honestate
amicicijs cunctis gratia fortunis que omnibus locupletissimus. qui
ex uxore claudia genitam eximie pulchritudinis lucretiam
habuit unicam spem honeste senectutis sue. Nam supra
prestantis forme claritudinem: qua omnes romanas virgines
antecellebat: tanta erat in ea vite modestia: tanta vis
ingenij, tanta literarum eruditio: ut nihil sibi deesset: quod
cum potero cuiusque eiusmodi etatis animo fas esset optare. Huius itaque
ardenti amore saucij inter complures reliquos romane
iuventutis vehementius incalescebant adolescentes
duo: quibus par forma et etas erat, dispares vero fortuna et
mores. Alter enim qui publius cornelius appellabatur illu-
stri ex familia Scipionum ortus omnibus pene fortune bonis
affluebat. Nam supra generis claritudinem ingentes sibi opes
erant: atque his consentanee semper amicicie clientele familie
potentatus hinc venandi cantandi psallendi universum
pene studium erat. Alter vero caius flaminius vocatus tem-

Plate 2 The *Controversia de nobilitate* on paper in a Humanistic cursive hand. Florence, Biblioteca Riccardiana, MS 671, f. 68v. By permission of / Su concessione del Ministero per i Beni e le Attività Culturali. Further reproduction prohibited.

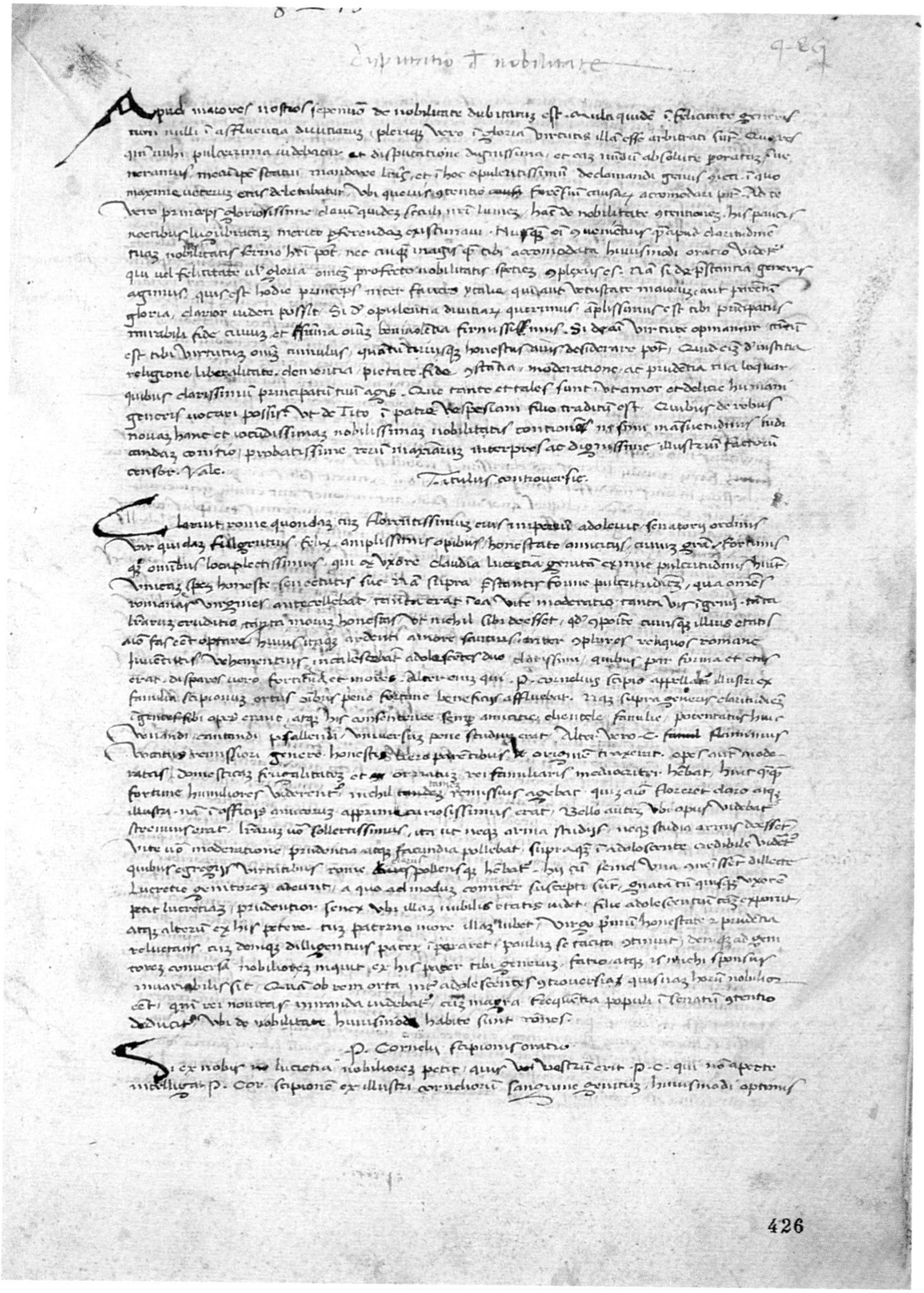

Plate 3 The *Controversia de nobilitate* on paper in a hybrid cursive hand. Note the use of both Gothic and Humanistic letter-forms. Florence, Biblioteca Riccardiana, MS 779, f. 426r. By permission of / Su concessione del Ministero per i Beni e le Attività Culturali. Further reproduction prohibited.

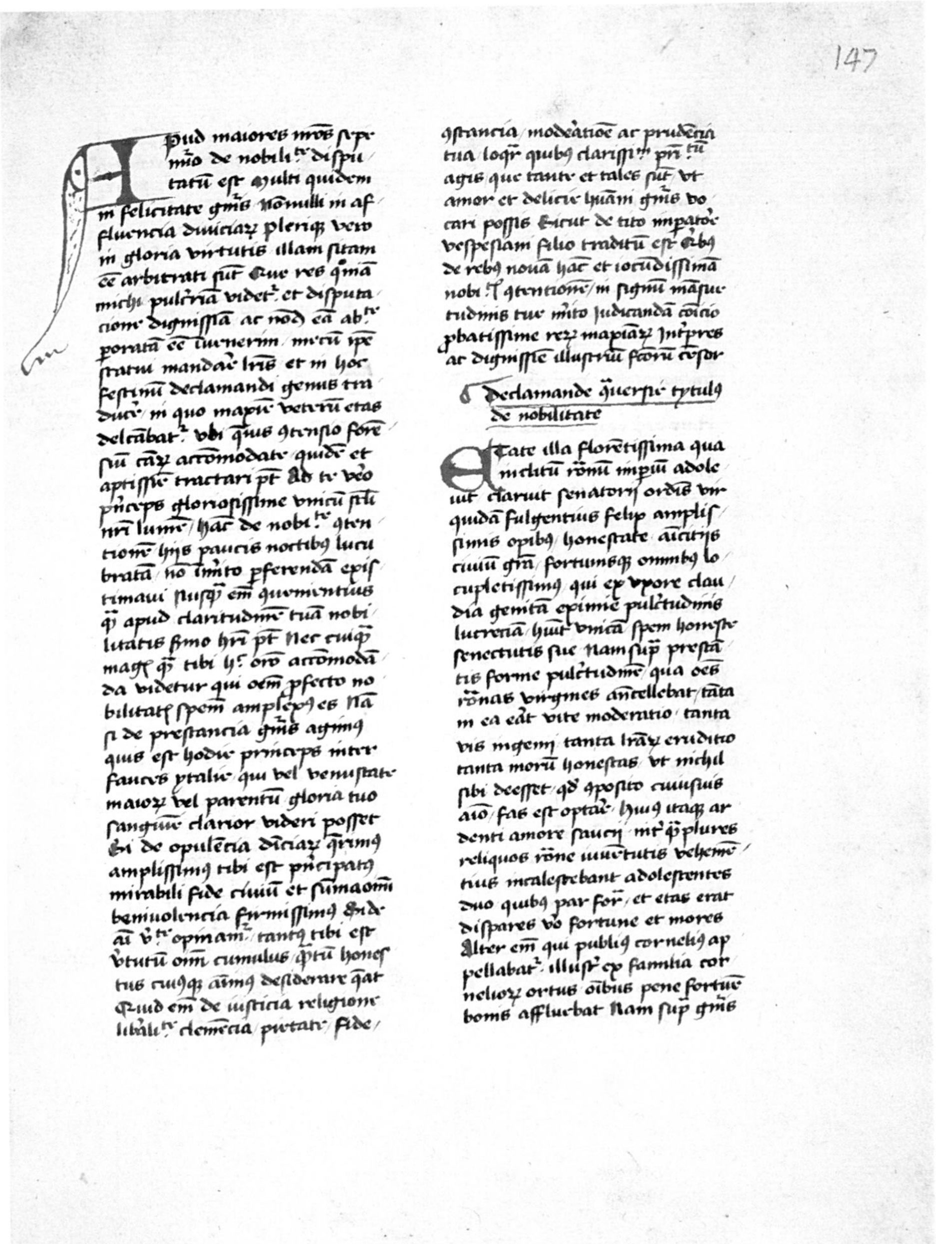

Plate 4 The *Controversia de nobilitate* on paper in a Gothic cursive hand. Note the two-columned layout. London, British Library, Harley 1883, f. 147r. Copyright © The British Library Board. All Rights Reserved.

Leonardi aretini opuſculum ad illu
ſtrē ac clarū pricipē Guidāthonium
montiſfereti comitem nobiliſſimum

a

Put maiores noſtros ſepe
nuēro de nobilitate dubita
tū ē. Multi qdē i claritate
geñris. nōnulli i affluēcia
diuiciaꝛ. pleriqꜫ uero i gloria uirtutis
illam eē ſitā arbitrati ſunt. Que r̄s qm̄
mihi pulcherrima uidet̄ et diſputatōe
digniſſima ac nedū eā abſolute perora
tā eē iueni mecum ipſe ſtatui mandare
litteris et in hoc feſtiuum declamandi
genus traducere in q° maxime noſtra
etas delectabat̄ ubi queuis contencio
forēſium cauſarum accomodate qdē
et aptiſſime tractari pōt. Ad te uero
princeps glorioſiſſime unicum noſtri
ſeculi lumen hanc ō nobilitate contro
uerſiā hijs paucis noctib⁹ lugubratam
non imerito perferendam exiſtimaui
Nuſquā etiam conueniencius q̃ aput
claritudinem tuam nobilitatis ſermo

cupiditati dedicent se ac deuoue
at tanqz deo. resipiscat ergo du
tempus dat et aliquam racione
habeant vite future. auscultent
sapientissimorum hominu sen
tencijs. pateant doctrium se uci
bus. Illamqz in primis M. tulij
inscripta animo habeant a pecto
ri infixam vocem: nichil esse tam
angusti tamqz parui animi qz a
mare diuicias. Nichil honestiꝰ
magnificecius qz pecuniam otep
nere si no habeas: si habeas ad
benificeciam libralitateqz oferre
Que cum dixiss leto: inqt an
thonius me pro auaris sensisse q
ista a te audirem9. Modo in
qt ille digna auribs vestris. Na
si probentur a uobis est vt non
pertimescam alioz iudiciu. Sed
cum satis collocuti sumus a nox
superuenerit abundum censeo.
Ita omnes consurrexerunt.

Pogij Floretini oratois diser
tissimi cenatissim9 atqz copiosis
simus in auariciam dyalog9 fe
liciter explicit.

Perpulchre ac elegantissi
me de nobilitate disputationis
prefatio inicium sumit.

Apud maiores no
stros sepenumero
de nobilitate dispu
tatum est. Multi
quidem i felicitate
generis: nonnulli in affluentia
diuiciaru: pleriqz vero in gloria
virtutis illam sitam esse arbitra
ti sunt. Que res quoniam michi
pulcherrima videt a disputacoe
dignissima: ac nondum ea abso
lute protata inuenerim: mecum
ipse statui mandare litteris a in
hoc festiuu declamandi genus
traducere. in quo maxime vetez
etas delectabat. vbi queuis ote
tio forensium causarum accom
modate quide a aptissime trac
tari pot. qd te vero pnceps glo
riosissime vniaz seculi nri lume
hanc de nobilitate otencionem
hijs paucis noctibs lucubratam
no immerito pferendam existima
ui. Nusqz enim ouenientius qz
apud claritudinem tuam nobili
tatis sermo haberi pot. nec aliqz
magis qz tibi hec oratio accom
modanda videt. qui omne pro
fecto nobilitatis spez ampler9 es.
Na si de pstancia gnis aginº qs
e hodie pnceps int fauces ytalie

Plate 6 The *Controversia de nobilitate* printed on paper. Note the two-columned layout and the influence of the Gothic hand. *Dialogi decem auctorum* [Cologne: Printer of *Flores S. Augustini*, 1473]. Cambridge, University Library, Inc.3.A.4.8 (501), f. 98v. By permission of the Syndics of Cambridge University Library. Further reproduction prohibited.

Trattato dinobilta composto perlo famosissimo
messere bonacorso damonte magnio :~

Nella florentissima eta nellaquale lomperio
deromani reggieua delsenatorio hordine·fu
huno clarissimo huomo nominato fulgienzio filicie
permolte richeze·edonesta damici digratia decipi
tadini·e abondantissimo ditutte fortune·Ilquale
dellasua donna nomata claudia ebbe huna figliuo
la chiamata lucrezia displendida belleza laquale
hera hunica & sola speranza della sua honesta
uechieza·perche incostei oltre allachiareza della
bella forma nellaquale trapassaua tutte lerom
ane uergini·tanto·hera honesta hornata &
temperata uita·tanta honesta dicostumi·tanta for
za dingiegnio & admaestramento dilettere·che
allei nonmanchaua alchuna chosa laquale sipote
sse desiderare nello hanimo diqualunque·heta
sifosse Infiammati adunque dello amore dicostei
intrapiu altri romani due giouani piu eficacemen
te sinfiamarono·Aiquali simile belleze hera eheta
mauati herono infortuna e incostumi·Luno a
dunque nominato publio cornelio della illustra
famiglia decorneli·quasi ditutti ebeni dellafor
tuna hera abondeuole & sopra la clarita della
nobilta della progienia aueua molte richeze
collequali aueua molte amicitie dipotenzia
dimolte famiglie costui dicacciare dicantare
disaltare·hera sollecito studiante·Laltro chia
mato gaio flaminio hunpocho dipiu basso

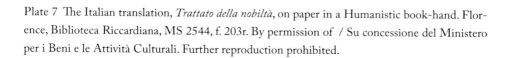

Plate 7 The Italian translation, *Trattato della nobiltà*, on paper in a Humanistic book-hand. Florence, Biblioteca Riccardiana, MS 2544, f. 203r. By permission of / Su concessione del Ministero
per i Beni e le Attività Culturali. Further reproduction prohibited.

Plate 8 The French translation, *La controversie de noblesse*, on parchment in a Gothic cursive hand. Note the miniature and decorated initial. Brussels, Bibliothèque royale de Belgique, MS 9278–80, f. 16r. Copyright © Bibliothèque royale de Belgique, Brussels, Department of Manuscripts. Further reproduction prohibited.

Plate 9 The French translation, *La controversie de noblesse*, on parchment in a Gothic cursive hand. Brussels, Bibliothèque royale de Belgique, MS 10977–9, f. 9r. Copyright © Bibliothèque royale de Belgique, Brussels, Department of Manuscripts. Further reproduction prohibited.

Ja commence la controuersie de noblesse
plaidoyee entre Publius Cornelius Sci
pion dunepart .Et Gapus flaminius de
autrepart .Laquelle a este faicte et compo.
see par vn notable docteur en loix et grant
orateur nomme Surse de pistoye .

Entre noz anciens maistres a este sou
uent dispute de noblesse .Car plu
seurs ont cuidie quelle fust scituee
en felicite de lignatge .Et les autres si ont affer
me quelle est influence de richesses .Et moult
dautres ont este dopinion quelle fust en gloire
de vertu (Mais pour ce q ce me semble estre
vne chose tresbelle et tresdigne destre disputee
et plaidoyee .et aussi pour ce que ie ne lay pas
aincoires trouuee souffisamment traittiee par
les orateurs :iay de moy mesmes entreprins
de la mettre par escript et le reduire en tele nou
uelle maniere de declamation : en laquelle no
blesse iadis se deluctoit souuerainement tout
leatge des plus anciens comme en ce ou quelcon
ques contention des causes foraines poit plus

Plate 10 The French translation in print. Note the influence of Gothic cursive in the letter-forms. Bonaccursius de Montemagno, *Controversie de noblesse, et Débat de trois chevaleureux princes* [Bruges: Colard Mansion, 1476]. Paris, Bibliothèque nationale de France, Rés. D-862, f. 2r. Copyright © Bibliothèque nationale de France. Further reproduction prohibited.

Plate 11 Illustrated title page of Vérard's printed edition of *Le gouvernement des princes*. Pseudo-Aristoteles, *Le gouvernement des princes* (Paris: Antoine Vérard, 1497). Paris, Bibliothèque nationale de France, Vélins 411, f. 1v. Copyright © Bibliothèque nationale de France. Further reproduction prohibited.

Plate 12 Illustrated title page of Vérard's printed edition of *Le trésor de noblesse*. Pseudo-Aristoteles, *Le gouvernement des princes* (Paris: Antoine Vérard, 1497). Paris, Bibliothèque nationale de France, Vélins 412, f. 1v. Copyright © Bibliothèque nationale de France. Further reproduction prohibited.

kern kündt/verpresten. So maynet auch etlich/ein weyl zůerziehen / vnd mich fragen
vñ verhören/vñ darnach viteylen. Als ich das marckt/do lieff ich für den obersten d stat
gähen/sond mich in sein behůtung zů nemen: biß er aygentlich erfůr/gstalt/herkomen
vñ warhayt dises dings. Auff das d Richter zů mir sprach: sag deinen/vñ deins vatters
vnd deiner freünden (ob du do etlich habest) vñ deiner stat daher du bürtig bist/namē.
Darzů ich antwort vñ sagt/mich haben ein vatter/genant Lucius/vñ ein brůd Gaiū/
sessen weren in einer statt/genant Patera/glegen in dem land Achaia. Do der Richter
dz erhört/sprach er. Du bist eins mañs sun/der mein liebster freünd ist/des gaste ich offt
gewesen/vnd von jm wol empfangen vnd gehalten worden bin: ich wayß das du nicht
leügst. Vnd stünde ab von seinem pferd/vnd vmbsieng mich küssende/vnd mich mit jm
inn sein hauß fürende. Jnn dem kam von geschicht mein brůder/mit silber vnd vil ande
rer gattung mit jm bringend. Mit dem selben saß ich nachmals inn ein schyff auff dem
Meere/durch glücklich wynd haym kam. Do ich den Göttern meines hayls/das sie mir
hetten geholffen/grossen danck sagen thet.

Die Vierdtzehent Translation/Zierliche red
vnd widerred von dem Adel/was der sey/vnd woher er kom. Mit
anzaigung mancherlay alter Exempel vnd Hysto-
rien/die frembd zů hören sind.

Em Hochgebornen Herrenn/ Herren Eberharten/Grauen zů
Wyrtenberg vnd zů Mümpelgart ꝛc. meinem gnädigen Herrn/ Ent
peüt ich Niclas von Weyl/mein vnderthänig willig dienst allzeyt zů
uor. Wiewol es gnädiger Herr: ein weyt ding ist vmb den Adel/ vñ das
der durch all welt/vnd in allen glauben für groß / vnd in hohen eeren
wyrden billich wirt gehalten : so ist noch dannocht bey vnsern altfor-
dern/vnd vor weysen hochgelerten mannen/offt inn frage vnd zwei-
sel gestanden/was der Adel an jhm selbs sey / vnnd woher der komme vnnd entspringe.

N iiij   Sonder

Plate 13 The German translation of the *Controversia de nobilitate*. Note woodcut, running titles, foliation, and use of different typefaces. Nicolaus von Wyle, *Translationen oder Deütschungen des hochgeachten Nicolai von Weil* (Augsburg: Heinrich Stayner, 1536). Cambridge, University Library, XII.1.1(4), f. 76r. By permission of the Syndics of Cambridge University Library. Further reproduction prohibited.

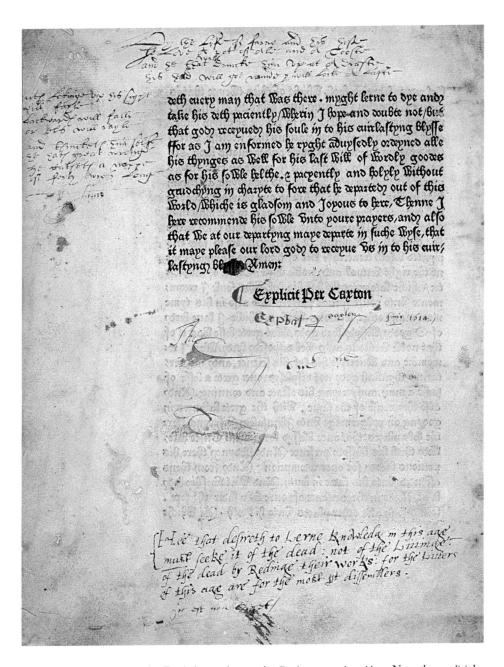

Plate 14 The epilogue to the English translation, the *Declamacyon de noblesse*. Note the *explicit* by William Caxton. Cicero, *Of Old Age* ([Westminster]: William Caxton, 12 August 1481). Cambridge, University Library, Inc.3.J.1.3 (3496), f. 120v. By permission of the Syndics of Cambridge University Library. Further reproduction prohibited.

Plate 15 Translator's prologue to *La controversie de noblesse* with depiction of scholar-scribe. Brussels, Bibliothèque royale de Belgique, MS 9278–80, f. 10r. Copyright © Bibliothèque royale de Belgique, Brussels, Department of Manuscripts. Further reproduction prohibited.

Plate 16 The Study of Federigo da Montefeltro, Duke of Urbino. Copyright © Palazzo Ducale, Urbino, Italy / The Bridgeman Art Library. Further reproduction prohibited.

be read from beginning to end. The CD-ROM offers another way in which the treatise might be understood. Because volume 2 preserves only didactic texts, *La controversie* is plainly identified as a participant in this genre. The *eLDB* thus follows the lead of fifteenth-century designers, reinscribing *La controversie* in the tradition of courtly romance, and further assigning it a subtype. In this way, *La controversie de noblesse* is not to be understood as a work of philosophy, theology, law, or classical literature, for the texts belonging to these subject areas are transmitted in the remaining four CD-ROMs. Instead, the nine pages of *La controversie* are explicitly understood and presented as courtesy literature and can be juxtaposed with each other for comparison or examined alongside others that have been similarly classified on the CD-ROM. Volume 2 of the *eLDB* enables the didactic texts of the Burgundian collection to coexist in the same space and time for the reader, despite their having been accumulated over the span of centuries.

The volumes of the *eLDB* cover a wide range of subject fields and are designed to draw attention to the extensiveness of the ducal collection. The pages of *La controversie* constitute integral components in a mission that seeks to provide evidence of the breadth of the ducal library and thereby document the Burgundian tradition of intellectual and artistic patronage. Understood in this way, the rationale behind the fragmentary presentation of *La controversie* begins to emerge; the digital pages communicate how they are designed to matter. The *eLDB* offers *La controversie* in a new light, recontextualizing, reconfiguring, editing, and even enhancing it.[27] The images of *La controversie* in the *eLDB* are not digital surrogates of medieval manuscripts, but are instead isolated moments that have been organized as a coherent body of evidence. These pages of *La controversie de noblesse* are arranged as historic representatives of a literary genre and, moreover, as artefacts of the fifteenth-century court of Burgundy. In offering this aestheticized vision of history, the CD-ROMs propose a cultural genealogy for Belgium, and link the medieval past with the modern day.[28]

The *eLDB* is a space that has been constructed to organize and transmit ideas according to a specific agenda; it has its own message, and the materials – including pages from *La controversie de noblesse* – have consequently been digitized and arranged in support of this message. Although over three hundred books from the library of the dukes of Burgundy still survive in institutions including the Royal Library of Belgium, the Bibliothèque nationale de France, the British Library, and the Österreichische Nationalbibliothek in Vienna, not all of these resources have been digitally encoded. The *eLDB* has restricted its exemplars to a subgroup of the manuscripts held in Brussels. The absence of examples from other national libraries implies that the connection between the ducal library of the fifteenth century and the Royal Library of Belgium of today is an exclusive one.[29] The designers of the *eLDB* have assembled together images of the manuscripts that will best and most persuasively demonstrate the historical and cultural importance of the library of the dukes of Burgundy and, it might be extrapolated by the reader, the Royal Library in Brussels, where the exemplars are now held. The careful adaptation of history is, of course, not unsurprising or new. The selection of particular items for reproduction frequently depends on political or economic considerations. As Michael Camille has observed more generally, 'It is neither the more historically interesting nor inaccessible examples that have been chosen [for facsimile reproduction].'[30] The principles that govern *La controversie* in the *eLDB* are dictated by the broader argument of the CD-ROMs about the significance of the ducal library and the modern-day Royal Library of Belgium. As the manuscripts of *La controversie* were commissioned by the dukes of Burgundy to help establish and consolidate a legacy in the fifteenth century, their pages were digitized four centuries later to harness the same legacy for the present. The images may therefore be understood as a refraction of history that has been forged out of modern concerns. Imbricated with contemporary agendas, they are an interpretation of, and assertion about, the past.

Encoded first by medieval designers and then by modern ones, the digital pages of *La controversie* are implicated in yet another phase in the history of the transmission of Buonaccorso's treatise and its translations. The digitized *La controversie* is configured by a particular narrative that enables the communication of the treatise while determining how the pages may circulate. Shaped by social forces of the twenty-first century, and marked with cultural, bibliographic, and computational codes of the past and present, the digitized pages are witness to their own course through time and space. They enjoy a tradition that is not the same as that of their medieval counterparts. The *eLDB* grants *La controversie* a new identity with which it can stimulate further developments in the history of Buonaccorso's treatise.[31] The digitally encoded pages can become cultural icons in their own right, taking up the position of exemplars and inspiring their own refractions; they will be downloaded and made into wallpaper for a computer screen, animated, or juxtaposed with other texts or images. These latest versions of *La controversie de noblesse* are one part the reproduction of Walter Benjamin with emancipatory power to free the manuscript from the confines of tradition, one part the self-referential illusion of Jean Baudrillard, and one part the cultural artefact of the past and present, diffusing an admixture of messages accrued over their extended process of production.[32]

Presented in this way, the digitized pages of *La controversie* might be thought to be purely original. However, their inclusion in the *eLDB* depends upon a critical relationship with extant fifteenth-century manuscripts. It is because of their link with the past that the pages of *La controversie* have been reincarnated in the *eLDB*. Indeed, Miélot's translation of Buonaccorso's treatise would not have been considered for inclusion in the project were it not for the surviving illustrated manuscripts. By supplying an important ancestry, the manuscripts KBR 9278–80 and KBR 10977–9 participate remotely in the discourse of their own digitally encoded images. The digital pages of *La controversie* are endowed with a historical authenticity because they can trace their origins back to relics from the Middle Ages. Conversely, the digitized pages help to secure the place of the manuscripts in the cultural heritage of Belgium. As each manuscript underwrites its own digital refractions on the CD-ROMs, credibility is conferred upon the entire project itself, and the assertion about the importance of the ducal collection and the Royal Library begins to gain a foothold in the national consciousness as an established historical fact.

In the foregoing discussion of the *Declamacyon de noblesse* and *La controversie de noblesse* in their digitally encoded forms, it is clear that the long-standing structures of the textual edition and the facsimile are continuing to shape the transmission of Buonaccorso's debate in the twenty-first century. As hybrid products of manuscript, print, and newer technologies, the digital pages are granted the authority – whether verbal, visual, or historical – to assume the position of exemplars and consequently propose new directions in the development of Buonaccorso's treatise and its translations. The dynamic of textual editing echoes the genealogical argument of Cornelius regarding his own character in some respects; nonetheless, the preceding exploration has discovered that digitized pages, like Cornelius's virtues, have a more complicated relationship with their ancestors than one that is strictly linear. The precise connection between the new incarnations of the *Controversia de nobilitate* and their medieval exemplars might be characterized as a tension across revelation and occlusion. There is always a critical reference, a gesture to the past, that makes these digitally encoded pages meaningful. At the same time, the digitized pages may conceal, obfuscate, or redirect attention as part of their way of making meaning. The pages of the *Declamacyon* in *EEBO* and *La controversie de noblesse* in the *eLDB* bear a striking resemblance to their forebears in the codex. But although these new pages are inspired by the past, each individual instantiation must be read for its own codes. The histories that are constructed upon the digitally encoded page are histories of the digitization, not of its exemplar. Every digital page has a specific materiality and therefore matters in its own way. Suffused with individual circumstances of production, circulation, and transmission, each page is witness to and participates in its own social history, even in the digital present.

Conclusion

The *Controversia de nobilitate* has been reimagined in a multitude of ways by designers and readers from the Middle Ages to the twenty-first century. The diverse incarnations continue to shape how Buonaccorso da Montemagno's treatise is understood and used: a parchment manuscript of the *Controversia* might be consulted in a darkened reading room by an expert scholar as evidence of fifteenth-century humanist thought; an early printed edition might be cherished by a collector of rare incunabula; meanwhile, digitally encoded images of both can be downloaded by an idle web surfer or a meticulous research assistant. Each page is, moreover, altered by its contact with readers and carries forward signs of the exchange. These signs may include an inadvertent smudge, an ironic illustration, or thoughtful marginalia. The marks reconfigure the expression of the page and change the significance of the treatise over time. Thus offering readers a variety of ways to make meaning, the pages of the *Controversia de nobilitate* play a central role in their own mattering.[1]

The page also influences how Buonaccorso's treatise is treated more generally in places and spaces of meaning-making. Based on the diversity of its manifestations, the *Controversia* has been called a work of rhetoric, literature, and theology, and packaged variously as materials for scholars and connoisseurs. Furthermore, particular editions have been distinguished according to their mode of production – manuscript, print, digital – as well as classified as printed-and-rare or printed-and-not-rare. Reinscribed in these categories over time, Buonaccorso's treatise has become an entrenched member of multiple disciplines and its instantiations incorporated into broader vectors in the representation of knowledge. The social and cultural impact of the page is therefore wide-ranging: in addition to helping determine the meaning of the text that it communicates, the page is also instrumental in shaping the character of its contiguous spaces. That is, the page of the *Controversia de nobilitate* can establish, confirm, or challenge the reputation of people and places with which it is associated, from designers to readers to collectors, from exhibitions to libraries to categories of knowledge.

The page has thus proved to be an important mechanism in the organization and transmission of ideas. Although dependent on a medium, the page is not specific to any particular one; its dynamic of matter and mattering transcends differences in time and technologies. After centuries of being linked almost exclusively with the printed book, the page has re-emerged in new media, where the hardware, software, and protocols that support the digital transmission of information now influence how meaning is made. The codes that underpin the digitally encoded page may be computational, but are nevertheless contingent and cultural, infusing the interface with a particular spirit that has been shaped by social, economic, and political pressures, and contemporary attitudes regarding the representation of ideas. Even in the digital environment, the page is generated from a unique set of circumstances and exhibits a distinct perspective.

How the Page Matters has tracked the entanglement of material and meaning in the page through five centuries of history. The exploration has focused on the movements of collection, recollection, recursion, influence, and inspiration in and around the page. By investigating the page as a cultural phenomenon, we have discovered that one set of materials and meanings has never entirely been supplanted by the next. Indeed, the *pagina* of the scroll was not eradicated by the parchment page of the medieval codex; the manuscript page was not replaced by the paper printed page; and none of these pages has been rendered obsolete by the page in digital form. Instead, the emergent page now calls upon multiple modes of production, including handwriting, printing, and computation; evokes multiple traditions of representation such as the diplomatic transcription, textual edition, and facsimile reproduction; and makes reference to the *paginae* of the scroll, the wax tablet, and the codex. Perhaps configured by the physicality of one mode, the graphic strategies of another, and the idiosyncratic dialect of a third, the page accommodates simultaneous and sometimes contradictory expressions as it encourages simultaneous and sometimes contradictory readings.

In fabricating new pages for the communication of ideas, we are also redefining the significance of their traditional counterparts. Ancient, medieval, and early modern pages now matter to us in different ways, our perception of them modified in light of how we are responding to more recent developments in culture and technology. The pages from the past are enriched by our efforts to transmit thought with innovative interfaces, even as we embrace or eschew millennia-old conventions. With the ability to mean differently through time, a page may reverberate in suggestive, novel, and influential ways long after its apparent obsolescence. The page is thus evidence of past conversations as it constitutes a forum for future ones, and reminds us of our own history as it inspires us to formulate new kinds of mattering and meaning in the world.

Notes

INTRODUCTION

1 A concise overview of the critical relationship between matter and mattering in the sciences is found in Barad, *Meeting the Universe Halfway*. On the same in the philosophy of computing and information, see Smith, 'From E&M to M&E,' 19–47.

2 *Selis*, in Greek. See discussions in Turner, *Greek Papyri*, 5; and Lewis, *Papyrus in Classical Antiquity*, 79–83. Most recently considered in Butler, *The Matter of the Page*, 7.

3 Similarly, see Drucker, 'Entity to Event.'

4 O'Donnell, *Avatars of the Word*; and Chartier, *Forms and Meanings*. For a critical overview of the field of book history, see Howsam, *Old Books and New Histories*, esp. 54–61.

5 Febvre and Martin, *The Coming of the Book*; and Eisenstein, *The Printing Press as an Agent of Change*, with an abridged version in Eisenstein, *The Printing Revolution in Early Modern Europe*, 2nd ed. (2005).

6 Eisenstein, *The Printing Revolution* (2005), 6–7.

7 McKenzie, *Bibliography and the Sociology of Texts*; and McGann, *The Textual Condition*.

8 Recently, Eisenstein, *Divine Art, Infernal Machine*; Pettegree, *The Book in the Renaissance*; and S.A. Baron, Lindquist, and Shevlin, *Agent of Change*. See the forum in the *American Historical Review* 107.1 (February 2002) between Eisenstein and Adrian Johns; and Johns, *The Nature of the Book*. Addressing the manuscript-print divide, see, for example, Kornicki, 'Manuscript, Not Print'; Crick and Walsham, *The Uses of Script and Print*; McKitterick, *Print, Manuscript and the Search for Order*; and Hindman, *Printing and the Written Word*.

9 Important characterizations include Landow, *Hypertext 3.0*; McGann, *Radiant Textuality*; Birkerts, *The Gutenberg Elegies*; and Lanham, *The Electronic Word*. Early analyses are found in Bolter, *Writing Space*; D. Small, 'Rethinking the Book'; and Nunberg, *The Future of the Book*. Also see the seminal works of Marshall McLuhan: 'The Medium Is the Message,' in *Understanding Media*, and *The Gutenberg Galaxy: The Making of Typographic Man*.

10 For a notable exception, see Stoicheff and Taylor, *The Future of the Page*. Some brief explora-

tions are found in Manguel, 'A Brief History of the Page'; Carruthers, *The Book of Memory*, 116–17 on the *pagina*; Duguid, 'Inheritance and Loss?'; Biddick, 'Introduction,' in *The Typological Imaginary*, 1–20; Bornstein, 'How to Read a Page,' in *Material Modernism*, 5–31; and Bray, Handley, and Henry, *Ma(r)king the Text*.

11 On the concurrent use of different technologies of writing, see, most recently, Stallybrass, *Printing-for-Manuscript*; and Hayles, 'The Future of Literature.' For an important study on the continued use of handwriting, see Hunger, *Schreiben und Lesen in Byzanz*.

12 Manguel, 'Turning the Page,' 27. See also Lapacherie, 'Typographic Characters,' 64.

CHAPTER 1: ARCHITECTURES OF THE PAGE

1 McKenzie, *Bibliography and the Sociology of Texts*, 8.

2 For papyrology, see, for example, Turner, *Greek Papyri*; and Lewis, *Papyrus in Classical Antiquity*. For codicology, see Derolez, 'Codicologie ou archéologie du livre?'; Gruijs, 'Codicology or the Archaeology of the Book?'; and Masai, 'Paléographie et codicologie.' For bibliography, see Fredson Bowers, *Principles of Bibliographical Description* (1949; repr. in New Castle, DE: Oak Knoll Press, 1994); and Thomas Tanselle, 'Issues in Bibliographical Studies since 1942,' in Davison, *The Book Encompassed*, 24–36.

3 For palaeography, see Ganz, 'Latin Palaeography since Bischoff'; and J. Brown, 'Latin Palaeography since Traube.' For print, see, for example, Gene Kannenberg, Jr, 'Graphic Text, Graphic Context: Interpreting Custom Fonts and Hands in Contemporary Comics,' in Gutjahr and Benton, *Illuminating Letters*, 163–92; and Drucker, *The Visible Word*.

4 Recent exceptions include McGrady, *Controlling Readers*; Hageman and Mostert, *Reading Images and Texts*; Dillon, *Medieval Music-Making*; and Brubaker, *Vision and Meaning*.

5 For example, Manovich, *Software Takes Command*; Montfort and Bogost, *Racing the Beam*; Harpold, *Ex-foliations*; Kirschenbaum, *Mechanism*; Hayles, *My Mother Was a Computer*; Liu, 'Transcendental Data'; and Ramsay, 'Toward an Algorithmic Criticism.'

6 In general, see J.P. Small, *Wax Tablets of the Mind*; Roberts and Skeat, *The Birth of the Codex*; E.G. Turner, *Greek Papyri* and *The Typology of the Early Codex*; and Lewis, *Papyrus in Classical Antiquity*.

7 E.G. Turner, 'The Terms *Recto* and *Verso*,' 62. See also Johnson, *Bookrolls and Scribes*, 58, 119–25; E.G. Turner, *Greek Papyri*, 173 n. 21, and *The Typology of the Early Codex*, 44. Cf. J.P. Small, *Wax Tablets of the Mind*, 151.

8 Kenyon, *Books and Readers in Ancient Greece and Rome*, 41, 53–4. Cf. Skeat, who writes that the standard roll was about three metres long, composed of about twenty papyrus sheets, in 'The Length of the Standard Papyrus Roll,' 170. See discussion in Johnson, *Bookrolls and Scribes*, 143–52.

9 On the vertical orientation of some scrolls, see E.G. Turner, 'The Terms *Recto* and *Verso*,' 26–53.

10 On the different dimensions of papyrus sheets, see Blanchard, 'Les papyrus littéraires grecs,' 38–9; and Kenyon, *Books and Readers*, 59.

11 Johnson, 'Is Oratory Written on Narrower Columns?' 423–7. See also Johnson, *Bookrolls and Scribes*, 100–19; Blanchard, 'Les papyrus littéraires grecs,' 40; and Kenyon, *Books and Readers*, 55–6.

12 See Johnson, *Bookrolls and Scribes*, 156 for luxury rolls; for sloped columns, 92. In general, see Sirat, *Writing as Handwork*, 280–4, 402–7.

13 Skeat discovers a 'psychological advantage' to reading in a scroll format, in 'Roll versus Codex,' 297–8.

14 See discussions of the Dunhuang manuscripts in Soymié, *Contributions aux études sur Touen-houang*, esp. J.-P. Drège, 'Les accordéons de Dunhuang,' 3: 195–204.

15 Recently on wax tablets, see Chartier, *Inscription and Erasure*, esp. chap. 1, 'Wax and Parchment: The Poems of Baudri de Bourgueil,' 1–12; Sirat, *Writing as Handwork*, 179–83; and J.P. Small, *Wax Tablets of the Mind*.

16 See the discussion in Roberts and Skeat, *The Birth of the Codex*, 5–10. On the construction of papyrus codices, see E.G. Turner, *The Typology of the Early Codex*; and Kenyon, *Books and Readers*, 99–109.

17 The process of making parchment is amply discussed in, among others, Hamel, *Scribes and Illuminators*, 8–16.

18 For a recent discussion on dye and parchment, see Porter, 'The Identification of Purple in Manuscripts.'

19 On the use of paper in general, see Gaskell, *A New Introduction to Bibliography*, 57–7.

20 For a more detailed codicological discussion, see J.P. Gumbert, 'Skins, Sheets and Quires,' in Pearsall, *New Directions in Later Medieval Manuscript Studies*, 81–90; Bozzolo and Ornato, *Pour une histoire du livre manuscrit au moyen âge*; and Gilissen, *Prolégomènes à la codicologie*.

21 For a recent discussion of page openings, see Hamburger, 'Openings.'

22 For a discussion of the shared task of copying books, see Hamel, *Glossed Books of the Bible*, 29. See also Jean Vezin, 'La fabrication du manuscrit,' in Chartier and Martin, *Histoire de l'édition française*, 1: 25–47.

23 Jean Vezin, 'Manuscrits "imposés,"' in Martin and Vezin, *Mise en page et mise en texte*, 423–5; and Gilissen, *Prolégomènes à la codicologie*, esp. chap. 3, 'Les formules de pliage,' 26–35. For printed books, see Richardson, *Printing, Writers and Readers*, 9–14; and Gaskell, *A New Introduction*.

24 See example in Hamel, *Scribes and Illuminators*, 20.

25 On non-Christian literature in scrolls, see Roberts and Skeat, *The Birth of the Codex*, 69.

26 For the continued use of papyrus, see Lewis, *Papyrus in Classical Antiquity*, 92.

27 On the traces of the roll in the codex, see Menci, 'L'impaginazione nel rotolo e nel codice'; and Weitzmann, *Illustrations in Roll and Codex*. On layout in general, see Sirat, *Writing as Handwork*, 253–300.

28 Kwakkel uses the phrase 'cultural residue' in 'The Cultural Dynamics of Medieval Book Production,' 244–5.

29 Drucker, *The Visible Word*, 4; Petrucci, *Public Lettering*; and Morison, *Politics and Script*. In general, see Gutjahr and Benton, *Illuminating Letters*.

30 Drucker, 'Graphical Readings and Visual Aesthetics of Textuality.'

31 Important discussions of layout are found in Parkes, *Their Hand before Our Eyes* and *Pause and Effect*.

32 For example, see Rouse and Rouse, '*Statim invenire*'; Parkes, 'The Influence of the Concepts of *Ordinatio* and *Compilatio*'; and Destrez, *La pecia dans les manuscrits universitaires*. See also Briggs, *Giles of Rome's 'De regimine principum.'*

33 Parkes, 'The Influence of the Concepts of *Ordinatio* and *Compilatio*,' 133. See also Illich, *In the Vineyard of the Text*.

34 On the significance of blank space, see Henry, 'Blank Emblems'; Stone Peters, *Theatre of the Book 1480–1880*, esp. chap. 1, 'Experimenting on the Page, 1480–1630,' 15–40; McCloud, *Understanding Comics*; Swanson, *Graphic Design & Reading*; Hardman, 'Windows into the Text,' 45, 70; and Braunmuller, 'Accounting for Absence.'

35 Rolf E. Rehe, 'Legibility,' in Swanson, *Graphic Design & Reading*, 99. See also Johns, *The Nature of the Book*, chap. 6, 'The Physiology of Reading,' 380–443.

36 P. Saenger, *Space between Words*. On the connection with memory, see Carruthers, *The Book of Memory*, 212–17.

37 A discussion of the critical relationship between image and medium is found in Belting, 'Image, Medium, Body,' 304.

38 Michael Camille, '"Seeing and Lecturing": Disputation in a Twelfth-Century Tympanum from Reims,' in Sears and Thomas, *Reading Medieval Images*, 76. See also Stafford, *Artful Science*; and Camille, *Image on the Edge*.

39 See, most recently, Duffy, *Marking the Hours*. See also P. Saenger, 'Books of Hours and Reading Habits'; and L.M.J. Delaissé, 'The Importance of Books of Hours for the History of the Medieval Book,' in McCracken, Randall, and Randall, *Gatherings in Honor of Dorothy E. Miner*, 203–25.

40 Genette, *Paratexts*; and McKenzie, *Bibliography and the Sociology of Texts*. Although Genette assumes that classical and medieval manuscripts circulated texts in their 'almost raw condition ... devoid of any formula of presentation' (3), this study instead argues that manuscripts, like their printed counterparts, are critically shaped by paratextual devices.

41 Chartier, *Forms and Meanings*, 1.

42 See, recently, Hayles, 'Traumas of Code'; Galloway and Thacker, 'Protocol, Control, and Networks'; and Ramsay, 'Toward an Algorithmic Criticism.'

43 Mackenzie, *Cutting Code*, 176.

44 The most recent discussion and translation of the treatise is found in Rabil, *Knowledge, Goodness, and Power*, 24–52. See also Vanderjagt, 'Qui sa la vertu anoblist.'

45 More biographical information can be found in Sabbadini, 'Buonaccorso da Montemagno il Giovane.'

46 Aristotle, *Nicomachean Ethics* 1.1099a5–a31; and *Politics* 5.1301a25–b29. Plato, *Laches* 186b–7b; *Menexenus*; and *Protagoras* 328b–c.

47 'Ibi primum confertissimam librarum bibliothecam meam videbis, in qua semper omnem spem meam detuli. Haec, splendidae quidem supellectiles.' Buonaccorso da Montemagno, *Prose e Rime*, ed. Casotti (1718), 92; English trans. in Rabil, *Knowledge, Goodness, and Power*, 51–2.

48 H.-J. Martin, *The History and Power of Writing*, 313.

49 McKenzie, *Bibliography and the Sociology of Texts*, 29. See also Drucker, 'Entity to Event'; and Certeau, *The Practice of Everyday Life*.

CHAPTER 2: READING THE PAGE

1 See Buonaccorso da Montemagno, *Orazioni di Buonaccorso da Montemagno*, ed. dello Russo (1862).

2 Jorde, *Cristoforo Landinos 'De vera nobilitate,'* 64–77; Tateo, *Tradizione e realità nel Umanesimo italiano*, 362 n. 8; and H. Baron, *The Crisis of the Early Italian Renaissance*, 420–3. On these forms, see Bloomer, 'Controversia and Suasoria'; and Lausberg, *Handbook of Literary Rhetoric*, §1146.

3 Marsh, *The Quattrocento Dialogue*, 14–15.

4 For an introduction, see, among others, Derolez, *Codicologie des manuscrits en écriture humanistique*; Ross, 'Salutati's Defeated Candidate for Humanistic Script'; Mare, *The Handwriting of Italian Humanists*; Wardrop, *The Script of Humanism*; and Ullman, *The Origin and Development of Humanistic Script*.

5 On the relationship between inscription and the creation of fact, see Latour and Woolgar, *Laboratory Life*, 106.

6 Measuring 224 × 155 mm; text block, 152 × 87 mm. For the purposes of clarity, the title *Controversia de nobilitate* will be used throughout this chapter and the rest of the book.

7 Similarly, see the *Controversia de nobilitate* in London, BL, Harley 3332; Florence, Bib. Ricc., MS 693; Milan, Bib. Ambrosiana, MS Suss. H52; Vatican City, BAV, Vat. lat. 3551; Vatican City, BAV, Ross. 492; and Vatican City, BAV, Ottob. lat. 1353. On the occurrence of Humanistic script in manuscripts made from parchment, see Derolez, *Codicologie*, 12–13.

8 Lieftinck, *Manuscrits datés conservés dans le Pays-bas*. Cf. Derolez, *The Palaeography of Gothic Manuscript Books*, 23.

9 M.P. Brown, *A Guide to Western Historical Scripts*, nos. 1–2; Wardrop, *The Script of Humanism*, 8, 13–14. On the influence of ancient inscriptions, see Stenhouse, *Reading Inscriptions and Writing Ancient History*, esp. chap. 1, 'Inscriptions and the Culture of Humanism,' 21–41.

10 Derolez, *The Palaeography of Gothic Manuscript Books*, 123ff; and Wardrop, *The Script of Humanism*, 11, 19–49.

11 See the *humanistica cursiva* in Lieftinck, *Manuscrits datés*, 1: pl. 428. Cf. the cursive of Niccolò Niccoli in Mare, *The Handwriting of Italian Humanists*, pll. X–XI.

12 Measuring 231 × 164 mm; text block, 145 × 96 mm. The text blocks of Florence, Bib. Ricc., MS 660 and Florence, Bib. Ricc., MS 671 are both composed of twenty-six long lines.

13 R.E. Rehe, 'Legibility,' in Swanson, *Graphic Design & Reading*, 101.

14 Derolez, *The Palaeography of Gothic Manuscript Books*, 10.

15 See also Rome, Bib. Casanatense, MS 303; and Rome, Bib. Vallicelliana, MS F.20.

16 Measuring 297 × 207 mm; text block, 224 × 140 mm. See the *cursiva fere humanistica* in Lieftinck, *Manuscrits datés*, 1: pl. 414.

17 Cf. the *hybrida* in Lieftinck, *Manuscrits datés*, 1: pll. 188, 207, and the *hybrida currens*, 1: pl. 211; and the *hybrida libraria* in Derolez, *The Palaeography of Gothic Manuscript Books*, pl. 124.

18 Measuring 290 × 210 mm; two columns, each 200 × 60 mm. Other examples include Vienna, Österreichische Nationalbibliothek, MS 3147. On the two-columned layout, see Geneviève Hasenohr, 'La prose,' in Martin, *Mise en page et mise en texte du livre français*, 265–87; and Bozzolo and Ornato, *Pour une histoire du livre manuscrit au moyen âge*, 18. For the connection between Humanistic scripts and layouts of a single text block of long lines, see Derolez, *Codicologie*, 68.

19 Derolez, *The Palaeography of Gothic Manuscript Books*, 37.

20 The precise relationship between manuscript and print in the fifteenth century continues to be debated. See Eisenstein, *Divine Art, Infernal Machine*; Pettegree, *The Book in the Renaissance*; Hobbins, *Authorship and Publicity before Print*; S.A. Baron, Lindquist, and Shevlin, *Agent of Change*; Crick and Walsham, *The Uses of Script and Print*; Dane, *The Myth of Print Culture*; McKitterick, *Print, Manuscript and the Search for Order*; Beal, *In Praise of Scribes*; and especially the forum in *American Historical Review* 107.1 (February 2002): 84–128; Johns, *The Nature of the Book*; and the seminal work by Eisenstein, *The Printing Press as an Agent of Change*.

21 Richardson, 'From Scribal Publication to Print Publication,' 687 and, later, in *Manuscript Culture in Renaissance Italy*. On this point, see also Love, *Scribal Publication in Seventeenth-Century England*, 35–46.

22 Leonardo Bruni [*sic*], *De nobilitate* [Florence: S. Jacopo di Ripoli?, 1480]. On the attribution to the Ripoli press, see Rouse and Rouse, *Cartolai, Illuminators, and Printers*, 94.

23 Measuring about 197 × 130 mm; text block, 134 × 78 mm. Cf. the external dimensions of the above examples in manuscript: 224 × 155 mm, 231 × 164 mm, and 297 × 207 mm respectively.

24 *Dialogi decem auctorum* [Cologne: Printer of *Flores S. Augustini*, 1473]. The printer of the *Flores S. Augustini* probably used type that was cut by Johannes Veldener, who moved from Cologne to Louvain around 1473. See Corsten, 'Caxton in Cologne'; Blake, *Caxton*, 78; and Ricci, 'Colard Mansion,' 96. Hessel notes that Veldener brought the *Kölner Bastarda* to

Louvain, in 'Von der Schrift zum Druck,' 95. Another example can be found in Dominicus Bonaccursius, *Orationes de vera nobilitate* [Leipzig: Conrad Kachelofen, 1494].

25 Measuring about 270 × 200 mm; two columns, each 190 × 58 mm.

26 Vanderjagt, 'Il pubblico dei testi umanistici'; Vanderjagt, *'Qui sa la vertu anoblist,'* 182; and R.J. Mitchell, *John Tiptoft*, 177. For more on Aurispa in general, see Cast, 'Aurispa, Petrarch, and Lucian'; and Sabbadini, *Carteggio di Giovanni Aurispa.*

27 For instance, Florence, Bib. Naz. Cent., Magl. Cl.VI.187; and Florence, Bib. Naz. Cent., Palat. 1105. See Martin, 'Politique et typographie: Le triomphe de la lettre romaine en France et ses conséquences,' in *Mise en page et mise en texte du livre français*, 162ff.

28 Measuring 234 × 155 mm; text block, 143 × 76 mm. See the *textualis humanistica* in Lieftinck, *Manuscrits datés*, 1: pl. 420, and *textualis humanistica formata*, 1: pl. 426.

29 Among others, Mare, 'Humanistic Script' and *The Handwriting of Italian Humanists*; Wardrop, *The Script of Humanism*; Ullman, *Humanistic Script*; and Morison, 'Early Humanistic Script and the First Roman Type.'

30 Among others, see Hankins, *Renaissance Civic Humanism*; Witt, 'In the Footsteps of the Ancients'; Huizinga, *The Autumn of the Middle Ages*; Grafton, *Defenders of the Text*; Bouwsma, *A Usable Past*; Grafton and Jardine, *From Humanism to the Humanities*; Kristeller, *Renaissance Concepts of Man*; H. Baron, *The Crisis of the Early Italian Renaissance*; and Burckhardt, *The Civilization of the Renaissance in Italy.*

31 Morison, 'Early Humanistic Script,' 24. On 'graphic bipolarism,' see Petrucci, *Writers and Readers in Medieval Italy*, 198, 218; and Derolez, *Codicologie*, 11.

32 Paul Saenger has noted the use of the Humanistic hand in manuscripts that transmit texts in the Italian vernacular, in *Space between Words*, 271.

33 Cf. Jed, *Chaste Thinking.*

34 On *La controversie de noblesse*, see Vanderjagt, *'Qui sa la vertu anoblist,'* in which a transcription is provided. An earlier transcription is found in Burger, *Eine französische Handschrift.* Although the treatise travels under other names, including *Le débat de la vraie noblesse*, the chapter and the rest of the book will refer to the French translation as *La controversie de noblesse* for the sake of clarity. On Miélot's production in general, see Perdrizet, 'Jean Miélot.'

35 On the graphic traditions of romance in general, see, among others, McGrady, *Controlling Readers*; Desmond and Sheingorn, *Myth, Montage, and Visuality in Late Medieval Manuscript Culture*; Hindman, *Sealed in Parchment*; Huot, *The Romance of the Rose and Its Medieval Readers*; and Hedeman, *The Royal Image.*

36 Vanderjagt, 'Il pubblico dei testi umanistici' and 'Between Court Literature and Civic Rhetoric.'

37 Vanderjagt, 'The Princely Culture of the Valois Dukes of Burgundy,' 76.

38 For a discussion and further bibliographical references, see Derolez, *The Palaeography of Gothic Manuscript Books*, 157–60. Examples are found in M.P. Brown, *A Guide to Western Historical Scripts*, no. 42; and Lieftinck, *Manuscrits datés*, 1: xv.

39 Conduct literature has been amply discussed in, for instance, Ashley and Clark, *Medieval Conduct*; Bryson, *From Courtesy to Civility*; Jaeger, *The Origins of Courtliness*; and Nicholls, *The Matter of Courtesy*.

40 On the circulation of treatises on nobility in northern Europe, see Oschema, 'Maison, noblesse et légitimité'; Vanderjagt, 'Princely Culture'; and Cannon Willard, 'The Concept of True Nobility at the Burgundian Court.'

41 Paris, BNF, fr. 12577. A third of Chrétien's manuscripts are illustrated. See Hindman, *Sealed in Parchment*, 3.

42 Mons, Bibliothèque municipale, MS 331/206; Montpellier, Bibliothèque de l'École de médecine, MS H249; Paris, BNF, fr. 12576; and Paris, BNF, fr. 1453.

43 Similarly, Grendler, 'Form and Function in Italian Renaissance Popular Books,' 479.

44 Buettner, 'Profane Illuminations, Secular Illusions,' 88. Similarly, see Bolzoni, *The Gallery of Memory*; Carruthers, *The Book of Memory*, esp. chap. 7, 'Memory and the Book,' 274–337; and Yates, *The Art of Memory*.

45 On the manuscripts of *La controversie de noblesse in general*, see Delaissé, *Medieval Miniatures from the Department of Manuscripts* and *Le siècle d'or de la miniature flamande*.

46 Measuring 405 × 275 mm; text block, 254 × 160 mm.

47 On the depiction of ancient figures in contemporary attire, see Hedeman, *Translating the Past*.

48 For a more detailed discussion of manuscript illumination, see Hamel, *The British Library Guide to Manuscript Illumination*; and Alexander, *Medieval Illuminators and Their Methods of Work*.

49 Measuring 275 × 190 mm; text block, 160 × 106 mm.

50 Orth, 'What Goes Around,' 189.

51 Bonaccursius de Montemagno, *Controversie de noblesse, et Débat de trois chevaleureux princes* [Bruges: Colard Mansion, 1476]. On Mansion, see P. Saenger, 'Colard Mansion'; and Ricci, 'Colard Mansion.' On the cursive in print in general, see Tinto, *Il corsivo nella tipografia del Cinquecento*. On the use of paper, see Kwakkel, 'A New Type of Book.'

52 Measuring about 269 × 185 mm; text block, 186 × 142 mm.

53 Paris, BNF, Rés. D-862.

54 See the discussion that follows in chapter 5, 'The Digital Page.' On the social construction of fact, see Latour and Woolgar, *Laboratory Life*, esp. 105–6, 176, 236–41. Similarly, see Poovey, *A History of the Modern Fact*.

55 Similarly, see Deeming, 'The Song and the Page'; and Zetzel, *Marginal Scholarship and Textual Deviance*.

CHAPTER 3: THE PARATEXT AND THE PAGE

1 Genette, *Paratexts*, 1–2.

2 See 'intratextuality,' in Grigely, *Textualterity*, 157.

3 Pseudo-Aristoteles, *Le gouvernement des princes* (Paris: Antoine Vérard, 1497), types 7 and 8. There is some question as to whether Vérard printed this edition himself or arranged for someone else to print it. See Winn, *Anthoine Vérard*.

4 In Paris, BNF, Vélins 411–13, 332 × 220 mm.

5 A recent discussion of title pages in printed books is found in Driver, *The Image in Print*. On Vérard's title pages, see M.M. Smith, *The Title-Page*, chap. 7, 'The Woodcut Title-Page,' 109–21; and Eleanor P. Spencer, 'Antoine Vérard's Illuminated Vellum Incunables,' in Trapp, ed., *Manuscripts in the Fifty Years after the Invention of Printing*, 62–5. See also Hirsch, 'Title Pages in French Incunables.'

6 Transcriptions can be found in Vanderjagt, 'Qui sa la vertu anoblist.' See also Prinet, 'Le Trésor de noblesse.' On titles, see Sharpe, *Titulus*.

7 On the politics of similar depictions, see C.J. Brown, 'Books in Performance'; Buettner, 'Past Presents'; C.J. Brown, *Poets, Patrons, and Printers*, esp. chap. 3, 'The Changing Image of the Poet,' 99–151; Chartier, 'Princely Patronage and the Economy of Dedication' in *Forms and Meanings*, 25–42; and Mortimer, *A Portrait of the Author in Sixteenth-Century France*. Similarly, on images representing the dedications of churches, see Bloch, 'Zum Dedikationsbild im Lob des Kreuzes des Hrabanus Maurus.'

8 For more on this point, see Richardson, *Printing, Writers and Readers in Renaissance Italy*, chap. 3, 'Publication in Print: Patronage, Contracts and Privileges,' 49–76.

9 On representations of sovereignship and patronage, see, among others, Ann M. Roberts, 'The Horse and the Hawk: Representations of Mary of Burgundy as Sovereign,' in Areford and Rowe, *Excavating the Medieval Image*, 137–50; Muir, *Reading Texts and Image*; Freeman Sandler, 'The Image of the Book-Owner in the Fourteenth Century'; and Hedeman, *The Royal Image*.

10 Kendrick, *Animating the Letter*, 205–6.

11 A longer discussion follows in chapter 4. See, recently, Elizabeth Sears, 'Portraits in Counterpoint: Jerome and Jeremiah in an Augsburg Manuscript,' in Sears and Thomas, *Reading Medieval Images*, 61–74; Thornton, *The Scholar in His Study*; and P. Saenger, 'Silent Reading,' 388–90, 407.

12 Macfarlane observes that the image of the book presentation was used in three other editions by Vérard between 1492 and 1494, two of which were destined for royal circles; *Antoine Vérard*, 135. On the reuse of images in general, see, recently, Dekeyzer and Van der Stock, *Manuscripts in Transition*; and Driver, *The Image in Print*.

13 London, BL, C.22.c.3.

14 Recent discussions of dedications are found in M. Saenger, *The Commodification of Textual Engagements*, chap. 2, 'The Antechambers of the English Book: A Survey of Front Matter,' 35–94; Buchtel, 'Book Dedications and the Death of a Patron'; Bernstein, *Print Culture and Music in Sixteenth-Century Venice*, chap. 5, 'Composers, Patrons, and the Venetian Music Press,' 99–113; and Chartier, 'Princely Patronage,' in *Forms and Meanings*, 25–42.

83

15 Genette, *Paratexts*, 134–5.

16 Buchtel, 'Book Dedications,' 10.

17 'Laquelle translacion je vous envoie sire qui par voz belles vertus et vaillances avez der-renierement travaillé a mettre bonne paix en vostre royaulme de France … Et ne sera pas forte chose a vous qui estes la droite sourse et l'estoq de noblesse et a qui tous les nobles non pas seulement de ce royaume mais de tous aultres doivent avoir recours de juger, determiner, decider et arrester lequel des deux doit estre dit le plus noble.' Vanderjagt, 'Qui sa la vertu anoblist,' 224, ll. 7–10, 12–17.

18 In the classical tradition of *laudando praecipere*, 'to teach by praising'; by telling people what virtues they possess, one teaches them the virtues that they ought to possess.

19 London, BL, Arundel 138. See Bertalot, 'Forschungen über Leonardo Bruni Aretino,' 308.

20 Among others, Oxford, Bodleian Library, D'Orville 530; Florence, Bib. Laur., Ash. 1657; Milan, Bib. Ambrosiana, MS D8 sup.; Rome, Bib. Casanatense, MS 1274; Vatican City, BAV, Reg. Lat. 1366; Vienna, Österreichische Nationalbibliothek, MS 3147.

21 Buchtel, 'Book Dedications,' 2.

22 Buonaccorso da Montemagno, *Prose e Rime*, ed. Casotti (1718).

23 The dedication to Carlo dominates twentieth-century discussions about the treatise. See Bertalot, *Studien zum italienischen und deutscher Humanismus*, 1: 143; Cannon Willard, 'The Concept of True Nobility at the Burgundian Court,' 37; R.J. Mitchell, *John Tiptoft*, 176; H. Baron, 'Forschungen über Leonardo Bruni Aretino'; Bertalot, 'Forschungen' and 'Drei Vorlesungsankündigungen des Paulus Niavis'; Bruni Aretino, *Humanistisch-philosophische Schriften*; and Cicero, *Caxton's Tully Of old age and Friendship*, 11.

24 Buonaccorso da Montemagno, 'De nobilitate / La nobiltà,' 139–66; and Rabil, *Knowledge, Goodness, and Power*, 32.

25 On the intellectual and rhetorical division of texts in the medieval and early-modern periods, see, among others, Enenkel and Neuber, *Cognition and the Book*; H.-J. Martin, *Mise en page et mise en texte du livre français*; Moss, *Printed Commonplace-Books*; Hamel, *Glossed Books of the Bible*; and Parkes, 'The Influence of the Concepts of *Ordinatio* and *Compilatio*,' esp. 125–35.

26 Similarly with the practice of *per cola et commata*. See Parkes, *Pause and Effect*; and P. Saenger, 'Silent Reading,' 374–5.

27 Genette, *Paratexts*, 294.

28 'Publii Cornelii Scipionis oratio.' Milan, Bib. Ambrosiana, MS N192 sup., f. 6r.

29 Parkes, *Pause and Effect*, 305, *s.v.* 'paraph,' and 307, *s.v.* 'virgula suspensiva.'

30 'Trattato che fecero due giovani Romani in presenzia del sanato [*sic*] Della Nobilita & come ognuno diceva esse piu Nobile dell altro.' Vatican City, BAV, Ross. 759, f. 28v.

31 'Oratione di plublio [*sic*] cornelio scipione Narrando di sua Nobilita.' Ibid., f. 31r.

32 'Essendo la quistione dianzi alli Senatori publio cornelio volendo di mostrare se essere piu nobile et pro allui doversi spectare lucretia per donna cosi comincia la sua oratione et parlare.' Florence, Bib. Naz. Cent., Palat. 1105, f. 30v.

33 'Uno altro archomento di publio cornelio scipione che nobilta sia per ricchezza.' Florence, Bib. Naz. Cent., Magl. Cl.VI.187, f. 56r.

34 'Exemplo di flamminio in fortificatione del suo argomento.' Florence, Bib. Naz. Cent., Palat. 1105, f. 42v.

35 'Argomento di flaminio dimonstrativo chella poverta non fa huomo virtuoso ingnobile [*sic*].' Florence, Bib. Naz. Cent., Palat. 1105, f. 43v.

85

36 Richardson, *Print Culture in Renaissance Italy*, 36; and Petrucci, *Writers and Readers in Medieval Italy*, esp. 174–89. On the vernacular curriculum in the late medieval and early modern period, see Grendler, *Schooling in Renaissance Italy*, chap. 10, 'Italian Literature,' 275–305.

37 Grendler, 'Form and Function in Italian Renaissance Popular Books,' 453–4, and *Schooling in Renaissance Italy*, 42–7, 78. See also Black, *Humanism and Education in Medieval and Renaissance Italy*; and Richardson, *Printing, Writers and Readers*, 135–55.

38 On these writers, see Bec, 'Lo statuto socio-professionale degli scrittori' and *Les marchands écrivains*.

39 Richardson, *Print Culture in Renaissance Italy*, 183. See also, Hirsch, *Printing, Selling, and Reading*, 133–7.

40 Florence, Bib. Ricc., MS 2546, ff. 63r–63v.

41 For instance, see Burke, *The Fortunes of the Courtier*.

42 Richardson, *Printing, Writers and Readers* (1999), 154–5.

43 In general, see H.-J. Martin, *Mise en page*; and P. Saenger, 'Silent Reading,' 408–10.

44 'Cy fine la prologue de lacteur et sensieult le title de ceste declamation de noblesse jadi plaidoie devant les senateurs de romme.' Paris, BNF, fr. 5413, f. 71r.

45 'Cy parle publius cornelius contre gayus flaminius devant les senateurs de Rome.' Brussels, KBR, MS 9278–80, f. 18r.

46 'Sensuit loroison de Gayus Flaminius.' Brussels, KBR, MS 10493–7, f. 86r. On this manuscript, see Byles, 'Caxton's *Book of the Ordre of Chyualry*.'

47 'Sensuit a ce propos la translation dune controversie et Debat de deux vaillans hommes contendans avoir la belle Lucresse en mariage.' London, BL, C.22.c.3, f. 41r, 1°.

48 On printing in red ink, see Scholderer, 'Red Printing in Early Books' and 'A Further Note on Red Printing in Early Books.'

49 Paris, BNF, Rés. D-862, and Paris, BNF, Vélins 411–13.

50 *Translationen*, also *Translatzen* or *Tütschungen*. For a complete transcription, see Wyle, *Translationen*, ed. von Keller (1861). On Wyle, see Flood, 'Niklas von Wyle'; Knape and Roll, *Rhetorica deutsch*, esp. 185–215; and Schwenk, *Vorarbeiten zu einer Biographie des Niklas von Wyle*. Manuscript copies of some individual translations are extant; however, the German version of the *Controversia* does not appear among these; see Strauss, *Der Übersetzer Nicolaus von Wyle*.

51 Wyle, *Translationen etlicher Bücher* [Esslingen: Conrad Fyner, after 5 April 1478]. In Boston, Public Library, Q.404.64, 285 × 210 mm; text block, 160 × 116 mm. See entry under

Conrad Fyner, in Voulliéme, *Die deutschen Drucker*, 46–66. Fyner's types show similarities with what is later called *Wittenbergerschrift* in the sixteenth century; see Crous and Kirchner, *Die gotischen Schriftarten*, figs. 79–80. See also Victor Scholderer, 'Notes on the Incunabula of Esslingen,' in *Fifty Essays in Fifteenth- and Sixteenth-Century Bibliography*, ed. Dennis E. Rhodes (Amsterdam: Menno Hertzberger, 1966), 224–8.

52 Genette, *Paratexts*, 316–18. On running titles in the early printed book, see Richardson, *Printing, Writers and Readers*, 130–1.

53 Wyle, *Transzlatzionen oder Tütschungen des hochgeachten Nicolai von Weil* (Strasbourg: Johannes Bryse, 1510). In London, BL, 12403.g.25, 294 × 200 mm; text block, 275 × 142 mm. In general, see Chrisman, *Lay Culture, Learned Culture*.

54 Wyle, *Translationen oder Deütschungen des hochgeachten Nicolai von Weil* (Augsburg: Heinrich Stayner, 1536). In London, BL, 837.L.19(2), 310 × 202 mm; text block, 245 × 160 mm.

55 On foliation, see M.M. Smith, 'Printed Foliation.' For a brief survey on the development of the Gothic in Germany see Kinross, *Modern Typography*, chap. 7, 'Cultures of Printing: Germany,' 67–79. See also H.-J. Martin, *Mise en page*, 62–81; Bain and Shaw, *Blackletter*; Crous and Kirchner, *Die gotischen Schriftarten*; Updike, *Printing Types*, chap. 4, 'Types of the Fifteenth Century in Germany,' 1: 58–69; and Voulliéme, *Die deutschen Drucker*.

56 Leclerq, *The Love of Learning and the Desire for God*, esp. 16–22, 89–90. In general, see Grotans, *Reading in Medieval St. Gall*, 30–3; and Beach, *Women as Scribes*.

57 For example, see Camille, *Image on the Edge*, 20–6. On universities in general, see, most recently, Grendler, *The Universities of the Italian Renaissance*; Black, *Humanism and Education in Medieval and Renaissance Italy*; and Courtenay and Miethke, *Universities and Schooling in Medieval Society*.

58 Robert Marichal, 'Les manuscrits universitaires,' and Richard H. Rouse and Mary A. Rouse, 'Concordances et index,' both in H.-J. Martin and J. Vezin, *Mise en page et mise en texte du livre manuscrit*, 211–17, 219–28.

59 Chrisman, 'Printing and the Evolution of Lay Culture in Strasbourg,' 74; Hackenberg, 'Books in Artisan Homes of Sixteenth-Century Germany,' 75. See also Chrisman, *Lay Culture, Learned Culture*.

60 Chrisman, 'Printing and the Evolution of Lay Culture,' 87, fig. 4.3. The importance of printing technology for religious reform in the early modern period has been the topic of much discussion; see, recently, Pettegree, *The Book in the Renaissance*; S.A. Baron, Lindquist, and Shevlin, *Agent of Change*; Lander, *Inventing Polemic*; Gilmont, *The Reformation and the Book*; and Edwards, *Printing, Propaganda, and Martin Luther*.

61 See Sharpe, *Titulus*, 31; and Roger Laufer, 'L'espace visuel du livre ancien,' in Chartier and H.-J. Martin, *Histoire de l'édition française*, 1: 479–97.

62 'la quelle a este faitte et composee par ung notable docteur en loix et grant orateur nomme bonne surse de pistoye. puis par le commandement de treshault trespuissant et tresexcellent prince Phelippe … A este la ditte controversie ou debat de noblesse translatee en francois.

Par Jo. Mielot le moindre des secretaires di cellui seigneur lan de grace mil iiiie xlix.' Vander-jagt, 'Qui sa la vertu anoblist,' 221–2, ll. 1235–44.

63 Cicero, *Of Old Age* ([Westminster]: William Caxton, 12 August 1481), types 2* and 3. A transcription of the *Declamacyon* is found in R.J. Mitchell, *John Tiptoft*, 215–41. On Caxton's epilogues in general, see Blake, 'Continuity and Change in Caxton's Prologues and Epi-logues'; and Caxton, *The Prologues and Epilogues of William Caxton*. See also Needham, *The Printer & The Pardoner.*

64 On Caxton's use of collaborative and accumulative authority, see Mayer, *Worlds Made Flesh*, 138–9. There is a large body of scholarly literature on Caxton and his role as printer, edi-tor, and translator. See, recently, Kuskin, *Caxton's Trace*. See also Duff, *William Caxton*; and Blades, *The Life and Typography of William Caxton*.

The role of the author has been the subject of much critical attention since the seminal essays of Barthes, 'The Death of the Author,' and Foucault, 'What Is an Author?' For the Middle Ages especially, see Gillespie, *Print Culture and the Medieval Author*, and Minnis, *Medieval Theory of Authorship.*

65 Caxton, *Prologues and Epilogues*, 46–7.

66 M.A. Amos, 'Violent Hierarchies: Disciplining Women and Merchant Capitalists in *The Book of the Knyght of the Towre*,' in Kuskin, *Caxton's Trace*, 94. See also Blake, *Caxton and His World*, 101ff.

67 On John Tiptoft, see R.J. Mitchell, *John Tiptoft*; on his involvement with the translation of the *Controversia de nobilitate*, see R.J. Mitchell, 'Italian "Nobilità" and the English Idea of the Gentleman.'

68 M. Saenger, *The Commodification of Textual Engagements*, 122.

69 Grigely, *Textualterity*, 163.

70 Wyle, *Translationen*, 283–4. On the disappearance of names of authors in translations of their works, see Brown, *Poets, Patrons, and Printers*, 156–7, 245–6.

71 Michael Saenger describes how authors may not be acknowledged in the text unless it was thought their name would add value to the book; *The Commodification of Textual Engage-ments*, 29.

CHAPTER 4: READING THE LIBRARY

1 A suggestive discussion of monuments is found in Choay, *The Invention of the Historic Monu-ment*, 165.

2 'Quae tanta, & talia sunt nobilitatis monimenta, quanta, & qualia cuique mortalium fas est optare. Est igitur mihi propria nobilitatis possessio relicta, quod a maioribus meis quasi haereditariae sun ingenitae illorum imagines. Hos illi gestabant habitus, haec facies in eorum vultibus lucebat. Ego illorum sanguinem, illorum membra, atque illorum formas in hac com-pagine corporis refero.' Buonaccorso da Montemagno, *Prose e Rime de'due Buonaccorso*

    da Montemagno, ed. Casotti, 28, 30. English trans. in Rabil, *Knowledge, Goodness, and Power*, 38.

3 Ruvoldt, 'Sacred to Secular, East to West,' 644–5. A survey of the recent scholarship on domestic spaces of the Renaissance is found in Ajmar-Wollheim, Dennis, and Matchette, 'Approaching the Italian Renaissance Interior.' See also Clercq, Dumolyn, and Haemers, '"Vivre Noblement"'; and McKeon, *The Secret History of Domesticity*. For a discussion of domestic and personal libraries in the modern era, see A. Black, 'Libraries.'

4 'Ego vero inter pacificos meos lares continentiam tuam, dulcis Lucretia, deducam, qui tametsi non supervacaneis ornatibus pleni sunt, tamen virtute, moribus, iocunditate, & omni pudicitia relucent. Ibi primum confertissimam librarum bibliothecam meam videbis, in qua semper omnem spem meam detuli. Haec, splendidae quidem supellectiles.' Buonaccorso da Montemagno, *Prose e Rime*, 90, 92; Rabil, *Knowledge, Goodness, and Power*, 51–2.

    On the notion of *supellex* and its connection with books in the early modern period, see, recently, Knight, '"Furnished" for Action'; and Eden, 'Intellectual Property and the *Adages* of Erasmus.'

5 'Tertio, havere nel primo solaro uno scriptoio habile alle facciende tue, et dextro che d'ogni banda si possa sedere et separato, senza dare inpaccio ala famiglia di casa per li forestieri che vengono a contare teco ... Et chi si dilecta di lectere non debbe tenere libri nello scriptoio commune, ma havere scriptoio separato in camera sua.' Cotrugli Raguseo, *Il libro dell'arte di mercatura*, 230–1; English trans. in Thornton, *The Scholar in His Study*, 32.

6 More can be found in Stock, 'Reading, Writing, and the Self,' 725–6. Petrarch's views on solitude have been discussed at length. See, among others, W.S. Blanchard, 'Petrarch and the Genealogy of Asceticism'; Lombardo, 'Vita Activa versus Vita Contemplativa'; and Constable, 'Petrarch and Monasticism.'

7 In general, see the essays in Leedham-Green and Webber, *The Cambridge History of Libraries in Britain and Ireland*, vol. 1; Francis Wormald, 'The Monastic Library,' in McCracken, Randall, and Randall, *Gatherings in Honor of Dorothy E. Miner*, 93–109; O'Gorman, *The Architecture of the Monastic Library in Italy*; Florence Edler de Roover, 'The Scriptorium,' in J.W. Thompson, *The Medieval Library*, 594–612; and Clark, *The Care of Books*.

8 'In vento minime pluvia nive sole sedere / Possumus in claustro nec scribere neque studere.' Cambridge, University Library, MS Hh.VI.ii. English trans. in Clark, *The Care of Books*, 71.

9 Alberti, *L'Architettura*, 10: 14.981. See also Serlio, *On Domestic Architecture*. In general, see Staikos, *Libraries*; Christ, *The Handbook of Medieval Library History*; Goldthwaite, 'The Florentine Palace as Domestic Architecture'; and Liebenwein, *Studiolo*.

10 Pearson Perry, 'Practical and Ceremonial Uses of Plants Materials as "Literary Refinements,"' 170, ll. 27–9.

11 On books and reading in the classical period, see, among others, Grafton and Williams, *Christianity and the Transformation of the Book*; Williams, *The Monk and the Book*; Casson, *Libraries in the Ancient World*; Snyder, *Teachers and Texts in the Ancient World*; Small, *Wax*

Tablets of the Mind; Roberts and Skeat, *The Birth of the Codex*; Dilke, *Roman Books and Their Impact*; and Kenyon, *Books and Readers in Ancient Greece and Rome*.

12 'Cubicula et bybliothecae ad orientem spectare debent; usus enim matutinum postulat lumen, item in bybliothecis libri non putrescent. nam quaecumque ad meridiem et occiden-tem spectant, ab tineis et umore libri vitiantur, quod venti umidi advenientes procreant eas et alunt infundentesque umidos spiritus pallore volumina corrumpunt.' Vitruvius, *On Archi-tecture*, 6: 4.1; English trans. in Vitruvius, *The Ten Books on Architecture*, trans. Morgan; both available at http://www.perseus.tufts.edu/cgi-bin/ptext?lookup=Vitr.+6.4.1.

13 'Postea vero quam Tyrannio mihi libros disposuit, mens addita videtur meis aedibus. qua qui-dem in re mirifica opera Dionysi et Menophili tui fuit, nihil venustius quam illa tua pegmata, postquam sittybae libros illustrarunt,' *Att.* 4.4a. Cicero, *Letters to Atticus*, 1: 309–11.

14 Discussions of the Ezra portrait and its influence abound. See, for example, Kendrick, *Animating the Letter*, 178–82; Kubiski, 'The Medieval "Home Office"'; and J.J.G. Alexander, 'Facsimiles, Copies, and Variations: The Relationship to the Model in Medieval and Renais-sance European Illuminated Manuscripts,' in Preciado, *Retaining the Original*, 64–5.

15 See Thornton, *The Scholar in His Study*; Warncke, *Ikonographie der Bibliotheken*; Hanebutt-Benz, *Die Kunst des Lesens*; Praz, *An Illustrated History of Furnishing*; and Prochno, *Das Schreiber- und Dedikationsbild in der deutschen Buchmalerei*.

16 See discussions in Harpold, *Ex-foliations*, 62; Williams, *The Monk and the Book*; Elizabeth Sears, 'Portraits in Counterpoint: Jerome and Jeremiah in an Augsburg Manuscript,' in Sears and Thomas, *Reading Medieval Images*, 61–72; Ridderbos, *Saint and Symbol*; and Meiss, 'Scholarship and Penitence in the Early Renaissance' and 'French and Italian Variations on an Early Fifteenth Century Theme.' Images of reading in later periods are discussed in Stewart, *The Look of Reading*.

17 Berger, *Fictions of the Pose*, 387.

18 Lane Ford, 'Private Ownership of Printed Books,' 218.

19 Elam, '"Studioli" and Renaissance Court Patronage,' 51–3. See also J.K. Lydecker, 'The Domestic Setting of the Arts in Renaissance Florence.'

20 On the date and attribution, see Cheles, *The Studiolo of Urbino*, 15; and Clough, 'Federigo da Montefeltro's Private Study.'

21 On the use of the panels as a stimulus for developing thought, see Kirkbride, 'On the Ren-aissance *Studioli* of Federico da Montefeltro and the Architecture of Memory' and *Archi-tecture and Memory*. In general, see Tenzer, 'The Iconography of the Studiolo of Federico da Montefeltro.'

22 Thornton, *The Scholar in His Study*, 99–127; and Findlen, *Possessing Nature*, 293–346.

23 Cheles, *The Studiolo of Urbino*, 45.

24 Attempts to reconstruct the order of the portraits are found in Cheles, *The Studiolo of Urbino*, 49; Clough, 'Federigo da Montefeltro's Private Study,' 281; Davies, *Early Netherlandish School*; and Gnudi, 'Lo Studiolo di Federico da Montefeltro,' 27, 30.

25 Dora Thornton has suggested that the *studiolo* was designed to host intimate social gatherings; *The Scholar in His Study*, 120. See also Elam, '"Studioli,"' 24–5. More on the linking of the home to museological space and the 'theatricalizing' of the audience is found in Furjàn, 'Scenes from a Museum,' esp. 74–6.

26 Measuring approximately 14 × 6.5 metres. Discussions of the space are found in Peruzzi, *Cultura, potere, immagine*; Paolo dal Poggetto, 'Nuova lettura di ambienti federiciani: Il Bagno cosidetto "della Duchessa" e la Biblioteca del duca Federico,' in Baiardi, Chittolini, and Floriani, *Federico da Montefeltro*, 2: 105–18, and 'Il restauro della Biblioteca del Duca e delle sale attigue'; and Rotondi, *The Ducal Palace of Urbino*.

27 'Le scanzie de'libri sono accostate alle mura, e disposte con molto bell'ordine'; in Baldi, *Memorie concernenti la città di Urbino*, 56. There are discussions of the contents of the library in Simonetta, *Federico da Montefeltro and His Library*; Luigi Michelini Tocci, 'La formazione della Biblioteca di Federico da Montefeltro: Codici contemporanei e libri a stampa,' in Cerboni Baiardi, Chittolini, and Floriani, *Federico da Montefeltro*, 3: 9–18; Herstein, 'The Library of Federigo da Montefeltro'; Clough, 'The Library of the Dukes of Urbino'; and Tocci, 'Agapito, Bibliotecario "Docto, Acorto et Diligente."'

28 By Lucas Holstenio, in the seventeenth century. Raffaelli, *La imparziale e veritiera istoria della unione della Biblioteca ducale di Urbino alla Vaticana di Roma*, 12.

29 Stornajolo suspects that this copy might be currently shelved as Vatican City, BAV, Urbin. lat. 1250; *Codices Urbinates Latini*, 3: 235.

30 In general, see Dorothy Robathan, 'Libraries of the Italian Renaissance,' in Thompson, *The Medieval Library*, 509–88; and Kibre, 'The Intellectual Interests Reflected in Libraries of the Fourteenth and Fifteenth Centuries.' On Francesco Gonzaga, see Chambers, *A Renaissance Cardinal and His Worldly Goods*; on Piero di Cosimo de' Medici, see Ames-Lewis, *The Library and Manuscripts of Piero di Cosimo de' Medici*.

31 Probably by Agapito. See Maria Moranti, 'Organizzazione della Biblioteca di Federico da Montefeltro,' in Cerboni Baiardi, Chittolini, and Floriani, *Federico da Montefeltro*, 3: 42–3, esp. n. 87. The *Indice vecchio* is transcribed in Stornajolo, *Codices Urbinates Graeci*, xx–ccii.

32 See Stornajolo, *Codices Urbinates Graeci* (1895), cxxxv, under the subheading 'Cosmographi, historici, poetae, grammatici, et reliqua.' The *Controversia de nobilitate* appears again in a later sixteenth-century catalogue, in Guasti, 'Inventario della libreria urbinata,' 148.

33 Lauro Quirini, 'Letter to Pietro Tommasi,' in Rabil, *Knowledge, Goodness, and Power*, 149–50. See also McLean, *The Art of the Network*, esp. chap. 3, 'The Socially Contested Concept of Honor.'

34 On the social function of manuscript circulation, see Richardson, 'From Scribal Publication to Print Publication.'

35 Trinkaus, *Adversity's Noblemen*, 50.

36   Murray, *Reason and Society in the Middle Ages*, 180–1; Skinner, *The Foundations of Modern Political Thought*, 1: 81; H. Baron, *The Crisis of the Early Italian Renaissance*, 420–3.

37 Vanderjagt, 'Between Court Literature and Civic Rhetoric,' 565. See also Martines, *Power and Imagination*.

38 Vanderjagt, 'Between Court Literature,' 569. See also Vanderjagt, 'Il pubblico dei testi umanistici nell'Italia settentrionale ed in Borgogna,' 486, and 'Three Solutions to Buonaccorso's *Disputatio de nobilitate*.'

39 In general, see discussion in Lefebvre, *The Production of Space*, 8–11, 319–21.

40 On the discipline of knowledge, see, among others, Foucault, *The Order of Things* and *The Archaeology of Knowledge*. Recent discussions are found in Garberson, 'Libraries, Memory, and the Space of Knowledge'; and McKeon, *The Secret History of Domesticity*.

41 Manuscripts in Latin: lat. 14177, 15087, 18534, 4329, 6098, 6254, 6711, 7808, 7862, 7167.A; printed editions in Latin: C-674, Rés. Z-478, Rés. E*-314, Rés. Z-1475; manuscripts in French: fr. 1968, fr. 5413, n. acq. fr. 10722; printed editions in French: Rés. D-862; Vélins 412, Rés. E*-46; printed edition in German: Rés. Z-543; printed edition in English: Rés. R-79.

42 Most fundamentally, see Eisenstein, *The Printing Press as an Agent of Change*; and Febvre and Martin, *The Coming of the Book*. The separation of manuscript and printed books in libraries was 'all but universally accepted' by the late seventeenth century. See David McKitterick, 'Libraries and the Organisation of Knowledge,' in Leedham-Green and Webber, *The Cambridge History of Libraries*, 1: 612.

43 On 'lived space,' see Lefebvre, *The Production of Space*, 35.

44 On the system of classification used by the BNF, see Durlik, 'The Bibliothèque nationale de France'; and Jouguelet, 'Various Applications of the Dewey Decimal Classification.' A recent discussion about digital catalogues is found in Markey, 'The Online Library Catalog.' See also Sharpe, *Titulus*, 33–4.

45 Grosz, *Architecture from the Outside*, 91–3.

46 In general, see Grosz, *Architecture from the Outside*. See also Deleuze, *Negotiations*; Derrida, 'Différance'; and Foucault, *The Order of Things*.

47 On this point, see Mandosio, *L'effondrement de la très grande bibliothèque de France*, 46. Other discussions are found in Dawson, 'The National Library of France'; Durlik, 'The Bibliothèque nationale de France'; and Vidler, 'Books in Space.'

48 Jacques, *Bibliothèque nationale de France*, 48, 75.

CHAPTER 5: THE DIGITAL PAGE

1 Vidler, 'Warped Space,' 289.

2 Kirschenbaum distinguishes between the formal and forensic materialities of digital technologies in *Mechanism*, 10–13.

3 Roger Chartier, 'From Mechanical Reproduction to Electronic Representation,' in Gumbrecht and Marrinan, *Mapping Benjamin*, 111.

4 See the explication in Bolter and Grusin, *Remediation*. The notion of remediation has been taken up most recently by Harpold, *Ex-foliations*, 83; Echard, *Printing the Middle Ages*, esp. 'Coda: The Ghost in the Machine: Digital Avatars of Medieval Manuscripts,' 198–216; Foys, *Virtually Anglo-Saxon*; and Stephen G. Nichols, 'An Artifact by Any Other Name: Digital Surrogates of Medieval Manuscripts,' in Blouin and Rosenberg, *Archives, Documentation, and Institutions of Social Memory*, 140.

5 On the development of textual editing in general, see Reynolds and Wilson, *Scribes and Scholars*, 137–62; on the stages of *recensio*, *examinatio*, and *emendatio*, 207–41. On the relationship between textual editing and textual criticism, see McGann, *A Critique of Modern Textual Criticism*.

6 Grigely, *Textualterity*, 28.

7 Tanselle, 'The Editorial Problem of Final Authorial Intention'; and Greg, 'The Rationale of Copy-Text.' New approaches to textual editing, including the sociological approach, new stemmatics, and genetic criticism, are moving away from intentionality and seek instead to reveal the processes by which a text came to be and continues to develop. Discussions are found in McCarty, *Humanities Computing*; Deppman, Ferrer, and Groden, *Genetic Criticism*; Schreibman, Siemens, and Unsworth, *A Companion to Digital Humanities*; Barbrook et al., 'The Phylogeny of *The Canterbury Tales*'; Hay, 'Does "Text" Exist?'; and McKenzie, *Bibliography and the Sociology of Texts*.

8 Traube, 'Geschichte der Paläographie,' in *Vorlesungen und Abhandlungen*, esp. 57ff. On the debate about facsimiles, see Buettner, 'Panofsky à l'ère de la reproduction mécanisée.'

9 At http://wwwlib.umi.com/eebo. Recent critiques include Kichuk, 'Metamorphosis'; Sherman, 'EEBO'; Jowett and Egan, 'Review of the Early English Books Online (EEBO)'; and Williams and Baker, '*Caveat Lector*.'

10 From the microfilm series *Early English Books, 1475–1640*; *Early English Books, 1641–1700*; the *Thomason Tracts (1640–1661)*; and the *Early English Books Tract Supplement*. On the development of *EEBO*, see S. Martin, 'EEBO, Microfilm, and Umberto Eco.' The images and citation files in *EEBO* are derived from the *Short-Title Catalogue*, which itself is not immune from error. On this point, see Gadd, 'The Use and Misuse of Early English Books Online'; McKitterick, '"Not in STC"'; Blayney, 'The Numbers Game'; and Pantzer, 'The Serpentine Progress of the STC Revision.'

11 The microfilmed version of the *Declamacyon* appears in the UMI collection, *Early English Books, 1475–1640*, reel 1571:04.

12 On diplomatic editions, see Masai, 'Principes et conventions de l'édition diplomatique.'

13 Ramsay, 'Toward an Algorithmic Criticism,' 171. See also Flanders, 'Detailism, Digital Texts, and the Problem of Pedantry'; and Liu, 'Transcendental Data.'

14 Robinson, 'Computer-Assisted Stemmatic Analysis,' 99.

15 Cerquiglini, *In Praise of the Variant*, 78–9.

16 Bolter and Grusin, *Remediation*, 23–31. See also Hayles, 'Traumas of Code'; Mackenzie, *Cutting Code*; Bolter, *Writing Space*; and Manovich, *The Language of New Media*.

17 Daston and Galison, 'The Image of Objectivity,' 82–3. See also B.C. Smith, 'Limits of Correctness in Computers,' 467.

18 There is more on this point in Drucker, 'The Virtual Codex from Page Space to E-Space'; and Salen and O'Mara, 'Dis[appearances].'

19 See the discussion of authenticity in W. Benjamin, 'The Work of Art in the Age of Mechanical Reproduction,' in *Illuminations*, 220.

20 Latour and Lowe, 'The Migration of the Aura.' See also B.C. Smith, 'Indiscrete Affairs.'

21 There are, of course, instances in manuscript and print in which the facing-page layout is designed to function as a single unit, such as for maps, plans, calendars, tables, and charts. See, for example, Macdonald and Morrison-Low, *A Heavenly Library*, item 3.5; and the numerous illustrations in Harley and Woodward, *The History of Cartography*, vol. 1, esp. pll. 9, 13, and 16. A recent discussion of the facing-page layout is found in Hamburger, 'Openings.'

22 See the Text Creation Partnership, at http://www.lib.umich.edu/tcp/eebo; esp. notes on production.

23 On recursion, see Hayles, *My Mother Was a Computer*, 211. On the allographic nature of digital objects, see, W.J. Mitchell, *The Reconfigured Eye*, 52.

24 Bousmanne, Johan, and van Hoorebeeck, *La librairie des ducs de Bourgogne*. Recent reviews include Hurlbut in *Speculum* 81.3 and Rudy in *H-ArtHist, H-Net Reviews* (January 2003).

25 See Lieve Watteeuw's introduction to Bousmanne, Hemelryck, and Hoorebeeck, *La librairie des ducs de Bourgogne*, vol. 3, esp. 19–20; Delaissé, *Medieval Miniatures from the Department of Manuscripts* and *Le siècle d'or de la miniature flamande*; and Marchal, *Catalogue des manuscrits de la Bibliothèque royale des ducs de Bourgogne*, 1: lxxxv–lxxxvi.

26 Here entitled *Le débat de la vraie noblesse*. For the sake of consistency and clarity, the title, *La controversie de noblesse* will be used throughout the chapter. A description of Brussels, KBR 9278–80 and KBR 10977–9 can be found in Bousmanne, van Hoorebeeck, and Arnould, *La librairie des ducs de Bourgogne*, 2: 78–82 and 202–5.

27 Nelson, 'The Slide Lecture, or the Work of Art "History,"' 432; and Daston and Galison, 'The Image of Objectivity,' 120. See also Klamt, 'Zur Reproduktionsgeschichte mittelalterlicher Schriftformen und Miniaturen.'

28 Arnold, 'Facts or Fragments?' 466. Cf. Dalbello, 'Institutional Shaping of Cultural Memory.' See also Baetens and van Looy, 'Digitising Cultural Heritage'; King, 'Historiography as Reenactment'; and Camille, *Mirror in Parchment*, 30, 80–1, and 'Sensations of the Page: Imaging Technologies and Medieval Illuminated Manuscripts,' in Bornstein and Tinkle, *The Iconic Page in Manuscript, Print, and Digital Culture*, 45–6.

29 Baudrillard, 'The System of Collecting,' 24.

30 Camille, 'The *Très Riches Heures*,' 105.

31 Desmond and Sheingorn, *Myth, Montage, & Visuality in Late Medieval Manuscript Culture*, 40; and Baudrillard, 'The Murder of the Real,' in *The Vital Illusion*, 59–83. See also Baudrillard, *Simulacra and Simulation* and *For a Critique of the Political Economy of the Sign*; and Panofsky, *Meaning in Visual Arts*.

32 Benjamin, 'The Work of Art,' in *Illuminations*, 224; and Baudrillard, 'Objects, Images, and the Possibilities of Aesthetic Illusion,' in *Jean Baudrillard, Art and Artefact*, 15.

CONCLUSION

1 Roger Chartier calls these 'new significations,' in 'Reading Matter and "Popular" Reading: From the Renaissance to the Seventeenth Century,' in Cavallo and Chartier, *A History of Reading in the West*, 278.

Bibliography

PRIMARY SOURCES

1. Manuscripts of the *Controversia de nobilitate*

Florence, Bib. Laur.: acq. e doni 450; Ash. 181, 273, 1657
Florence, Bib. Naz. Cent.: Conv. Sop. J.IX.4
Florence, Bib. Ricc.: MSS 162, 660, 671, 693, 779
London, BL: Arundel 138; Harley 1883, 2580, 3332
Milan, Bib. Ambrosiana: MSS C69 inf., D8 sup., N192 sup., O71 sup., S21 sup., Suss. H52
Oxford, Bodleian Library: d'Orville 530
Rome, Bib. Casanatense: MSS 303, 1274
Rome, Bib. Corsiniana: MSS 36.D.28, 45.C.18
Rome, Bib. Vallicelliana: MS F.20
Vatican City, BAV: Barb. lat. 1952; Chigi J.V.160, J.VI.215; Ottob. lat. 1153, 1353, 2290; Reg. lat. 602, 1366; Ross. 492; Urbin. 1167; Vat. lat. 2906, 3551, 4510, 4514, 6875, 6898
Vienna, Österreichische Nationalbibliothek: MS 3147

2. Printed Editions of the *Controversia de nobilitate*

(1) *Dialogi decem auctorum* [Cologne: Printer of *Flores S. Augustini*, 1473]. Also attributed to [Louvain: Johannes Veldener, 1473].
    H.C. 6107; Pr. 1101; Pell. 4212; Oates 584–5; Polain 1262; BMC I.235; BSB-Ink D-103; *ISTC* id00145700.

    Cambridge, University Library: Inc. 3.A.4.8
    London, BL: G.8988 (olim IB.3752)
    Oxford, Bodleian Library: Auct. 2.Q.inf.II.71; Auct. 6.Q.inf.I.34

Bibliography

(2) Leonardo Bruni, *De nobilitate* [Florence: S. Jacopo di Ripoli? 1480]. Also attributed to [Milan: Bonus Accursius, c. 1480].
H. 1576; R. IV.118; Goff M-845; *IGI* 1878; *ISTC* im00845000.

London, BL: IA.26571

(3) Dominicus Bonaccursius, *Orationes de vera nobilitate* [Leipzig: Conrad Kachelofen, 1494]. Also attributed to [Moritz Brandis, c. 1488].
H.C. 3459; Pr. 2882; R. IV.150; Oates 1274; Goff M-846; *ISTC* im00846000

Cambridge, University Library: Inc. 5.A.27.2
Chicago, Newberry Library: Inc. 2882
The Hague, KB: 151.D.37
Oxford, Bodleian Library: Auct. 2.Q.5.88
Vatican City, BAV: Inc. IV.151

3. Manuscripts of the *Trattato della nobiltà*

Florence, Bib. Naz. Cent.: Magl. Cl.VI.187; Palat. 51, 1105; Panciatich. 126; II.II.39
Florence, Bib. Ricc.: MSS 2313, 2544, 2546
Vatican City, BAV: Ross. 759

4. Manuscripts of *La controversie de noblesse*

Brussels, KBR: 9278–80, 10493–97, 10977–79, 14821–40
London, BL: Harley 4402
Oxford, Bodleian Library: Lyell 48
Paris, BNF: fr. 1968, 5413
Paris, BNF: n.acq. fr. 10722

5. Printed Editions of *La controversie de noblesse*

(1) Bonaccursius de Montemagno, *Controversie de noblesse, et Débat de trois chevaleureux princes.* [Bruges: Colard Mansion, 1476.]
H.C. 15187; Pr. 9317; Polain 924; BMC IX.132; *ISTC* im00846200

Paris, BNF: Rés. D-862
London, BL: IB.49406

(2) Pseudo-Aristoteles, *Le gouvernement des princes, Le trésor de noblesse, Les Fleurs de Valere le grant.* Paris: Antoine Vérard, 1497.

H.C. 1784; Macfarlane, *Antoine Vérard*, no. 50; Pr. 8440; Pell. 1253; BMC VIII.87; CIBN A-557; *ISTC* ia01051000

London, BL: C.22.c.3
Paris, BNF: Vélins 412

6. Printed Editions of the *Von dem Adel aus alten Hystorien*

(1) Nicolaus von Wyle, *Translationen etlicher Bücher* [Esslingen: Conrad Fyner, after 5 April 1478].
H. 16224; Goff W-72; *IGI* 10402; CIBN W-41; *ISTC* iw00072000

Boston, Public Library: Q.404.64
London, BL: IB.8933
Paris, BNF: Rés. Z-543
San Marino, HEHL: 99566

(2) Nicolaus von Wyle, *Transzlatzionen oder Tütschungen des hochgeachten Nicolai von Weil.* Strasbourg: Johannes Bryse, 1510.

London, BL: 12403.g.25

(3) Nicolaus von Wyle, *Translationen oder Deütschungen des hochgeachten Nicolai von Weil.*

Augsburg: Heinrich Stayner, 1536.
Cambridge, University Library: XII.1.1
London, BL: 837.L.19(2)

7. Printed Editions of the *Declamacyon de noblesse*

Cicero, *Of Old Age.* [Westminster]: William Caxton, 12 August 1481.
H.C. 5311; Pr. 9640; Pell. 3683; *GW* 6992; Duff 103; Oates 4075–7; Goff C-627; de Ricci 31; *STC* 5293; *ISTC* ic00627000; *ESTC* 006178233

Cambridge, St. John's College: A.1.4, Ii.1.49
Cambridge, University Library: Inc. 3.J.1.1 (3495), 3.J.1.1 (3496), 3.J.1.1 (3497)
Chicago, Newberry Library: Inc. 9640
London, BL: IB.55045, IB.55047
Oxford, Queen's College: Sel.a.111
San Marino, HEHL: 82872, 82873
Windsor, Eton College: Df.7.7

8. Modern Editions

Bousmanne, Bernard, Frédérique Johan, and Céline van Hoorebeeck, eds. *La librairie des ducs de Bourgogne: Manuscrits conservés à la Bibliothèque royale de Belgique*. CD-ROM. Vol. 2: Textes didactiques. Turnhout, Belgium: Brepols, 2004.

Buonaccorso da Montemagno. 'De nobilitate / La nobiltà.' In *Prosatori latini del Quattrocento*, edited by Eugenio Garin, 139–66. Milan: R. Ricciardi, 1952.

– *Orazioni di Buonaccorso da Montemagno il giovane, con rime di Buonaccorso da Montemagno il vecchio*. Edited by Michele dello Russo. Naples: F. Ferrante, 1862.

– *Prose e Rime de'due Buonaccorso da Montemagno*. Edited by Giovanni Casotti. Florence: G. Manni, 1718.

Cicero, Marcus Tullius. *hEre begynneth the prohemye vpon the reducynge, both out of latyn as of frensshe in to our englyssh tongue, of the polytyque book named Tullius de senectute* … [Westminster: William Caxton, (12 Aug. [– ca. Sept.]) 1481]. In *Early English Books Online*. http://gateway.proquest.com/openurl?ctx_ver=Z39.88-2003&res_id=xri:eebo&rft_id=xri:eebo:citation:99842238.

SECONDARY SOURCES

Ajmar-Wollheim, Marta, Flora Dennis, and Ann Matchette. 'Approaching the Italian Renaissance Interior: Sources, Methodologies, Debates.' *Renaissance Studies* 20.5 (November 2006): 623–8.

Alberti, Leon Battista. *L'Architettura [De re aedificatoria]*. Edited and translated by Giovanni Orlandi. 2 vols. Milan: Polifilo, 1966.

Alexander, J.J.G. 'Facsimiles, Copies, and Variations: The Relationship to the Model in Medieval and Renaissance European Illuminated Manuscripts.' In *Retaining the Original: Multiple Originals, Copies, and Reproductions*, edited by Kathleen Preciado, 61–72. Washington: National Gallery of Art, 1989.

– *Medieval Illuminators and Their Methods of Work*. New Haven, CT: Yale University Press, 1992.

Ames-Lewis, Frances. *The Library and Manuscripts of Piero di Cosimo de' Medici*. New York: Garland, 1984.

Amos, Mark Addison. 'Violent Hierarchies: Disciplining Women and Merchant Capitalists in *The Book of the Knyght of the Towre*.' In *Caxton's Trace: Studies in the History of English Printing*, edited by William Kuskin, 69–100. Notre Dame: University of Notre Dame Press, 2006.

Arnold, Dana. 'Facts or Fragments? Visual Histories in the Age of Mechanical Reproduction.' *Art History* 25.4 (September 2002): 450–68.

Ashley, Kathleen, and Robert L.A. Clark, eds. *Medieval Conduct*. Minneapolis: University of Minnesota Press, 2001.

Baetens, Jan, and Jan van Looy. 'Digitising Cultural Heritage: The Role of Interpretation in

Cultural Preservation.' *Image [&] Narrative* 17 (April 2007). http://www.imageandnarrative
.be/digital_archive/baetens_vanlooy.htm.

Bain, Peter, and Paul Shaw, eds. *Blackletter: Type and National Identity.* New York: Cooper Union
for the Advancement of Science and Art, 1998.

Baldi, Bernardino. *Memorie concernenti la città di Urbino.* 1578. Reprinted in Bologna: Arnaldo
Forni, 1978.

Barad, Karen. *Meeting the Universe Halfway: Quantam Physics and the Entanglement of Matter
and Meaning.* Durham, NC: Duke University Press, 2007.

Barbrook, Adrian C., Christopher J. Howe, Norman Blake, and Peter Robinson. 'The Phylogeny
of *The Canterbury Tales.*' *Nature* 394 (27 August 1998): 839.

Barney, Stephen A., ed. *Annotation and Its Texts.* New York: Oxford University Press, 1991.

Baron, Hans. *The Crisis of the Early Italian Renaissance.* Princeton, NJ: Princeton University Press,
1966.

– 'Forschungen über Leonardo Bruni Aretino, Eine Erwiderung.' *Archiv für Kulturgeschichte*
22.3 (1932): 352–71.

Baron, Sabrina Alcorn, Eric N. Lindquist, and Eleanor F. Shevlin, eds. *Agent of Change: Print
Culture Studies after Elizabeth L. Eisenstein.* Amherst: University of Massachusetts Press, 2007.

Barthes, Roland. 'The Death of the Author.' In *Image – Music – Text,* translated by Stephen
Heath, 142–8. London: Fontana, 1987.

Baudrillard, Jean. *For a Critique of the Political Economy of the Sign.* Translated by Charles Levin.
St Louis, MO: Telos Press, 1981.

– *Jean Baudrillard, Art and Artefact.* Edited by Nicholas Zurbrugg. London: Sage, 1997.

– *Simulacra and Simulation.* Translated by Sheila F. Glaser. Ann Arbor: University of Michigan
Press, 1994.

– 'The System of Collecting.' In *The Cultures of Collecting,* edited by John Elsner and Roger
Cardinal, 7–24. Cambridge, MA: Harvard University Press, 1994.

– *The Vital Illusion.* Edited by Julia Witwer. New York: Columbia University Press, 2000.

Beach, Alison I. *Women as Scribes: Book Production and Monastic Reform in Twelfth-Century
Bavaria.* Cambridge: Cambridge University Press, 2004.

Beal, Peter. *In Praise of Scribes: Manuscripts and Their Makers in Seventeenth-Century England.*
Oxford: Clarendon Press, 1998.

Bec, Christian. *Les marchands écrivains: Affaires et humanisme à Florence (1375–1434).* Paris:
Mouton, 1967.

– 'Lo statuto socio-professionale degli scrittori (Trecento e Cinquecento).' In *Letteratura italiana,* edited by Alberto Asor Rosa, 2: 230–62. Turin: G. Einaudi, 1983.

Belting, Hans. 'Image, Medium, Body: A New Approach to Iconology.' *Critical Inquiry* 31
(Winter 2005): 302–19.

Benjamin, Walter. *Illuminations.* Edited by Hannah Arendt. Translated by Harry Zohn. New
York: Schocken, 1968.

Bibliography

Berger, Jr, Harry. *Fictions of the Pose: Rembrandt against the Italian Renaissance*. Stanford, CA: Stanford University Press, 2000.

Bernstein, Jane A. *Print Culture and Music in Sixteenth-Century Venice*. New York: Oxford University Press, 2001.

Bertalot, Ludwig. 'Drei Vorlesungsankündigungen des Paulus Niavis in Leipzig 1489.' *Archiv für Kulturgeschichte* 20 (1929): 370–5.

– 'Forschungen über Leonardo Bruni Arentino.' *Archivum Romanicum* 15.2 (1931): 284–323.

– *Studien zum italienischen und deutscher Humanismus*. Edited by Paul O. Kristeller. 2 vols. Rome: Edizioni di Storia e Letteratura, 1975.

Biddick, Kathleen. *The Typological Imaginary: Circumcision, Technology, History*. Philadelphia: University of Pennsylvania Press, 2003.

Birkerts, Sven. *The Gutenberg Elegies: The Fate of Reading in an Electronic Age*. Boston: Faber and Faber, 1994.

Black, Alistair. 'Libraries.' In *The Encyclopedia of the Novel*, edited by Peter Logan, 472. Oxford: Blackwell, 2010.

Black, Robert. *Humanism and Education in Medieval and Renaissance Italy: Tradition and Innovation in Latin Schools from the Twelfth to the Fifteenth Century*. Cambridge: Cambridge University Press, 2001.

Blades, William. *The Life and Typography of William Caxton, England's First Printer*. 2 vols. 1861. Reprinted in New York: Burt Franklin, 1965.

Blake, Norman. *Caxton: England's First Publisher*. New York: Barnes & Noble, 1976.

– *Caxton and His World*. London: Andre Deutsch, 1969.

– 'Continuity and Change in Caxton's Prologues and Epilogues: The Bruges Period.' *Gutenberg-Jahrbuch* 64 (1979): 72–7.

Blanchard, Alain. 'Les papyrus littéraires grecs extraits de Cartonnages: Études de bibliologie.' In *Ancient and Medieval Book Materials and Techniques*, edited by Marilena Maniaci and Paola F. Munagò, 1: 15–40. Vatican City: Biblioteca Apostolica Vaticana, 1993.

Blanchard, W. Scott. 'Petrarch and the Genealogy of Asceticism.' *Journal of the History of Ideas* 62.3 (July 2001): 401–23.

Blayney, Peter W.M. 'The Numbers Game: Appraising the Revised *Short-Title Catalogue*.' *Papers of the Bibliographical Society of America* 88.3 (1994): 353–407.

Bloch, Peter. 'Zum Dedikationsbild im Lob des Kreuzes des Hrabanus Maurus.' In *Das erste Jahrtausend: Kultur und Kunst im werdenden Abendland an Rhein und Ruhr*, edited by Victor H. Elbern, 1: 471–94. Düsseldorf: L. Schwann, 1962.

Bloomer, W. Martin. 'Controversia and Suasoria.' In *Encyclopedia of Rhetoric*, edited by Thomas Sloane, 168–9. New York: Oxford University Press, 2001.

Bolter, J. David. *Writing Space: Computers, Hypertext, and the Remediation of Print*. 2nd ed. Mahwah, NJ: L. Erlbaum, 2001.

Bolter, J. David, and Richard Grusin. *Remediation: Understanding New Media*. Cambridge, MA: MIT Press, 1999.

Bolzoni, Lina. *The Gallery of Memory: Literary and Iconographic Models in the Age of the Printing Press*. Translated by Jeremy Parzen. Toronto: University of Toronto Press, 2001.

Bornstein, George. *Material Modernism: The Politics of the Page*. Cambridge: Cambridge University Press, 2001.

Bousmanne, Bernard, Tania van Hemelryck, and Céline van Hoorebeeck, eds. *La librairie des ducs de Bourgogne: Manuscrits conservés à la Bibliothèque royale de Belgique*. Vol. 3: Textes littéraires. Turnhout, Belgium: Brepols, 2007.

Bousmanne, Bernard, Frédérique Johan, and Céline van Hoorebeeck, eds. *La librairie des ducs de Bourgogne: Manuscrits conservés à la Bibliothèque royale de Belgique*. Vol. 2: Textes didactiques. Turnhout, Belgium: Brepols, 2003.

– *La librairie des ducs de Bourgogne: manuscrits conservés à la Bibliothèque royale de Belgique*. CD-ROM. Vols. Turnhout, Belgium: Brepols, 2001–.

Bouwsma, William. *A Usable Past: Essays in European Cultural History*. Berkeley and Los Angeles: University of California Press, 1990.

Bozzolo, Carla, and Ezio Ornato. *Pour une histoire du livre manuscrit au moyen âge: Trois essais de codicologie quantitative*. Paris: Centre National de la Recherche Scientifique, 1983.

Braunmuller, A.R. 'Accounting for Absence: The Transcription of Space.' In *New Ways of Looking at Old Texts: Papers of the Renaissance English Text Society, 1985–1991*, edited by W. Speed Hill, 47–56. Binghamton, NY: Center for Medieval and Early Renaissance Studies, 1993.

Bray, Joe, Miriam Handley, and Anne C. Henry, eds. *Ma(r)king the Text: The Presentation of Meaning on the Literary Page*. Aldershot, England: Ashgate, 2000.

Briggs, Charles F. *Giles of Rome's 'De regimine principum': Reading and Writing Politics at Court and University, c.1275–c.1525*. Cambridge: Cambridge University Press, 1999.

Brown, Cynthia J. 'Books in Performance: The Parisian Entry (1504) and Funeral (1514) of Anne of Brittany.' *Yale French Studies* 110 (2006): 75–91.

– *Poets, Patrons, and Printers: Crisis of Authority in Late Medieval France*. Ithaca, NY: Cornell University Press, 1995.

Brown, Julian. 'Latin Palaeography since Traube.' In *A Palaeographer's View: Selected Writings of Julian Brown*, edited by Janet Bately, Michelle P. Brown, and Jane Roberts, 17–37. London: Harvey Miller, 1993.

Brown, Michelle P. *A Guide to Western Historical Scripts from Antiquity to 1600*. Toronto: University of Toronto Press, 1990.

Brubaker, Leslie. *Vision and Meaning in Ninth-Century Byzantium: Image as Exegesis in the Homilies of Gregory of Nazianzus*. Cambridge: Cambridge University Press, 1999.

Bruni Aretino, Leonardo. *Humanistisch-philosophische Schriften. Mit einer Chronologie seiner Werke und Briefe*. Edited by Hans Baron. Leipzig: Teubner, 1928.

Bryson, Anna. *From Courtesy to Civility: Changing Codes of Conduct in Early Modern England*. Oxford: Clarendon Press, 1998.

Buchtel, John A. 'Book Dedications and the Death of a Patron: The Memorial Engraving in Chapman's *Homer*.' *Book History* 7 (2004): 1–29.

Bibliography

Buettner, Brigitte. 'Panofsky à l'ère de la reproduction mécanisée. Une question de perspective.' *Cahiers du Musée national d'art moderne* 53 (Autumn 1995): 57–77.

– 'Past Presents: New Year's Gifts at the Valois Courts, ca. 1400.' *Art Bulletin* 83.4 (December 2001): 598–625.

– 'Profane Illuminations, Secular Illusions: Manuscripts in Late Medieval Courtly Society.' *Art Bulletin* 74.1 (March 1992): 75–90.

Burckhardt, Jacob. *The Civilization of the Renaissance in Italy.* New York: Harper, 1958.

Burger, Emil. *Eine französische Handschrift der Breslauer Stadtbibliothek.* Breslau: Grass, Barth, 1901.

Burke, Peter. *The Fortunes of the Courtier: The European Reception of Castiglione's Cortegiano.* University Park, PA: Pennsylvania State University Press, 1995.

Butler, Shane. *The Matter of the Page: Essays in Search of Ancient and Medieval Authors.* Madison: University of Wisconsin Press, 2011.

Byles, Alfred T.P. 'Caxton's *Book of the Ordre of Chyualry*: A French Manuscript in Brussels.' *Review of English Studies* 6.23 (July 1930): 305–8.

Camille, Michael. *Image on the Edge: The Margins of Medieval Art.* Cambridge, MA: Harvard University Press, 1992.

– *Mirror in Parchment: The Luttrell Psalter and the Making of Medieval England.* Chicago: University of Chicago Press, 1998.

– '"Seeing and Lecturing": Disputation in a Twelfth-Century Tympanum from Reims.' In *Reading Medieval Images: The Art Historian and the Object*, edited by Elizabeth Sears and Thelma K. Thomas, 75–90. Ann Arbor: University of Michigan Press, 2002.

– 'Sensations of the Page: Imaging Technologies and Medieval Illuminated Manuscripts.' In *The Iconic Page in Manuscript, Print, and Digital Culture*, edited by George Bornstein and Theresa Tinkle, 33–53. Ann Arbor: University of Michigan Press, 1998.

– 'The *Très Riches Heures*: An Illuminated Manuscript in the Age of Mechanical Reproduction.' *Critical Inquiry* 17 (Autumn 1990): 72–107.

Cannon Willard, Charity. 'The Concept of True Nobility at the Burgundian Court.' *Studies in the Renaissance* 14 (1967): 33–48.

Carruthers, Mary. *The Book of Memory: A Study of Memory in Medieval Culture.* 2nd ed. Cambridge: Cambridge University Press, 2008.

Casson, Lionel. *Libraries in the Ancient World.* New Haven, CT: Yale University Press, 2001.

Cast, David. 'Aurispa, Petrarch, and Lucian: An Aspect of Renaisance Translation.' *Renaissance Quarterly* 27 (1974): 157–73.

Caxton, William. *The Prologues and Epilogues of William Caxton.* Edited by W.J.B. Crotch. London: Oxford University Press, 1928.

Cerquiglini, Bernard. *In Praise of the Variant: A Critical History of Philology.* Translated by Betsy Wing. Baltimore, DE: Johns Hopkins University Press, 1999.

Certeau, Michel de. *The Practice of Everyday Life.* Translated by Steven Rendall. Berkeley and Los Angeles: University of California Press, 2002.

Chambers, D.S. *A Renaissance Cardinal and His Worldly Goods: The Will and Inventory of Francesco Gonzaga (1444–1483).* London: Warburg Institute, 1992.

Chartier, Roger. *Forms and Meanings: Text, Performance, and Audience from Codex to Computer.* Translated by Lydia Cochrane. Philadelphia: University of Pennsylvania Press, 1995.

– 'From Mechanical Reproduction to Electronic Representation.' In *Mapping Benjamin: The Work of Art in the Digital Age,* edited by Hans Ulrich Gumbrecht and Michael Marrinan, 109–13. Stanford, CA: Stanford University Press, 2003.

– *Inscription and Erasure: Literature and Written Culture from the Eleventh to the Eighteenth Century.* Translated by Arthur Goldhammer. Philadelphia: University of Pennsylvania Press, 2007.

– 'Reading Matter and "Popular" Reading: From the Renaissance to the Seventeenth Century.' In *A History of Reading in the West,* edited by Guglielmo Cavallo and Roger Chartier, 269–83. Translated by Lydia Cochrane. Cambridge: Polity Press, 1999.

Chartier, Roger, and Henri-Jean Martin, eds. *Histoire de l'édition française.* 4 vols. Paris: Éditions du Cercle de la Librairie-Promodis, 1982–6.

Cheles, Luciano. *The Studiolo of Urbino: An Iconographic Investigation.* Wiesbaden: L. Reichert, 1986.

Choay, Françoise. *The Invention of the Historic Monument.* Translated by Lauren M. O'Connell. Cambridge: Cambridge University Press, 2001.

Chrisman, Miriam U. *Lay Culture, Learned Culture: Books and Social Change in Strasbourg, 1480–1599.* New Haven, CT: Yale University Press, 1982.

– 'Printing and the Evolution of Lay Culture in Strasbourg 1480–1599.' In *The German People and the Reformation,* edited by R. Po-Chia Hsia, 74–100. Ithaca, NY: Cornell University Press, 1988.

Christ, Karl. *The Handbook of Medieval Library History.* Revised by Anton Kern. Edited and translated by Theophil Otto. Metuchen, NJ: Scarecrow Press, 1984.

Cicero, Marcus Tullius. *Caxton's Tully Of old age and Friendship, 1481, now for the first time collated.* Edited by E. Gordon Duff. London: J. Pearson & Co., 1912.

– *Letters to Atticus.* Edited and translated by D.R. Shackleton Bailey. Vol. 1. Cambridge, MA: Harvard University Press, 1999.

Clark, J.W. *The Care of Books.* 2nd ed. 1902. Reprinted in Bristol: Thoemmes, 1997.

Clercq, Wim de, Jan Dumolyn, and Jelle Haemers. '"Vivre Noblement": Material Culture and Elite Identity in Late Medieval Flanders.' *Journal of Interdisciplinary History* 38.1 (Summer 2007): 1–31.

Clough, Cecil M. 'Federigo da Montefeltro's Private Study in His Ducal Palace of Gubbio.' *Apollo* 86 (1967): 278–87.

– 'The Library of the Dukes of Urbino.' *Librarium* 9 (1966): 101–5.

Constable, Giles. 'Petrarch and Monasticism.' In *Francesca Petrarca: Citizen of the World. Proceedings of the World Petrarch Congress,* edited by Aldo S. Bernardo, 53–99. Albany: State University of New York Press, 1980.

Bibliography

Corsten, Severin. 'Caxton in Cologne.' *Journal of the Printing Historical Society* 11 (1976/7): 1–18.

Cotrugli Raguseo, Benedetto. *Il libro dell'arte di mercatura*. Edited by Ugo Tucci. Venice: Arsenale, 1990.

Courtenay, William J., and Jürgen Miethke, eds. *Universities and Schooling in Medieval Society*. Leiden: Brill, 2000.

Crick, Julia, and Alexandra Walsham, eds. *The Uses of Script and Print, 1300–1700*. Cambridge: Cambridge University Press, 2004.

Crous, Ernst, and Joachim Kirchner. *Die gotischen Schriftarten*. 2nd ed. Braunschweig, Germany: Klinkhardt and Biermann, 1970.

Dalbello, Marija. 'Institutional Shaping of Cultural Memory: Digital Library as Environment for Textual Transmission.' *Library Quarterly* 74.3 (July 2004): 265–98.

Dane, Joseph A. *The Myth of Print Culture: Essays on Evidence, Textuality, and Bibliographic Method*. Toronto: University of Toronto Press, 2003.

Daston, Lorraine, and Peter Galison. 'The Image of Objectivity.' *Representations* 40 (Autumn 1992): 81–128.

Davies, Martin. *Early Netherlandish School*. 2nd ed. London: National Gallery, 1955.

Dawson, Robert L. 'The National Library of France: A Patron Reflects.' *Libraries & Culture* 39.1 (Winter 2004): 76–88.

Deeming, Helen. 'The Song and the Page: Experiments with Form and Layout in Manuscripts of Medieval Latin Song.' *Plainsong and Medieval Music* 15.1 (2006): 1–27.

Dekeyzer, Brigitte, and Jan Van der Stock, eds. *Manuscripts in Transition: Recycling Manuscripts, Texts and Images. Proceedings of the International Congres [sic] held in Brussels, 5–9 November 2002*. Leuven: Uitgeverij Peeters, 2005.

Delaissé, L.M.J. 'The Importance of Books of Hours for the History of the Medieval Book.' In *Gatherings in Honor of Dorothy E. Miner*, edited by Ursula E McCracken, Lilian M.C. Randall, and Richard H. Randall, Jr, 203–25. Baltimore, MD: Walters Art Gallery, 1974.

Delaissé, L.M.J., ed. *Le siècle d'or de la miniature flamande: Le mécénat de Philippe le Bon*. Brussels: Bibliothèque Royale de Belgique[?], 1959.

– *Medieval Miniatures from the Department of Manuscripts (formerly the 'Library of Burgundy'), The Royal Library of Belgium*. New York: Henry N. Abrams, 1965.

Deleuze, Gilles. *Negotiations, 1972–1990*. Translated by Martin Joughin. New York: Columbia University Press, 1995.

Deppman, Jed, Daniel Ferrer, and Michael Groden, eds. *Genetic Criticism: Texts and Avant-textes*. Philadelphia: University of Pennsylvania Press, 2004.

Derolez, Albert. 'Codicologie ou archéologie du livre?' *Scriptorium* 28 (1973): 47–9.

– *Codicologie des manuscrits en écriture humanistique sur parchemin*. 2 vols. Turnhout: Brepols, 1984.

– *The Palaeography of Gothic Manuscript Books: From the Twelfth to the Early Sixteenth Century*. Cambridge: Cambridge University Press, 2003.

Derrida, Jacques. 'Différance.' In *Margins of Philosophy*, translated by Alan Bass, 3–27. Chicago: University of Chicago Press, 1982.

Desmond, Marilynn, and Pamela Sheingorn. *Myth, Montage, and Visuality in Late Medieval Manuscript Culture: Christine de Pizan's 'Epistre Othea.'* Ann Arbor: University of Michigan Press, 2003.

Destrez, Jean. *La pecia dans les manuscrits universitaires du XIIe et du XIVe siècle*. Paris: Jacques Vautrain, 1935.

Dilke, O.A.W. *Roman Books and Their Impact*. Leeds: Elmete Press, 1977.

Dillon, Emma. *Medieval Music-Making and the Roman de Fauvel*. Cambridge: Cambridge University Press, 2002.

Drège, J.-P. 'Les accordéons de Dunhuang.' In *Contributions aux études sur Touen-houang*, edited by Michel Soymié, 3: 195–204. Paris: École française d'Extrême-Orient, 1984.

Driver, Martha W. *The Image in Print: Book Illustration in Late Medieval England and Its Sources*. London: The British Library, 2004.

Drucker, Johanna. 'Entity to Event: From Literal, Mechanistic Materiality to Probabilistic Materiality.' *Parallax* 15.4 (2009): 7–17.

– 'Graphical Readings and Visual Aesthetics of Textuality.' *TEXT: An Interdisciplinary Annual of Textual Studies* 16 (2006): 267–76.

– 'The Virtual Codex from Page Space to E-Space.' Lecture. History of the Book Seminar. Syracuse University, Syracuse, New York, 25 April 2003. http://www.philobiblon.com/drucker/.

– *The Visible Word: Experimental Typography and Modern Art, 1909–1923*. Chicago: University of Chicago Press, 1994.

Duff, E. Gordon. *William Caxton*. 1905. Reprinted New York: Burt Franklin, 1970.

Duffy, Eamon. *Marking the Hours: English People and Their Prayers 1214–1570*. New Haven, CT: Yale University Press, 2006.

Duguid, Paul. 'Inheritance and Loss? A Brief Survey of Google Books.' *First Monday* 12.8 (6 August 2007). http://firstmonday.org/htbin/cgiwrap/bin/ojs/index.php/fm/article/view/1972/1847.

Durlik, Andrzej. 'The Bibliothèque nationale de France: My French Experience.' *Libraries & Culture* 37.3 (Summer 2002): 256–68.

Echard, Siân. *Printing the Middle Ages*. Philadelphia: University of Pennsylvania Press, 2008.

Eden, Kathy. 'Intellectual Property and the *Adages* of Erasmus: *Coenobium v. Ercto non cito*.' In *Rhetoric and Law in Early Modern Europe*, edited by Victoria Kahn and Lorna Hutson, 269–84. New Haven, CT: Yale University Press, 2001.

Edwards, Mark U. *Printing, Propaganda, and Martin Luther*. Berkeley and Los Angeles: University of California Press, 1994.

Eisenstein, Elizabeth. *Divine Art, Infernal Machine: The Reception of Printing in the West from First Impressions to the Sense of an Ending*. Philadelphia: University of Pennsylvania Press, 2010.

– *The Printing Press as an Agent of Change: Communications and Cultural Transformations in Early Modern Europe*. 2 vols. Cambridge: Cambridge University Press, 1979. Abridged version in *The Printing Revolution in Early Modern Europe*, 2nd ed.

Bibliography

- *The Printing Revolution in Early Modern Europe.* 2nd edition. Cambridge: Cambridge University Press, 2005.
- 'Reply' [to Adrian Johns, q.v.]. *American Historical Review* 107.1 (February 2002): 126–8.
- 'An Unacknowledged Revolution Revisited.' *American Historical Review* 107.1 (February 2002): 87–105.

Elam, Caroline. '"Studioli" and Renaissance Court Patronage.' MA report, Courtauld Institute of Art, May 1970.

Enenkel, Karl A.E., and Wolfgang Neuber, eds. *Cognition and the Book: Typologies of Formal Organisation of Knowledge in the Printed Book of the Early Modern Period.* Leiden: Brill, 2005.

Febvre, Lucien, and Henri-Jean Martin. *The Coming of the Book: The Impact of Printing 1450–1800.* Translated by David Gerard. New York: Verso, 1976.

Findlen, Paula. *Possessing Nature: Museums, Collecting, and Scientific Culture in Early Modern Italy.* Berkeley and Los Angeles: University of California Press, 1994.

Flanders, Julia. 'Detailism, Digital Texts, and the Problem of Pedantry.' *TEXT Technology* 14.2 (2005): 41–70.

Flood, John L. 'Niklas von Wyle.' In *German Writers of the Renaissance and Reformation, 1280–1580,* edited by James Hardin and Max Reinhart, 332–7. Detroit: Gale Research, 1997.

Foot, Mirjam. *The History of Bookbinding as a Mirror of Society.* London: British Library, 1998.

Foucault, Michel. *The Archaeology of Knowledge.* Translated by A.M. Sheridan Smith. London: Tavistock Publications, 1972.

- *The Order of Things: An Archaeology of the Human Sciences.* New York: Vintage, 1973.
- 'What Is an Author?' In *The Foucault Reader.* Edited by Paul Rabinow, 101–20. New York: Pantheon, 1984.

Foys, Martin. *Virtually Anglo-Saxon: Old Media, New Media, and Early Medieval Studies in the Late Age of Print.* Gainesville: University Press of Florida, 2007.

Freeman Sandler, Lucy. 'The Image of the Book-Owner in the Fourteenth Century: Three Cases of Self-Definition.' In *England in the Fourteenth Century: Proceedings of the 1991 Harlaxton Symposium,* edited by Nicholas Rogers, 58–80. Stamford, England: P. Watkins, 1993.

Furjàn, Helene. 'Scenes from a Museum.' *Grey Room* 17 (Fall 2004): 64–81.

Gadd, Ian. 'The Use and Misuse of *Early English Books Online.' Literature Compass* 6.3 (May 2009): 680–92.

Galloway, Alexander, and Eugene Thacker. 'Protocol, Control, and Networks.' *Grey Room* 17 (Fall 2004): 6–29.

Ganz, David. 'Latin Palaeography since Bischoff.' In *'Omnia disce': Medieval Studies in Memory of Leonard Boyle, O.P.,* edited by Anne J. Duggan, Joan Greatrex, and Brenda Bolton, 91–107. Aldershot, England: Ashgate, 2005.

Garberson, Eric. 'Libraries, Memory, and the Space of Knowledge.' *Journal of the History of Collections* 18.2 (2006): 105–36.

Gaskell, Philip. *A New Introduction to Bibliography.* Oxford: Clarendon Press, 1972.

Genette, Gérard. *Paratexts: Thresholds of Interpretation*. Translated by Jane Lewin. Cambridge: Cambridge University Press, 1997.

Gilissen, Léon. *Prolégomènes à la codicologie: Recherches sur la construction des cahiers et la mise en page des manuscrits médiévaux*. Gand: Story-Scientia, 1977.

Gillespie, Alexandra. *Print Culture and the Medieval Author: Chaucer, Lydgate, and Their Books, 1473–1557*. New York: Oxford University Press, 2006.

Gilmont, Jean-François, ed. *The Reformation and the Book*. Translated by Karin Maag. Aldershot, England: Ashgate, 1998.

Gnudi, Cesare. 'Lo Studiolo di Federico da Montefeltro nel Palazzo Ducale di Urbino.' In *Mostra di Melozzo e del quattrocento romagnolo*, edited by Luisa Becherucci and Cesare Gnudi, 25–38. Bologna: Stabilimenti Poligrafici, 1938.

Goldthwaite, Richard A. 'The Florentine Palace as Domestic Architecture.' *American Historical Review* 77.4 (October 1972): 977–1012.

Grafton, Anthony. *Defenders of the Text: The Traditions of Scholarship in an Age of Science, 1450–1800*. Cambridge, MA: Harvard University Press, 1991.

Grafton, Anthony, and Lisa Jardine. *From Humanism to the Humanities: Education and the Liberal Arts in Fifteenth- and Sixteenth-century Europe*. Cambridge, MA: Harvard University Press, 1986.

Grafton, Anthony, and Megan Williams. *Christianity and the Transformation of the Book: Origen, Eusebius, and the Library of Caesarea*. Cambridge, MA: Belknap Press of Harvard University Press, 2006.

Grau, Oliver. *Virtual Art: From Illusion to Immersion*. Cambridge, MA: MIT Press, 2003.

Greg, W.W. 'The Rationale of Copy-Text.' *Studies in Bibliography* 3 (1950–1): 20–37.

– 'What Is Bibliography?' In *Collected Papers*, edited by J.C. Maxwell, 73–88. Oxford: Clarendon Press, 1966.

Grendler, Paul F. 'Form and Function in Italian Renaissance Popular Books.' *Renaissance Quarterly* 46.3 (Autumn 1993): 451–85.

– *Schooling in Renaissance Italy: Literacy and Learning, 1300–1600*. Baltimore, MD: Johns Hopkins University Press, 1989.

– *The Universities in the Italian Renaissance*. Baltimore, MD: Johns Hopkins University Press, 2002.

Grigely, Joseph. *Textualterity: Art, Theory, and Textual Criticism*. Ann Arbor: University of Michigan Press, 1995.

Grosz, Elizabeth. *Architecture from the Outside: Essays on Virtual and Real Space*. Cambridge, MA: MIT Press, 2001.

Grotans, Anna. *Reading in Medieval St Gall*. Cambridge: Cambridge University Press, 2006.

Gruijs, Albert. 'Codicology or the Archaeology of the Book? A False Dilemma.' *Quaerendo* 2 (1972): 87–108.

Guasti, Cesare. 'Inventario della libreria urbinata compilato nel secolo XV da Federigo Veterano.' *Giornale storico degli archivi toscani* 7 (1863): 45–55, 130–54.

Bibliography

Gumbert, J.P. 'Skins, Sheets and Quires.' In *New Directions in Later Medieval Manuscript Studies: Essays from the 1998 Harvard Conference*, edited by Derek Pearsall, 81–90. York, Eng.: York Medieval Press, 2000.

Gutjahr, Paul, and Megan Benton, eds. *Illuminating Letters: Typography and Literary Interpretation.* Amherst: University of Massachusetts Press, 2001.

Hackenberg, Michael. 'Books in Artisan Homes of Sixteenth-Century Germany.' *Journal of Library History* 21.1 (Winter 1986): 72–91.

Hageman, Mariëlle, and Marco Mostert, eds. *Reading Images and Texts: Medieval Images and Texts as Forms of Communication. Papers from the Third Utrecht Symposium on Medieval Literacy, Utrecht, 7–9 December 2000.* Turnhout: Brepols, 2005.

Hamburger, Jeffrey F. 'Openings.' In 'Imagination, Books & Community in Medieval Europe.' *Papers of a conference held at the State Library of Victoria, Melbourne, Australia, 29–31 May 2008 in conjunction with an exhibition, 'The Medieval Imagination,' 28 March–15 June 2008*, edited by Gregory Kratzmann], 51–143. Melbourne, Australia: MacMillan, 2010.

Hamel, Christopher de. *The British Library Guide to Manuscript Illumination: History and Techniques.* Toronto: University of Toronto Press, 2001.

– *Glossed Books of the Bible and the Origins of the Paris Booktrade.* Bury St Edmunds: Rowland, 1984.

– *Scribes and Illuminators.* 1992. Reprinted Toronto: University of Toronto Press, 1997.

Hanebutt-Benz, Eva-Maria. *Die Kunst des Lesens.* Frankfurt: Museum für Kunsthandwerk, 1985.

Hankins, James, ed. *Renaissance Civic Humanism: Reappraisals and Reflections.* Cambridge: Cambridge University Press, 2000.

Hardman, Phillippa. 'Windows into the Text: Unfilled Spaces in Some Fifteenth-Century English Manuscripts.' In *Texts and Their Contexts: Papers from the Early Book Society*, edited by John Scattergood and Julia Boffey, 44–70. Portland, OR: Four Courts Press, 1997.

Harley, J.B., and David Woodward, eds. *The History of Cartography.* Vol. 1. Chicago: University of Chicago Press, 1987.

Harpold, Terry. *Ex-foliations: Reading Machines and the Upgrade Path.* Minneapolis: University of Minnesota Press, 2008.

Hasenohr, Geneviève. 'La prose.' In *Mise en page et mise en texte du livre français: La naissance du livre moderne (XIVe–XVIIe siècles)*, edited by Henri-Jean Martin, 265–87. Paris: Éditions du Cercle de la Librairie, 2000.

Hay, Louis. 'Does "Text" Exist?' Translated by Matthew Jocelyn. Revised by Hans Walter Gabler. *Studies in Bibliography* 41 (1988): 64–76.

Hayles, N. Katherine. 'The Future of Literature.' Plenary lecture, inaugural session for the New Media and Culture Research Network, University of British Columbia, Vancouver, 13 January 2006.

– *My Mother Was a Computer: Digital Subjects and Literary Texts.* Chicago: University of Chicago Press, 2005.

– 'Traumas of Code.' *Critical Inquiry* 33 (Autumn 2006): 136–57.

Hedeman, Anne D. *The Royal Image: Illustrations of the Grandes Chroniques de France, 1274–1422*. Berkeley and Los Angeles: University of California Press, 1991.

– *Translating the Past: Laurent de Premierfait and Boccaccio's 'De casibus.'* Los Angeles: Getty Publications, 2008.

Henry, Anne C. 'Blank Emblems: The Vacant Page, the Interleaved Book and the Eighteenth-Century Novel.' *Word & Image* 22.4 (October–December 2006): 363–71.

Herstein, Sheila. 'The Library of Federigo da Montefeltro, Duke of Urbino: Renaissance Book Collecting at Its Height.' *The Private Library* 4 (1971): 113–28.

Hessel, Alfred. 'Von der Schrift zum Druck.' *Zeitschrift des deutschen Vereins für Buchwesen* 6 (1923): 89–101.

Hindman, Sandra. *Printing and the Written Word: The Social History of Books, circa 1450–1520*. Ithaca, NY: Cornell University Press, 1991.

– *Sealed in Parchment: Rereadings of Knighthood in the Illuminated Manuscripts of Chrétien de Troyes*. Chicago: University of Chicago Press, 1994.

Hirsch, Rudolf. *Printing, Selling, and Reading, 1450–1550*. Wiesbaden: Harrassowitz, 1967.

– 'Title Pages in French Incunables, 1486–1500.' *Gutenberg-Jahrbuch* 63 (1978): 63–6.

Hobbins, Daniel. *Authorship and Publicity Before Print: Jean Gerson and the Transformation of Late Medieval Learning*. Philadelphia: University of Pennsylvania Press, 2009.

Howsam, Leslie. *Old Books and New Histories: An Orientation to Studies in Book and Print Culture*. Toronto: University of Toronto Press, 2006.

Huizinga, Johan. *The Autumn of the Middle Ages*. Translated by Rodney Payton and Ulrich Mammitzsch. Chicago: University of Chicago Press, 1996.

Hunger, Herbert. *Schreiben und Lesen in Byzanz: Die byzantinische Buchkultur*. Munich: C.H. Beck, 1989.

Huot, Sylvie. *The Romance of the Rose and Its Medieval Readers: Interpretation, Reception, Manuscript Transmission*. Cambridge: Cambridge University Press, 1993.

Hurlbut, Jesse D. 'Review of Bernard Bousmanne, Céline van Hoorebeeck, and Alain Arnould, eds., *La librairie des ducs de Bourgogne: manuscrits conservés à la Bibliothèque royale de Belgique, 1: Textes liturgiques, ascétiques, théologiques, philosophiques et moraux*. Turnhout: Brepols, 2000, and Bernard Bousmanne, Céline van Hoorebeeck, and Alain Arnould, eds., *La librairie des ducs de Bourgogne: manuscrits conservés à la Bibliothèque royale de Belgique, 2: Textes didactiques*. CD-ROM. Turnhout: Brepols, 2004.' *Speculum* 81.3 (July 2006): 813–15.

Illich, Ivan. *In the Vineyard of the Text: A Commentary to Hugh's 'Didascalicon.'* Chicago: University of Chicago Press, 1993.

Jacques, Michel, ed. *Bibliothèque nationale de France 1989–1995*. Paris: Artemis, 1995.

Jaeger, C. Stephen. *The Origins of Courtliness: Civilizing Trends and the Formation of Courtly Ideals, 939–1210*. Philadelphia: University of Pennsylvania Press, 1985.

Jardine, Lisa, and Anthony Grafton. '"Studied for Action": How Gabriel Harvey Read His Livy.' *Past and Present* 129 (November 1990): 30–78.

Jed, Stephanie H. *Chaste Thinking: The Rape of Lucretia and the Birth of Humanism.* Bloomington: Indiana University Press, 1989.

Johns, Adrian. 'How to Acknowledge a Revolution.' *American Historical Review* 107.1 (February 2002): 106–25. *See* Eisenstein, 'An Unacknowledged …'

– *The Nature of the Book: Print and Knowledge in the Making.* Chicago: University of Chicago Press, 1998.

Johnson, William A. *Bookrolls and Scribes in Oxyrhynchus.* Toronto: University of Toronto Press, 2004.

– 'Is Oratory Written on Narrower Columns? A Papyrological Rule of Thumb Reviewed.' In *Proceedings of the 20th International Congress of Papyrologists, Copenhagen, 23–29 August, 1992,* compiled by Adam Bülow-Jacobsen, 423–7. Copenhagen: Museum Tusculanum Press and University of Copenhagen, 1994.

Jorde, Tilmann. *Cristoforo Landinos 'De vera nobilitate': Ein Beitrag zur Nobilitas-Debatte in Quattrocento.* Stuttgart: Teubner, 1995.

Jouguelet, Suzanne. 'Various Applications of the Dewey Decimal Classification at the Bibliothèque Nationale de France.' *Library Review* 47.4 (1998): 206–10.

Jowett, John, and Gabriel Egan. 'Review of the Early English Books Online (EEBO).' *Interactive Early Modern Literary Studies* (January 2001): 1–13. http://purl.oclc.org/emls/iemls/reviews/jowetteebo.htm.

Kannenberg, Jr, Gene. 'Graphic Text, Graphic Context: Interpreting Custom Fonts and Hands in Contemporary Comics.' In *Illuminating Letters: Typography and Literary Interpretation,* edited by Paul Gutjahr and Megan Benton, 163–92. Amherst: University of Massachusetts Press, 2001.

Kendrick, Laura. *Animating the Letter: The Figurative Embodiment of Writing from Late Antiquity to the Renaissance.* Columbus: Ohio State University Press, 1999.

Kenyon, Frederic G. *Books and Readers in Ancient Greece and Rome.* 2nd ed. Oxford: Clarendon Press, 1951.

Kibre, Pearl. 'The Intellectual Interests Reflected in Libraries of the Fourteenth and Fifteenth Centuries.' *Journal of the History of Ideas* 7.3 (June 1946): 257–97.

Kichuk, Diana. 'Metamorphosis: Remediation in *Early English Books Online (EEBO).*' *Literary and Linguistic Computing* 22.3 (2007): 291–303.

King, Katie. 'Historiography as Reenactment: Metaphors and Literalizations of TV Documentaries.' *Criticism* 46.3 (2004): 459–75.

Kinross, Robin. *Modern Typography: An Essay in Critical History.* London: Hyphen Press, 1994.

Kirkbride, Robert. *Architecture and Memory: The Renaissance Studioli of Federico da Montefeltro.* New York: Columbia University Press, 2008.

– 'On the Renaissance *Studioli* of Federico da Montefeltro and the Architecture of Memory.' In *Chora 4,* edited by Alberto Pérez-Gómez and Stephen Parcell, 128–76. Montreal: McGill-Queen's University Press, 2004.

Kirschenbaum, Matthew G. *Mechanism: New Media and the Forensic Imagination*. Cambridge, MA: MIT Press, 2008.

Klamt, Johann-Christian. 'Zur Reproduktionsgeschichte mittelalterlicher Schriftformen und Miniaturen in der Neuzeit.' *Quaerendo* 23.3 (1999): 169–207; part 2 in *Quaerendo* 29.4 (1999): 247–74.

Knape, Joachim, and Bernhard Roll, eds. *Rhetorica deutsch: Rhetorikschriften des 15. Jahrhunderts*. Wiesbaden: Harrassowitz, 2002.

Knight, Jeffrey Todd. '"Furnished" for Action: Renaissance Books as Furniture.' *Book History* 12 (2009): 37–73.

Kornicki, Peter F. 'Manuscript, not Print: Scribal Culture in the Edo Period.' *Journal of Japanese Studies* 32.1 (Winter 2006): 23–52.

Kristeller, P.O. *Renaissance Concepts of Man and Other Essays*. New York: Harper, 1972.

Kubiski, Joyce. 'The Medieval "Home Office": Evangelist Portraits in the Mount Athos Gospel Book, Stavronikita Monastery, MS 43.' *Studies in Iconography* 22 (2001): 21–53.

Kuskin, William, ed. *Caxton's Trace: Studies in the History of English Printing*. Notre Dame: University of Notre Dame Press, 2006.

Kwakkel, Erik. 'The Cultural Dynamics of Medieval Book Production.' In *Manuscripten en miniaturen: Studies aangeboden aan Anne S. Korteweg bij haar afscheid van de Koninklijke Bibliotheek*, edited by Jos Biemans, Klaas van der Hoek, Kathryn M. Rudy, and Ed van der Vlist, 243–52. Zutphen, The Netherlands: Walburg Pers, 2007.

– 'A New Type of Book for a New Type of Reader: The Emergence of Paper in Vernacular Book Production.' *The Library* 4.3 (2003): 219–48.

Lander, Jesse M. *Inventing Polemic: Religion, Print, and Literary Culture in Early Modern England*. Cambridge: Cambridge University Press, 2006.

Landow, George P. *Hypertext 3.0: Critical Theory and New Media in an Era of Globalization*. 3rd ed. Baltimore, MD: Johns Hopkins University Press, 2006.

Lane Ford, Margaret. 'Private Ownership of Printed Books.' In *Cambridge History of the Book in Britain*, edited by Lotte Hellinga and J.B. Trapp, 3: 205–28. Cambridge: Cambridge University Press, 1999.

Lanham, Richard. *The Electronic Word: Democracy, Technology, and the Arts*. Chicago: University of Chicago Press, 1993.

Lapacherie, Jean-Gérard. 'Typographic Characters: Tension between Text and Drawing.' Translated by Anna Lehmann. *Yale French Studies* 84 (1994): 63–77.

Latour, Bruno, and Adam Lowe. 'The Migration of the Aura, or How to Explore the Original through Its Fac Similes.' In *Switching Codes: Thinking through New Technology in the Humanities and the Arts*, edited by Thomas Bartscherer and Roderick Coover, 275–97. Chicago: University of Chicago Press, 2011.

Latour, Bruno, and Steven Woolgar. *Laboratory Life: The Social Construction of Scientific Facts*. Beverly Hills, CA: Sage Publications, 1979.

Bibliography

Laufer, Roger. 'L'espace visuel du livre ancien.' In *Histoire de l'édition française*, edited by Roger Chartier and Henri-Jean Martin, 1: 479–97. Paris: Éditions du Cercle de la Librairie-Promodis, 1982.

Lausberg, Heinrich. *Handbook of Literary Rhetoric: A Foundation for Literary Study.* Edited by D.E. Orton and R.D. Anderson. Translated by M.T. Bliss, A. Jansen, and D.E. Orton. Leiden: Brill, 1998.

Leclerq, Jean. *The Love of Learning and the Desire for God: A Study of Monastic Culture.* Translated by Catharine Misrahi. New York: Fordham University Press, [1961].

Leedham-Green, Elisabeth, and Teresa Webber, eds. *The Cambridge History of Libraries in Britain and Ireland.* Vol. 1. Cambridge: Cambridge University Press, 2006.

Lefebvre, Henri. *The Production of Space.* Translated by Donald Nicholson-Smith. Oxford: Blackwell Publishing, 1991.

Lewis, Naphtali. *Papyrus in Classical Antiquity.* Oxford: Clarendon Press, 1974.

Liebenwein, Wolfgang. *Studiolo: Die Entstehung eines Raumtyps und seine Entwicklung bis um 1600.* Berlin: Gebr. Mann, 1977.

Lieftinck, G.I. *Manuscrits datés conservés dans le Pays-bas.* Vol. 1. Amsterdam: North Holland Publishing, 1964.

Liu, Alan. 'Transcendental Data: Toward a Cultural History and Aesthetics of the New Encoded Discourse.' *Critical Inquiry* 31.1 (Autumn 2004): 49–84.

Lombardo, Paul A. 'Vita Activa versus Vita Contemplativa in Petrarch and Salutati.' *Italica* 59.2 (Summer 1982): 83–92.

Love, Harold. *Scribal Publication in Seventeenth-Century England.* Oxford: Clarendon Press, 1993.

Lydecker, J.K. 'The Domestic Setting of the Arts in Renaissance Florence.' PhD diss., Johns Hopkins University, 1987.

Mandosio, Jean-Marc. *L'effondrement de la très grande bibliothèque de France: Ses causes, ses conséquences.* Paris: L'Encyclopédie des nuisances, 1999.

Manguel, Alberto. 'A Brief History of the Page.' In *A Reader on Reading*, 120–7. New Haven, CT: Yale University Press, 2010.

– 'Turning the Page.' In *The Future of the Page*, edited by Peter Stoicheff and Andrew Taylor, 27–36. Toronto: University of Toronto Press, 2004.

Manovich, Lev. *The Language of New Media.* Cambridge, MA: MIT Press, 2001.

– *Software Takes Command.* Cambridge, MA: MIT Press, forthcoming.

Marchal, Joseph. *Catalogue des manuscrits de la Bibliothèque royale des ducs de Bourgogne.* Vol. 1. Brussels: C. Muquardt, 1842.

Mare, Albinia de la. *The Handwriting of Italian Humanists.* Oxford: University Press for the Association internationale de bibliophilie, 1973.

– 'Humanistic Script: The First Ten Years.' In *Das Verhältnis der Humanisten zum Buch*, edited by Fritz Krafft and Dieter Wuttke, 89–108. Boppard: Boldt, 1977.

Marichal, Robert. 'Les manuscrits universitaires.' In *Mise en page et mise en texte du livre manuscrit*, edited by Henri-Jean Martin and Jean Vezin, 211–17. Paris: Éditions du Cercle de la Librairie-Promodis, 1990.

Markey, Karen. 'The Online Library Catalog: Paradise Lost and Paradise Regained?' *D-Lib Magazine* 13.1/2 (January/February 2007). http://www.dlib.org/dlib/january07/markey/01markey.html.

Marsh, David. *The Quattrocento Dialogue: Classical Tradition and Humanist Innovation*. Cambridge, MA: Harvard University Press, 1980.

Martin, Henri-Jean. *The History and Power of Writing*. Translated by Lydia Cochrane. Chicago: University of Chicago Press, 1994.

Martin, Henri-Jean, ed. *Mise en page et mise en texte du livre français: La naissance du livre moderne (XIVe–XVIIe siècles)*. Paris: Éditions du Cercle de la Librairie, 2000.

Martin, Henri-Jean, and Jean Vezin, eds. *Mise en page et mise en texte du livre manuscrit*. Paris: Éditions du Cercle de la Librairie-Promodis, 1990.

Martin, Shawn. '*EEBO*, Microfilm, and Umberto Eco: Historical Lessons and Future Directions for Building Electronic Collections.' *Microform and Imaging Review* 36.4 (Fall 2007): 159–64.

Martines, Lauro. *Power and Imagination: City-States in Renaissance Italy*. 1979. Reprinted Baltimore, MD: Johns Hopkins University Press, 1988.

Masai, François. 'Paléographie et codicologie.' *Scriptorium* 4 (1950): 279–93.

– 'Principes et conventions de l'édition diplomatique.' *Scriptorium* 4 (1950): 177–93.

Mayer, Lauryn S. *Worlds Made Flesh: Reading Medieval Manuscript Culture*. New York: Routledge, 2004.

McCarty, Willard. *Humanities Computing*. New York: Palgrave, 2005.

McCloud, Scott. *Understanding Comics*. [New York]: Paradox, 2000.

Macdonald, Angus, and A.D. Morrison-Low, eds. *A Heavenly Library: Treasures from the Royal Observatory's Crawford Collection*. Edinburgh: Macdonald Lindsay Pindar, 1994.

Macfarlane, John. *Antoine Vérard*. 1900. Reprinted in Geneva: Slatkine Reprints, 1971.

McGann, Jerome. *A Critique of Modern Textual Criticism*. Charlottesville: University Press of Virginia, 1983.

– *Radiant Textuality: Literature after the World Wide Web*. New York: Palgrave, 2001.

– *The Textual Condition*. Princeton, NJ: Princeton University Press, 1991.

McGrady, Deborah. *Controlling Readers: Guillaume de Machaut and His Late Medieval Audience*. Toronto: University of Toronto Press, 2006.

Mackenzie, Adrian. *Cutting Code: Software and Sociality*. New York: Peter Lang, 2006.

McKenzie, D.F. *Bibliography and the Sociology of Texts*. London: British Library, 1986.

McKeon, Michael. *The Secret History of Domesticity: Public, Private, and the Division of Knowledge*. Baltimore, MD: Johns Hopkins University Press, 2005.

McKitterick, David. 'Libraries and the Organisation of Knowledge.' In *The Cambridge History of*

Libraries in Britain and Ireland, vol. 1, edited by Elisabeth Leedham-Green and Teresa Webber, 592–615. Cambridge: Cambridge University Press, 2006.

'"Not in STC": Opportunities and Challenges in the ESTC.' *The Library*, ser. 7, 6.2 (June 2005): 178–94.

– *Print, Manuscript and the Search for Order 1450–1830*. Cambridge: Cambridge University Press, 2003.

McLean, Paul D. *The Art of the Network: Strategic Interaction and Patronage in Renaissance Florence*. Durham, NC: Duke University Press, 2007.

McLuhan, Marshall. *The Gutenberg Galaxy: The Making of Typographic Man*. Toronto: University of Toronto Press, 1962.

– *Understanding Media: The Extensions of Man*. New York: MacGraw-Hill, 1964.

Meiss, Millard. 'French and Italian Variations on an Early Fifteenth Century Theme: St Jerome in His Study.' *Gazette des beaux-arts* 6.62 (September 1963): 147–70.

– 'Scholarship and Penitence in the Early Renaissance: The Image of St Jerome.' *Pantheon* 32 (1974): 134–40.

Menci, Giovanna. 'L'impaginazione nel rotolo e nel codice: Alcune note.' In *Akten des 21.Internationalen Papyrologenkongresses, Berlin 13.–19.8.1995*, edited by Bärbel Kramer, Wolfgang Luppe, Herwig Maehler, and Günther Poethke, 2: 682–90. Teubner: Stuttgart, 1997.

Minnis, A.J. *Medieval Theory of Authorship: Scholastic Literary Attitudes in the Later Middle Ages*. London: Scolar Press, 1984.

Mitchell, R.J. 'Italian "Nobilità" and the English Idea of the Gentleman in the XV Century.' *English Miscellany* 9 (1958): 23–37.

– *John Tiptoft (1427–1470)*. New York: Longmans, 1938.

Mitchell, W.J. *The Reconfigured Eye: Visual Truth in the Post-Photographic Era*. Cambridge, MA: MIT Press, 1992.

Montfort, Nick, and Ian Bogost. *Racing the Beam: The Atari Video Computer System*. Cambridge, MA: MIT Press, 2009.

Moranti, Maria. 'Organizzazione della Biblioteca di Federico da Montefeltro,' In *Federico da Montefeltro: Lo stato, le arti, la cultura*, edited by Giorgio Cerboni Baiardi, Giorgio Chittolini, and Piero Floriani, 3: 19–49. Rome: Bulzoni, 1986.

Morison, Stanley. 'Early Humanistic Script and the First Roman Type.' *The Library* 4.24 (1943): 1–29.

– *Politics and Script: Aspects of Authority and Freedom in the Development of Graeco-Latin Script from the Sixth Century BC to the Twentieth Century AD*. Edited by Nicolas Barker. Oxford: Clarendon Press, 1972.

Mortimer, Ruth. *A Portrait of the Author in Sixteenth-Century France*. Chapel Hill, NC: Hanes Foundation, 1980.

Moss, Ann. *Printed Commonplace-Books and the Structuring of Renaissance Thought*. Oxford: Clarendon Press, 1996.

Muir, Bernard James, ed. *Reading Texts and Images: Essays on Medieval and Renaissance Art and Patronage: In Honour of Margaret M. Manion.* Exeter: University of Exeter Press, 2002.

Murray, Alexander. *Reason and Society in the Middle Ages.* New York: Oxford University Press, 1978.

Needham, Paul. *The Printer & The Pardoner.* Washington: Library of Congress, 1986.

Nelson, Robert S. 'The Slide Lecture, or the Work of Art "History" in the Age of Mechanical Reproduction.' *Critical Inquiry* 26.3 (Spring 2000): 414–34.

Nicholls, Jonathan. *The Matter of Courtesy: Medieval Courtesy Books and the Gawain-Poet.* Woodbridge, England: D.S. Brewer, 1985.

Nichols, Stephen G. 'An Artifact by Any Other Name: Digital Surrogates of Medieval Manuscripts.' In *Archives, Documentation, and Institutions of Social Memory: Essays from the Sawyer Seminar,* edited by Francis X. Blouin and William G. Rosenberg, 134–43. Ann Arbor: University of Michigan Press, 2006.

Nunberg, Geoffrey, ed. *The Future of the Book.* Berkeley: University of California Press, 1996.

O'Donnell, James J. *Avatars of the Word: From Papyrus to Cyberspace.* Cambridge, MA: Harvard University Press, 1998.

O'Gorman, James. *The Architecture of the Monastic Library in Italy, 1300–1600.* New York: New York University Press, 1972.

Ong, Walter. *Orality and Literacy: The Technologizing of the Word.* New York: Metheun, 1982.

Orth, Myra D. 'What Goes Around: Borders and Frames in French Manuscripts.' *Journal of the Walters Art Gallery* 54 (1996): 189–201.

Oschema, Klaus. 'Maison, noblesse et légitimité: Aspects de la notion d'"hérédité" dans le milieu de la cour bourguignonne (XVème siècle).' In *L'hérédité entre Moyen Âge et Époque Moderne: Perspectives historiques,* edited by Charles de Miramon and Maaike van der Lugt, 211–44. Florence: SISMEL, 2008.

Panofsky, Erwin. *Meaning in Visual Arts: Papers in and on Art History.* Woodstock, NY: Overlook Press, 1974.

Pantzer, Katherine F. 'The Serpentine Progress of the *STC* Revision.' *Papers of the Bibliographical Society of America* 62.3 (1968): 297–311.

Parkes, Malcolm. 'The Influence of the Concepts of *Ordinatio* and *Compilatio* on the Development of the Book.' In *Medieval Learning and Literature: Essays Presented to Richard William Hunt,* edited by J.J.G. Alexander and M.T. Gibson, 115–41. Oxford: Clarendon Press, 1976.

– *Pause and Effect: An Introduction to Punctuation in the West.* Berkeley and Los Angeles: University of California Press, 1993.

– *Their Hand before Our Eyes: A Closer Look at Scribes.* Aldershot, England: Ashgate, 2008.

Pearsall, Derek, ed. *New Directions in Later Medieval Manuscript Studies: Essays from the 1998 Harvard Conference.* York, England: York Medieval Press, 2000.

Pearson Perry, Jon. 'Practical and Ceremonial Uses of Plants Materials as "Literary Refinements" in the Libraries of Leonello d'Este and His Courtly Literary Circle (Angelo Decembrio's *De politia litteraria*, Book 1, Part 3, and Book 2, Part 21).' *La Bibliofilia* 91.2 (1989): 121–73.

Perdrizet, Paul. 'Jean Miélot, l'Un des Traducteurs de Philippe le Bon.' *Revue d'Histoire Littéraire de la France* 14 (1907): 472–82.

Peruzzi, Marcella. *Cultura, potere, immagine: La biblioteca di Federico di Montefeltro*. Urbino: Accademia Raffaello, 2004.

Pettegree, Andrew. *The Book in the Renaissance*. New Haven, CT: Yale University Press, 2010.

Petrucci, Armando. *Public Lettering: Script, Power, and Culture*. Translated by Linda Lappin. Chicago: University of Chicago Press, 1993.

– *Writers and Readers in Medieval Italy: Studies in the History of Written Culture*. Edited and Translated by Charles Radding. New Haven, CT: Yale University Press, 1995.

Poggetto, Paolo dal. 'Nuova lettura di ambienti federiciani: Il Bagno cosidetto "della Duchessa" e la Biblioteca del duca Federico.' In *Federico da Montefeltro: Lo stato, le arti, la cultura*, edited by Giorgio Cerboni Baiardi, Giorgio Chittolini, and Piero Floriani, 2: 105–18. Rome: Bulzoni, 1986.

– 'Il restauro della Biblioteca del Duca e delle sale attigue.' In *Il Palazzo di Federico da Montefeltro*, edited by Maria Luisa Polichetti, 1: 699–705. Urbino: Quattroventi, 1985.

Poovey, Mary. *A History of the Modern Fact: Problems of Knowledge in the Sciences of Wealth and Society*. Chicago: University of Chicago Press, 1998.

Porter, Cheryl. 'The Identification of Purple in Manuscripts.' *Dyes in History and Archaeology* 21 (2007): 59–64.

Praz, Mario. *An Illustrated History of Furnishing, from the Renaissance to the Twentieth Century*. New York: Braziller, 1964.

Prinet, Max. 'Le Trésor de noblesse.' *Le Bibliographe moderne* 14 (1910): 84–9.

Prochno, Joachim. *Das Schreiber- und Dedikationsbild in der deutschen Buchmalerei*. 2 vols. Leipzig: B.G. Teubner, 1929.

Rabil, Jr, Albert, ed. and trans. *Knowledge, Goodness, and Power: The Debate over Nobility among Quattrocento Italian Humanists*. Binghamton, NY: Medieval & Renaissance Texts & Studies, 1991.

Raffaelli, Filippo. *La imparziale e veritiera istoria della unione della Biblioteca ducale di Urbino alla Vaticana di Roma*. Fermo: Bucher, 1877.

Ramsay, Stephen. 'Toward an Algorithmic Criticism.' *Literary and Linguistic Computing* 18.2 (2003): 167–74.

Rehe, Rolf E. 'Legibility.' In *Graphic Design & Reading: Explorations of an Uneasy Relationship*, edited by Gunnar Swanson, 97–110. New York: Allworth, 2000.

Reynolds, L.D., and N.G. Wilson. *Scribes and Scholars: A Guide to the Transmission of Greek and Latin Literature*. 3rd ed. New York: Oxford University Press, 1991.

Ricci, Seymour de. 'Colard Mansion.' *The Library* 4.1 (1920): 95–6.

Richardson, Brian. 'From Scribal Publication to Print Publication: Pietro Bembo's *Rime*, 1529–1535.' *Modern Language Review* 95.3 (July 2000): 684–95.

– *Manuscript Culture in Renaissance Italy*. Cambridge: Cambridge University Press, 2009.

– *Print Culture in Renaissance Italy: The Editor and the Vernacular Text, 1470–1600*. Cambridge: Cambridge University Press, 1994.

– *Printing, Writers and Readers in Renaissance Italy*. Cambridge: Cambridge University Press, 1999.

Ridderbos, Bernhard. *Saint and Symbol: Images of Saint Jerome in Early Italian Art*. Translated by P. de Waard-Dekking. Groningen: Bouma's Boekhuis, 1984.

Robathan, Dorothy. 'Libraries of the Italian Renaissance.' In *The Medieval Library*, edited by James Westfall Thompson, 509–88. 1939. Reprinted New York: Hafner, 1957.

Roberts, Ann M. 'The Horse and the Hawk: Representations of Mary of Burgundy as Sovereign.' In *Excavating the Medieval Image: Manuscripts, Artists, Audiences. Essays in Honor of Sandra Hindman*, edited by David S. Areford and Nina A. Rowe, 137–50. Burlington, VT: Ashgate, 2004.

Roberts, Colin, and T.C. Skeat. *The Birth of the Codex*. London: Oxford University Press, 1983.

Robinson, Peter. 'Computer-Assisted Stemmatic Analysis and "Best-Text" Historical Editing.' In *Studies in Stemmatology*, edited by Pieter Th. van Reene, Margot van Mulken, and Janet Dyk, 71–104. Amsterdam: J. Benjamins, 1996.

Roover, Florence Edler de. 'The Scriptorium.' In *The Medieval Library*, edited by James Westfall Thompson, 594–612. 1939. Reprinted New York: Hafner, 1957.

Ross, Braxton. 'Salutati's Defeated Candidate for Humanistic Script.' *Scrittura e Civiltà* 5 (1981): 186–98.

Rotondi, Pasquale. *The Ducal Palace of Urbino: Its Architecture and Decoration*. New York: Transatlantic Arts, 1969.

Rouse, Mary A., and Richard H. Rouse. *Cartolai, Illuminators, and Printers in Fifteenth-Century Italy: The Evidence of the Ripoli Press*. Los Angeles: Department of Special Collections, University Research Library, University of California, 1988.

– '*Statim invenire*: Schools, Preachers and New Attitudes to the Page.' In *Renaissance and Renewal in the Twelfth Century*, edited by Robert L. Benson and Giles Constable with Carol D. Lanham, 201–25. Cambridge, MA: Harvard University Press, 1982.

Rouse, Richard H., and Mary A. Rouse. 'Concordances et index.' In *Mise en page et mise en texte du livre manuscrit*, edited by Henri-Jean Martin and Jean Vezin, 219–28. Paris: Éditions du Cercle de la Librairie-Promodis, 1990.

Rudy, Kathryn M. 'Review of Bernard Bousmanne, Céline van Hoorebeeck, and Alain Arnould, eds., *La librairie des ducs de Bourgogne: manuscrits conservés à la Bibliothèque royale de Belgique, Vol. 1: Textes liturgiques, ascétiques, théologiques, philosophiques et moraux*. Turnhout: Brepols, 2000.' *H-ArtHist, H-Net Reviews* (January 2003). http://www.h-net.org/mmreviews/showrev.cgi?path=286.

Ruvoldt, Maria. 'Sacred to Secular, East to West: The Renaissance Study and Strategies of Display.' *Renaissance Studies* 20.5 (November 2006): 640–57.

Bibliography

Sabbadini, Remigio. 'Buonaccorso da Montemagno il Giovane.' *Giornale storico della letteratura italiana* 50 (1907): 43–9.

Sabbadini, Remigio, ed. *Carteggio di Giovanni Aurispa*. Rome: Tipografia del Senato, 1931.

Saenger, Michael. *The Commodification of Textual Engagements in the English Renaissance*. Aldershot, England: Ashgate, 2006.

Saenger, Paul. 'Books of Hours and the Reading Habits of the Later Middle Ages.' In *The Culture of Print: Power and the Uses of Print in Early Modern Europe*, edited by Roger Chartier, 141–73. Oxford: Polity Press, 1989.

– 'Colard Mansion and the Evolution of the Printed Book.' *Library Quarterly* 45.4 (1975): 405–18.

– 'Silent Reading: Its Impact on Late Medieval Script and Society.' *Viator* 13 (1982): 367–414.

– *Space between Words: The Origins of Silent Reading*. Stanford, CA: Stanford University Press, 1997.

Salen, Katie, and Sharyn O'Mara. 'Dis[appearances]: Representational Strategies and Operational Needs in Codexspace and Screenspace.' *Visible Language* 31.3 (1997): 260–85.

Scholderer, Victor. *Fifty Essays in Fifteenth- and Sixteenth-Century Bibliography*. Edited by Dennis E. Rhodes. Amsterdam: Menno Hertzberger, 1966.

– 'A Further Note on Red Printing in Early Books.' *Gutenberg-Jahrbuch* 34 (1959): 59–60.

– 'Red Printing in Early Books.' *Gutenberg-Jahrbuch* 33 (1958): 105–7.

Schreibman, Susan, Ray Siemens, and John Unsworth, eds. *A Companion to Digital Humanities*. Oxford: Blackwell, 2004. http://www.digitalhumanities.org/companion/.

Schwenk, Rolf. *Vorarbeiten zu einer Biographie des Niklas von Wyle und zu einer kritischen Ausgabe seiner ersten Translatze*. Göppingen: Kümmerle, 1978.

Sears, Elizabeth. 'Portraits in Counterpoint: Jerome and Jeremiah in an Augsburg Manuscript.' In *Reading Medieval Images: The Art Historian and the Object*, edited by Elizabeth Sears and Thelma K. Thomas, 61–74. Ann Arbor: University of Michigan Press, 2002.

Serlio, Sebastiano. *On Domestic Architecture: The Sixteenth-Century Manuscript of Book VI in the Avery Library of Columbia University*. New York: Architectural History Foundation, 1978.

Sharpe, Richard. *Titulus: Identifying Medieval Latin Texts. An Evidence-Based Approach*. Turnhout: Brepols, 2003.

Sherman, Willam. 'EEBO: The Missing Manual.' Conference paper. The 52nd Annual Meeting of the Renaissance Society of America. San Francisco, CA, 25 March 2006.

Simonetta, Marcello, ed. *Federico da Montefeltro and His Library*. Milan: Y. Press and Biblioteca Apostolica Vaticana, 2007.

Sirat, Colette. *Writing as Handwork: A History of Handwriting in Mediterranean and Western Culture*. Turnhout: Brepols, 2006.

Skeat, T.C. 'The Length of the Standard Papyrus Roll and the Cost-Advantage of the Codex.' *Zeitschrift für Papyrologie und Epigraphik* 45 (1982): 169–75.

– 'Roll versus Codex – A New Approach?' *Zeitschrift für Papyrologie und Epigraphik* 84 (1990): 297–8.

Skinner, Quentin. *The Foundations of Modern Political Thought*. Vol. 1. Cambridge: Cambridge University Press, 1978.

Small, David. 'Rethinking the Book.' PhD diss., Massachusetts Institute of Technology, 1999.

Small, Jocelyn Penny. *Wax Tablets of the Mind: Cognitive Studies of Memory and Literacy in Classical Antiquity*. New York: Routledge, 1997.

Smith, Brian Cantwell. 'From E&M to M&E. A Journey through the Landscape of Computing.' In *The Philosophy of Computing and Information: Five Questions*, edited by Luciano Floridi, 19–47. [S.I.]: Automatic Press/VIP, 2008.

– 'Indiscrete Affairs.' Unpublished paper. Indiana University–Bloomington, 1998.

– 'Limits of Correctness in Computers.' In *Computers, Ethics & Social Values*, edited by Deborah G. Johnson and Helen Nissenbaum, 456–69. Upper Saddle River, NJ: Prentice Hall, 1995.

Smith, Margaret M. 'Printed Foliation: Forerunner to Printed Page-Numbers?' *Gutenberg Jahrbuch* (1988): 54–70.

– *The Title-Page: Its Early Development, 1460–1510*. New Castle, DE: Oak Knoll Press, 2000.

Snyder, H. Gregory. *Teachers and Texts in the Ancient World: Philosophers, Jews, and Christians*. New York: Routledge, 2000.

Soymié, Michel, ed. *Contributions aux études sur Touen-houang*. Vol. 3. Paris: École française d'Extrême-Orient, 1984.

Spencer, Eleanor P. 'Antoine Vérard's Illuminated Vellum Incunables.' In *Manuscripts in the Fifty Years after the Invention of Printing*, edited by J.B. Trapp, 62–5. London: Warburg Institute, 1983.

Stafford, Barbara Maria. *Artful Science: Enlightenment Education and the Eclipse of Visual Education*. Cambridge, MA: MIT Press, 1994.

Staikos, Konstantinos, ed. *Libraries: From Antiquity to the Renaissance and Major Humanist and Monastery Libraries (3000 BC – AD 1600)*. Translated by David Hardy. New Rochelle, NY: A. Caratzas, 1997.

Stallybrass, Peter. *Printing-for-Manuscript*. Philadelphia: University of Pennsylvania Press, forthcoming.

Stenhouse, William. *Reading Inscriptions and Writing Ancient History: Historical Scholarship in the Late Renaissance*. Institute of Classical Studies, School of Advanced Study, University of London, 2005.

Stewart, Garrett. *The Look of Reading: Book, Painting, Text*. Chicago: University of Chicago Press, 2006.

Stock, Brian. 'Reading, Writing, and the Self: Petrarch and His Forerunners.' *New Literary History* 26.4 (1995): 717–30.

Bibliography

Stoicheff, Peter, and Andrew Taylor, eds. *The Future of the Page*. Toronto: University of Toronto Press, 2004.

Stone Peters, Julie. *Theatre of the Book 1480–1880: Print, Text, and Performance in Europe*. Oxford: Oxford University Press, 2000.

Stornajolo, Cosimo. *Codices Urbinates Graeci Bibliothecae Vaticanae*. Rome: Typis Vaticanis, 1895.

– *Codices Urbinates Latini*. Vol. 3. Rome: Typis Vaticanis, 1921.

Strauss, Bruno. *Der Übersetzer Nicolaus von Wyle*. 1912. Reprinted New York: Johnson Reprint, 1970.

Swanson, Gunnar, ed. *Graphic Design & Reading: Explorations of an Uneasy Relationship*. New York: Allworth, 2000.

Tanselle, G. Thomas. 'The Editorial Problem of Final Authorial Intention.' *Studies in Bibliography* 29 (1976): 168–212.

– 'Issues in Bibliographical Studies since 1942.' In *The Book Encompassed: Studies in Twentieth-Century Bibliography*, edited by Peter Davison, 24–36. Cambridge: Cambridge University Press, 1992.

Tateo, Francesco. *Tradizione e realtà nel Umanesimo italiano*. Bari: Dedalo libri, 1974.

Tenzer, Virginia. 'The Iconography of the Studiolo of Federico da Montefeltro in Urbino.' PhD diss., Brown University, 1985.

Thompson, James Westfall, ed. *The Medieval Library*. 1939. Reprinted New York: Hafner, 1957.

Thornton, Dora. *The Scholar in His Study: Ownership and Experience in Renaissance Italy*. New Haven, CT: Yale University Press, 1997.

Tinto, Alberto. *Il corsivo nella tipografia del Cinquecento*. Milan: Il Polifio, 1972.

Tocci, Luigi Michelini. 'Agapito, Bibliotecario "Docto, Acorto et Diligente" della Biblioteca Urbinate alla fine del Quattrocento.' *Collectanea Vaticana in honorem Anselmi M. Card. Albareda, Studi e Testi* 220 (1962): 243–80.

– 'La formazione della Biblioteca di Federico da Montefeltro: Codici contemporanei e libri a stampa.' In *Federico da Montefeltro: Lo stato, le arti, la cultura*, edited by Giorgio Cerboni Baiardi, Giorgio Chittolini, and Piero Floriani, 3: 9–18. Rome: Bulzoni, 1986.

Traube, Ludwig. *Vorlesungen und Abhandlungen*. Vol. 1. Munich: C.H. Beck, 1909.

Trinkaus, Charles. *Adversity's Noblemen: The Italian Humanists on Happiness*. New York: Columbia University Press, 1940.

Turner, E.G. *Greek Papyri: An Introduction*. Oxford: Clarendon Press, 1980.

– 'The Terms *Recto* and *Verso*: The Anatomy of the Papyrus Roll.' In *Actes du XVe Congrès International de Papyrologie*, 1: 7–71 (Brussels: Fondation égyptologique Reine Élisabeth, 1978).

– *The Typology of the Early Codex*. Philadelphia: University of Pennsylvania Press, 1977.

Ullman, B.L. *The Origin and Development of Humanistic Script*. Rome: Edizioni di Storia e Letteratura, 1960.

Updike, D.B. *Printing Types: Their History, Forms, and Use*. 3rd ed. 2 vols. Cambridge, MA: Harvard University Press, 1966.

Vanderjagt, A.J. 'Between Court Literature and Civic Rhetoric: Buonaccorso da Montemagno's *Controversia de nobilitate.*' In *Courtly Literature: Culture and Context*, edited by Keith Busby and Erik Cooper, 561–72. Philadelphia: J. Benjamins, 1990.

– 'The Princely Culture of the Valois Dukes of Burgundy.' In *Princes and Princely Culture 1450–1650*, edited by Martin Gosman, Alasdair MacDonald, and Arjo Vanderjagt, 1: 51–79. Leiden: Brill, 2003.

– 'Il pubblico dei testi umanistici nell'Italia settentrionale ed in Borgogna: Buonaccorso da Montemagno e Giovanni Aurispa.' *Aevum* 70 (1996): 477–86.

– '*Qui sa la vertu anoblist': The Concepts of noblesse and chose publicque in Burgundian Political Thought.* Groningen: J. Miélot, 1981.

– 'Three Solutions to Buonaccorso's *Disputatio de nobilitate.*' In *Non Nova, Sed Nove: Mélanges de civilisation médiévale*, edited by Martin Gosman and Jaap van Os, 247–59. Groningen: Bouma's Boekhuis, 1984.

Vezin, Jean. 'La fabrication du manuscrit,' In *Histoire de l'édition française*, edited by Roger Chartier and Henri-Jean Martin, 1: 25–47. Paris: Éditions du Cercle de la Librairie-Promodis, 1982.

– 'Manuscrits "imposés."' In *Mise en page et mise en texte du livre manuscrit*, edited by Henri-Jean Martin and Jean Vezin, 423–5. Paris: Éditions du Cercle de la Librairie-Promodis, 1990.

Vidler, Anthony. 'Books in Space: Tradition and Transparency in the Bibliothèque de France.' *Representations. Special Issue: Future Libraries* 42 (Spring 1993): 115–34.

– 'Warped Space: Architectural Anxiety in Digital Culture.' In *Impossible Presence: Surface and Screen in the Photogenic Era*, edited by Terry Smith, 285–303. Chicago: University of Chicago Press, 2001.

Vitruvius. *On Architecture*. Edited by F. Krohn. Vol. 6. Leipzig: B.G. Teubner, 1912.

– *The Ten Books on Architecture*. Translated by Morris Hicky Morgan. Cambridge, MA: Harvard University Press, 1914. http://www.perseus.tufts.edu/cgi-bin/ptext?lookup=Vitr.

Voulliéme, Ernst. *Die deutschen Drucker des fünfzehnten Jahrhunderts*. 2nd ed. Berlin: Reichsdruckerei, 1922.

Wardrop, James. *The Script of Humanism: Some Aspects of Humanistic Script, 1460–1560*. Oxford: Clarendon Press, 1963.

Warncke, Carsten-Peter, ed. *Ikonographie der Bibliotheken*. Wiesbaden: Harrassowitz, 1992.

Weitzmann, Kurt. *Illustrations in Roll and Codex: A Study of the Origin and Method of Text Illustration*. 1947. Reprinted, with addenda, Princeton, NJ: Princeton University Press, 1970.

Williams, Megan Hale. *The Monk and the Book: Jerome and the Making of Christian Scholarship*. Chicago: University of Chicago Press, 2006.

Williams, William Proctor, and William Baker. '*Caveat Lector*: English Books 1475–1700 and the Electronic Age.' *Analytical & Enumerative Bibliography* 12 (2001): 1–29.

Winn, Mary Beth. *Anthoine Vérard: Parisian Publisher, 1485–1512*. Geneva: Droz, 1997.

Bibliography

Witt, Ronald. *'In the Footsteps of the Ancients': The Origins of Humanism from Lovato to Bruni.* Leiden: Brill, 2000.

Wormald, Francis. 'The Monastic Library.' In *Gatherings in Honor of Dorothy E. Miner*, edited by Ursula E. McCracken, Lilian M.C. Randall, and Richard H. Randall, Jr, 93–109. Baltimore, MD: Walters Art Gallery, 1974.

Wyle, Niclas von. *Translationen.* Edited by Adelbert von Keller. Stuttgart: Litterarischer Verein, 1861.

Yates, Frances. *The Art of Memory.* Chicago: University of Chicago Press, 1966.

Zetzel, James E.G. *Marginal Scholarship and Textual Deviance: The 'Commentum Cornuti' and the Early Scholia on Persius.* London: Institute of Classical Studies, School of Advanced Study, University of London, 2005.

Index

Index

Index

127

STUDIES IN BOOK and PRINT CULTURE
General Editor: Leslie Howsam

Dean Irvine, *Editing Modernity: Women and Little-Magazine Cultures in Canada, 1916–1956*

Janet Friskney, *New Canadian Library: The Ross-McClelland Years, 1952–1978*

Janice Cavell, *Tracing the Connected Narrative: Arctic Exploration in British Print Culture, 1818–1860*

Elspeth Jajdelska, *Silent Reading and the Birth of the Narrator*

Martyn Lyons, *Reading Culture and Writing Practices in Nineteenth-Century France*

Robert A. Davidson, *Jazz Age Barcelona*

Gail Edwards and Judith Saltman, *Picturing Canada: A History of Canadian Children's Illustrated Books and Publishing*

Miranda Remnek, ed., *The Space of the Book: Print Culture in the Russian Social Imagination*

Adam Reed, *Literature and Agency in English Fiction Reading: A Study of the Henry Williamson Society*

Bonnie Mak, *How the Page Matters*

Eli MacLaren, *Dominion and Agency: Copyright and the Structuring of the Canadian Book Trade, 1867–1918*

Ruth Panofsky, *The Literary Legacy of the Macmillan Company of Canada: Making Books and Mapping Culture*

Archie L. Dick, *The Hidden History of South Africa's Book and Reading Cultures*

Darcy Cullen, ed., *Editors, Scholars, and the Social Text*